THE EASTERN ORTHODOX CHURCH

The Eastern Orthodox Church

A New History

JOHN ANTHONY McGUCKIN

Yale

UNIVERSITY PRESS

New Haven and London

Published with assistance from the foundation established in memory of Calvin Chapin of the Class of 1788, Yale College.

Yale University Press books may be purchased in quantity for educational, business, or promotional use. For information, please e-mail sales.press@yale.edu (U.S. office) or sales@yaleup.co.uk (U.K. office).

Set in Janson type by IDS Infotech Ltd.
Printed in the United States of America.

Library of Congress Control Number: 2019948578
ISBN 978-0-300-21876-3 (hardcover : alk. paper)

A catalogue record for this book is available from the British Library.

This paper meets the requirements of ANSI/NISO Z39.48-1992 (Permanence of Paper).

10 9 8 7 6 5 4 3 2 1

For the Family of Saint Gregory's Orthodox Chaplaincy,
Manhattan

Contents

CONTENTS

The Naming of Parts

H ENRY REED (1914–1986), a friend of the poets W. H. Auden and Louis MacNeice, was a witty and acutely intelligent twenty-seven-year-old when he was conscripted into the British armed forces during World War II. He was set to work (with no previous facility or experience) to serve as a translator of Japanese, and would later quip that the brightest benefit of peacetime was that he would never have to study another word of the language as long as he lived. His most famous poem is his satire on British Army officious inefficiency, "Naming of Parts." Even when the recruits had no actual equipment with which to fight, they were required, in a formal daily drill, to learn names of all the broken-down parts of their (nonexistent) guns, from the example of the one weapon the drill sergeant showed to them: "Today we have naming of parts. Yesterday, / We had daily cleaning. And tomorrow morning, / We shall have what to do after firing."

The naming of parts is a tedious business at the best of times, and the mind would always prefer to flit to more glistening bits—Japonica, coral, gardens with fragile blossoms, which Reed immediately goes on to talk about in his poem—but when it comes to highly controverted terms and concepts, it is maybe a good place to start.

Even the title of *The Eastern Orthodox Church: A New History* will introduce several such parts. Ninety-six thousand words may not be short enough for some, but we must let that pass. A workably brief history of something as old as two millennia in so short a space may be inconceivable for others. The designation "Eastern" may itself be confusing; when I, for example, who am a member of the Eastern Church, come from Wallsend in the North of England and formerly served a community in New York's Harlem neighborhood. I myself was much confused when, dressed in the robes of an Orthodox archpriest at an ecumenical convention, I was approached by some well-meaning Protestant minister delegate who wished me Happy Passover and wondered why I was not wearing *payot* sidelocks and a hat. It took me a few moments to realize he had confused his Orthodoxes. But today we have the naming of parts—for what I wish to begin with is a few comments on what that last little word "Church" might mean; and that is a question that underlies both the logic of how I might make a short historical account of Orthodox Christianity in the first place, and also how the Orthodox Church can be rightly placed among the other, perhaps more well-known, forms of Christian tradition.

Why I think it is necessary to have this shuffling of feet at the very outset is because Eastern Orthodoxy refuses to call itself, or see itself, as a denomination. I used to have regular fun at faculty meetings when the dean would turn the discussion around to ecumenism and ask how we might all contribute to an interdenominational approach to various questions. My hand raised to register a point of order became a regular moment of humor.[1] But the serious aspect to it was that a very common modern approach to the history of the Christian Church takes its beginnings from the present-day great diversity of churches. Denominationalism is a preferred way in our time of dealing with the fractions of Christendom that occurred especially after (but existing long before) the era of the Reformation. Today, without the notion of denominations and the idea that there are multiplicities of Christian churches, most can hardly comprehend the idea of what the word "church" might mean. The fundamental creed of Christendom, the Nicene-Constantinopolitan statement of faith that most Christians acknowledge, and some churches recite regularly at worship, states as one of its articles of faith that the Church of Christ is: "One, holy, catholic, and apostolic." But even those Christians who publicly profess those words, week after week, would be hard put to say how Christianity reconciles the concept of fundamental unity (that the church is one) with the multiplicity we see with our eyes. So Orthodoxy's claim not to be "one of" the Christian churches but rather "the Church" of Christ is a rather big one that needs addressing up front.

So let me state up front that this will be a focused history of the Byzantine Orthodox tradition—the definition of Eastern Orthodox Christianity that includes, today, the Greek, Russian, and Romanian Orthodox Churches (the big communities), as well as the Serbs, the Bulgarians, the Georgians, the Orthodox churches of Antioch and Jerusalem, of Poland,

of the Czech lands and Slovakia, of Albania, the churches of
Cyprus and Sinai, and the Orthodox churches in communion
with these in Finland, China, and Japan. This is not to mention the large communities of the diaspora: those faithful
originally from these Eastern European and Eastern Mediterranean countries who by dint of centuries of immigration
have now moved all over the globe in significant Orthodox
communities even in such places (which could hardly be
called Eastern any more) as England, America, and Oceania,
for example. For ready-reckoner recognition: this is the Orthodox Church that recognizes the high doctrinal authority
(as do the Roman Catholics and Episcopalians) of the seven
Ecumenical Councils.[2] For this reason the present account
looks only very cursorily at the so-called Oriental Orthodox
churches. In the latter case the word "Oriental" refers to
the *Provincia Orientalis* of the late Roman Empire (not the
manner in which English language used to use the word "Ori-
entalism" pejoratively), because these churches in ancient
times used to be located mainly there, in what is now Syria,
Egypt, and Ethiopia, and nowadays we would add to that
communion the Armenian Church. These are collectively
also described as the Non-Chalcedonian Orthodox churches,
for they recognize the high authority only of the first three
Ecumenical Councils.

To tell the story of the ancient Eastern Orthodox Church,
incarnated in a scintillating array of local churches of different language groups and national traditions, is a task of no
small order. But as the old saying goes, "A journey of a thousand miles begins with a small step," and this book is best
begun by walking down the road that takes us from Jesus to
the classical patristic age in the fourth and fifth centuries. By

that time many of the more recognizable forms of Eastern Orthodox tradition are set in place and become familiar. Western Catholicism, after Cardinal Newman, often likes to talk about its history and culture in developmental terms and images. Orthodoxy prefers to understand itself in terms of organic wholeness. If we compare the church to a piece of great music, the early centuries within the first half of the first millennium are like the establishment of the major themes: subthemes commenting on the primary themes of the Gospels. The later centuries are like the variations, all trying to be faithful to the spirit and intelligence (the ethos) set up by the primary inspiration—but carried on with equal inspiration (the music endures with authority) even to the end that is still to come.

Anyway, let us begin that task, since it is a long journey, with a protohistory of the church, as it were, for a commonly held theory among some scholars today is that the church never existed as a single coherent unit or factor; such was its diversity that unity and uniformity had to be an anachronistic concept foisted on it retrospectively, and so Orthodoxy's claim to be this church is impossible. This is a view partly behind the great delight in reclaiming suspiciously lost Gospels: as if they represented viable forms of alternative Christianity pushed aside by an oppressive orthodoxy. Where this supposed oppressive power came from in the pre-third-century church is never explained, of course. Against the myth that these allegedly lost Gospels (which the church had generally preserved in its record anyway) were of fundamental significance and offered a powerful alternative, I always used to say to students: "Read them for yourselves and then tell me which, if you had to buy one, would you prefer: the Gospel of

John or the Gospel of Truth?" The Gnostic literature and the apocryphal literature were rejected by the church at large well before there was any universal authority structure in place to ostracize them. They were rejected for exactly the same reasons our contemporary bookshops carrying remaindered books are able to find their stock. They are, in short, the remaindered literature of Christian antiquity and (as is generally the case) remaindered for good reason. To the claim that there never was a single Christian Church with coherent unified doctrinal positions, Orthodoxy answers, of course: "Yes there was, and we are it; and our history demonstrates that core and essential history of the unified church." This attitude, I would maintain, is universally typical of Orthodox churchmen and -women when asked to characterize or discuss their church. Such a stance often causes confusion and maybe even some degree of offense among other Christians who hear it; thinking, perhaps, that this claim that they themselves "are the church" somehow implies that all others are not recognized as Christians in their own right; as Roman Catholics or Protestants, for example. But this latter implication is not intended by most Orthodox, who in this robust and singular sense of being church, and professing to be the direct and unbroken continuance of the early church, are more concerned with maintaining and stating what they regard themselves as being, rather than defining, what a widely differentiated Western Christianity has become.

On the issue of the modern relations of churches, Orthodoxy currently has no universally agreed answer to offer: a result, mainly, of its profound isolation from Western Christendom over most of the formative centuries that saw contemporary church relations being formed in the years after the Western Reformation. Orthodoxy regards the Great Church in antiquity (for most of the first millennium) as comprising, on one side, the Eastern Orthodox world (the Byzantine patriarchates presided over by the hierarch of the Church of Constantinople together with the Slavic Orthodox churches); and, on the other side, the Western Catholic Church, presided over by the hierarch of the Church of Rome. To define what is meant by authenticity as a church, Orthodoxy raises up as a canon (or set of tick boxes) a synopsis of a whole set of characteristics that once defined the church of old and have been maintained intact into the present. We can look at these later in more detail, but briefly stated they would include being closely attentive to biblical prescripts, especially the evangelical charter, observant of the decrees and creedal definitions of the Ecumenical Councils, careful of the spirit and forms of the ancient liturgical life of the Christians, reverent toward the practices and teachings of the great saints of its foundational history; and perhaps in a most homely statement of the crux of the matter: being contemporaneously demonstrative of the radiant life of the Spirit of God in the church's ongoing quest for purification and holiness of life.

The lack of a common agreement among the Eastern churches on matters of present-day ecumenicity is why today one sees many Orthodox leaders happy to engage in ecumenical dialogues with institutions such as the World Council of Churches, but others who are vehemently opposed to such engagement, some of whom have labeled even the slightest form of ecumenical rapprochement with other Christians as the "pan-heresy of the age."[3] The latter leaders often tend to be zealous monastics, and they represent some of the most conservative and literalist forces of the Orthodox world. For some of them, their very deep conservatism leads them to believe that they thereby speak for all of world Orthodoxy, which is a delusion. But at the heart of this strong division of opinion lies the crux of the Orthodox conception of what church means, and who represents it within the present world order.

There were, roughly speaking, two practical systems of identifying church belonging in the ancient Christian world. One was an exclusionist one, identified with Saint Cyprian of Carthage: arguing that the church is one, and if you are not identified with it by being in that oneness, then you are not in it at all. Cyprian summed up this sharp no-nonsense view in lawyer's Latin as: *Extra Ecclesiam nulla salus.* It is often translated (by those who wish to overstress its exclusionist qualities) as "Outside the Church there is no salvation." But it equally, and properly, translates as: "Outside the Church there is no safety," which is a very different matter and highlights what Cyprian wanted to insist on in his own time and from within his own bitterly divided Christian environment: that schisms among Christian believers are a very serious and sobering matter in relation to the spiritual life.[4] The other practical system was represented by, among others, Saints Dionysius the Great of Alexandria and Basil the Great of Caesarea, who both produced what are now known as "canonical epistles" in an attempt to reconcile the schismatic groups of dissidents that had already risen up in the early centuries; groups we know from history, such as Gnostics, Marcionites, Arians, Novatians, Photinians, and others. Working from a very practical emphasis on restoring Christians to communion around one bishop presiding over one priestly council that celebrated the Eucharist in the local churches, these pastorally minded leaders simply reverted to the question: How close are these divided believers to the central confession of Orthodox faith? What would be necessary to restore them to communion? Would it require simply a statement of proper faith? A blessing ritual of forgiveness? Or (for those who differed in great matters of substance) a new—and first—baptismal ceremony, one that clearly did not accept them as having been "really baptized" at all in their prior liturgical ceremonies.

Perhaps this issue of why the Orthodox see themselves as the church, simply stated, might be better clarified if we simply start to narrate the story, because Orthodox tradition gives great weight to the Roman legal concepts of tradition and authoritative precedent. So, let us begin to chart the history, then, of what the Great Church, or the Orthodox Church, or the Church Catholic and the Apostolic Church (for all these titles are claimed as *propria*, that is, as defining identifier marks by the Eastern Orthodox), looked like in its earliest iterations. In that case we need to begin, now, with the Apostolic Age, before our story can pick up with increasingly fuller sets of identifying ecclesial characteristics in the so-called patristic age, which will be the focus of chapters 2 and 3.[5] The later ages of Christian history called for increasingly explicit qualifications of important things that had to be witnessed if the church was to be authentically the Great Church. Many of these issues were determined at the highest level of episcopal and imperial consultation, and so they were much more in the light of public debate than the earliest formulations of Christian faith we find in the New Testament and the apostolic fathers in the first two centuries. These later meetings, from the fourth century onward, have come to be known as the Ecumenical Councils and form a later part of this book.[6]

THE RESURRECTION ORIGIN OF THE CHURCH

To understand how Orthodoxy defines itself as church, it is necessary to begin with the Gospels. It might be thought, as an initial reflection, that the Christian movement began with the preaching ministry of Jesus, when he assembled apostles (*shaliachim*) as missionaries and began to gather around him crowds to hear the message, attended by an inner circle of followers (other than the apostles) who were called disciples (*mathetai*, or students).[7] This would clearly make sense; even if the movement in the lifetime of Jesus should more or less be seen as entirely enclosed within the confines of Jewish geography, culture, and theological precedent.[8] So we could say that the church begins with Jesus's calling (vocation) of the apostles. This is exactly why the Gospel of Mark begins its account of the Good News with the vocational stories of the chief apostles (Mk. 1.14–20).

It has, however, been customary among Christians from ancient times to say that the church, in a fuller sense, began at Pentecost. The classic account of this is given in the prelude to Luke-Acts. Here the apostle tells the story of how the resurrection power of Jesus was extended in two dramatic acts that had the effect of establishing his earthly congregation.[9] The first of these events was the Ascension; the second was the descent of the Spirit in the form of tongues of fire (Acts 1.1–11; Acts 2.1–4). The first event, Jesus's triumphal ascent to the right-hand side of the Father's throne is one of the biblical ways of speaking about his posthumous glorification, or exaltation. The scriptural words to denote this glory are manifold. Chief among them are: *doxa, anastasis, hypsosis, anabasis:* New Testament words for: glory, rising up, being lifted up, and ascending. These are collectively words that connote the exaltation of the triumphant hero. Most modern readers of the New Testament tend to speak collectively about this aspect simply as the Resurrection story—understanding that the term "resurrection" means more than just the literal semantic of the rising up of the dead body but expands to include all the various motifs of glorification which the New Testament refers to in regard to Jesus's post-Crucifixion state.

But so to focus on the Resurrection word alone, to collate the whole complex of biblical narratives of Jesus's post-death glorification, misreads the New Testament teaching. This is because even the events of Transfiguration (*metamorphosis,* Mk. 9.1–10), Ascension (*analêpsis, anabasis,* Acts 1.2–11), and Pentecostal outpouring of the Spirit (*ekpempsis pneumatos,* Acts 2.1–36) are meant, in the New Testament writings, to be understood as the wider nexus of the glorification events following on Jesus's sacrifice.[10] It would take a much longer book to go through the New Testament theology and show how this is the case: so let me take but one example. What Saint Luke, for example, in his typical historicizing style of Gospel writing, presents as a linear sequence of post-Crucifixion glory events (first the Resurrection, then the appearances of the risen Jesus, then the Ascension, and then the descent of the Spirit), Saint John's Gospel offers to the reader distinctively differently all as radiant aspects of the self-same event: the return of Jesus to the Father after his death. So in the hands of the Fourth Gospel theologian, Jesus rises from the dead on the first paschal Sunday, appears to the disciples that same day, tells Mary Magdalene in the garden that he is "ascending" to the Father, and again on the same day bestows the gift of the Spirit on his apostles with the command to reconcile the world (the church's foundational mission, Jn. 20.1–23). Everything that Luke has tried to spread out on the table in a linear way, so that one could consider the historical sequencing of the parts, John has compressed in a manner that insists they are all aspect events of one and the same "eschatological mystery": that is, a primary event that is not bound within the sequence of time limitations but rather stands as the cause or explanation of that very sequence.

New Testament eschatology is a profound theory, or philosophy, of time transcendence that permeates the Gospel and apostolic writings. It sees in the sacred events of Christ's life and death and glory the definitive movements that have given time its meaning, and thus in a real sense transcended it—given it an end, a *telos* in the Greek—a word that English finds difficult to evoke, insofar as it means both a terminal end and a goal, or end object, that is, a fulfillment. The New Testament writers consider eschatology as a completion (*teleiosis*) of history, and this is why John cannot agree with Luke's linearization and fragmentation into history of what is more rightly understood as an eschatological mystery. In short, rather than talk about the Resurrection of Jesus, which is but one part of a wider nexus of events, the New Testament would have us think about the collective of those events that together form the divine Glorification (doxa, hypsosis) of Jesus. These are difficult ideas to convey quickly, but as the Gospel writings are the foundation of Christian ideas about the church, and especially crucial to the Orthodox understanding of the authoritative sources of Christian consciousness, it is important to try to bring one's mind around to the fact that the New Testament theologians were generally a lot more sophisticated than we have often given them credit for being; and that they speak in idioms and analogies that are Semitic and often alien to our presuppositions.

The overall sense among the earliest canonical writers about the death and exaltation of Jesus is that there is an antithesis of response from God the Father to the sacrificial witness of Jesus's life. Just as Jesus poured himself out in self-sacrificing obedience to the Father's will in a bitter *kenosis* (a word that means "emptying out"), so too God gave him in return the fullness (*pleroma*) of glory after his sufferings, raised him up to the right-hand side of the heavenly throne, and acclaimed him with the inexpressible (divine) name of "Lord." The New Testament writers customarily use images of a royal throne to express this, with its power and glory now being manifested as shared. The Resurrected and Glorified Jesus is now shown to the whole cosmos as Lord, who was once regarded as a slave. The clearest example of this way of thinking and writing is given in a very early Christian hymn, possibly written within two decades of the Crucifixion, which Saint Paul himself quotes (he does not compose it) in Philippians 2.1–11: "Have this mind among yourselves, which is yours in Christ Jesus, who, though he was in the form of God, did not count equality with God a thing to be grasped, but emptied himself, taking the form of a servant, being born in the likeness of men. And being found in human form he humbled himself and became obedient unto death, even death on a cross. Therefore God has highly exalted him and bestowed on him the name which is above every name, that at the name of Jesus every knee should bow, in heaven and on earth and under the earth, and every tongue confess that Jesus Christ is Lord, to the glory of God the Father."[11] Here the emptiness of kenosis is clearly balanced antithetically against the glorious fullness (pleroma) of exaltation Jesus received.

What, then, does this woefully brief synopsis of New Testament teaching on the glory of Christ tell us about church? In short, I would say, this: We are meant to deduce that the Apostolic preaching that flows from the Pentecostal Spirit, and that first initiates the church's mission of reconciliation on earth, is itself presented by the New Testament as a fundamental part of Jesus's resurrectional glory.[12] This is partly because the prime arena of where the dominion of Jesus as Lord (his doxa) is manifested in history is the church, his special communion of followers and disciples, who thus form an abiding presence in this world of the dawning Kingdom of righteousness and peace he promised throughout his preaching. The New Testament teaches, then, two significant things in relation to the church. The first is that it is a mysterious and transcendent part of Jesus's Lordly glory: an eschatological reality, not entirely reducible to a historical or sociological phenomenon (the number of people at any given time who claim to be Christians). The second is that it is per se the fundamental sign, or witness, of the dawning advent of the Kingdom of God on earth: that Kingdom of God's perfected will that would one day accomplish history and terminate it, when God's intent for his creation would be all in all. This latter aspect could be summed up as concluding that the New Testament doctrine of church defines the church community as an extension of the Risen Lord's exalted body. It is often called, especially as based on the formative writings of the apostle Paul, the "Mystical Body of Christ"; and just as Christ was himself a sign, or sacrament, of the Kingdom in the world throughout his ministry, the church too has the destiny to be a sacrament of reconciliation and hope in its own historical journey through the ages.

A SPECIFIC PHILOSOPHY OF

CHURCH HISTORY

What does it mean, then, to consider church as first and foremost a part of the resurrection glory given to Jesus? Like the divine doxa itself, which in part we can see and feel, and which in larger part escapes our grasp because it is an ineffable mystery, the church shares in that character of being visible and approachable, and yet also mysterious and ungraspable. It is like the Risen Jesus himself, who appears to his disciples, speaks and drinks with them—but then mysteriously disappears; or having proved his embodiment by eating fish before their eyes, then walks through the door of the Upper Room and disappears as mysteriously as he came. He cannot quite be grasped even when he reveals himself to Mary in the garden. The Orthodox have always understood the church, therefore, to be fundamentally a mystery (*mysterion*), an energy in the world of Jesus as Risen Lord, the active grace of his presence (*parousia*) in history, made present there by the divine Spirit; but not primarily an association of people (like a club, a philosophical or philanthropic society) who align themselves with Jesus's values. It is an earthly and mystical *sacrament* (for this is the deeper sense of what the Orthodox mean when they speak of *mystery*—not a conundrum but a sacramental sign that has deeper connotations than appear). It is a sacrament of the presence of Christ in the world by virtue of the ever-active working of the Spirit, still being outpoured among men and women for their restoration to life.

And so, where the spirit of the Risen Jesus is present and active, there is either the seed or the deep root of the church; a perennial aspect of the glory of Christ and his outpouring of the Spirit on the world. This is why Jesus promised that his church would last until the end of time (Mt. 16.18; Mt. 28.19–20). It is also why the Orthodox see the church as essentially "catholic" in character: *katholike* is a Greek word that means universal: having universal extension, worldwide recognizability, and all-embracing significance for the salvation of the world.[13] The term "catholic" has often been used in the media to denote Roman Catholicism simply put, but this is a misuse of the word. Roman (a localizing adjective) sits ill with the concept of catholicity, which it here qualifies. "Roman Catholic" arose as a nomenclature especially after the Reformation divides of Western Christendom. But catholicity does not belong to a denomination, it belongs to the whole Church of Christ wherever catholicity of belief and its concomitant practices are represented.

I have written another, much larger book about the Orthodox Church, and in that volume such theological notions as these have had pride of place.[14] This book, being a short history in its scope, is not the place to develop profound theological discussions as such. But this very brief review of what the New Testament writers suggest about the nature of the church as a sign of the glory of the Risen Lord explains a very characteristic thing about how Orthodox Christians have approached the nature of church from the beginning to the present day; and in this they tend to appear as quite different from most other Christians in the West. This is because the Orthodox approach the concept of church transcendentally before they do so sociologically. Orthodox writers throughout history have seen the church as a congregation of the living that includes, as still active participants, the angels and the saints of earlier ages, as well as the believers who are currently alive on earth. The living faithful are seen, therefore, not as the owners of the corporation but rather as junior members of a communion that extends far beyond them in space and time, and that is only partially embodied within time and space in any historical locality.

Christians of the present age, then, are not seen as having either the power or the ability to alter the charter of what the church is, in order, for example, to update the scriptures' prescripts to modern conditions and attitudes. The Orthodox take seriously the apostolic injunction "Do not conform yourselves to this present age but be transformed by the renewal of your mind, that you may prove what is the will of God, what is good and acceptable and perfect" (Rom. 12.2). The Orthodox Church is not worried that it might not be sufficiently adapted to modern attitudes: it worries only that it might not fulfill its core mission of adapting society's disparate values to those of the Gospel it has been commissioned to preach to the world. This goes a long way to explaining the deeply conservative nature of Orthodox theological, moral, and institutional teachings. But it also raises another significant question for us at the outset of this book: What characterizes the division, or distinction, between what is a theological fact and what is a historical fact?

Christians would surely proclaim the Resurrection of Jesus as a historical fact. But it is also quite clearly an event that stands above history, not contained within it. Being that which Christians apply as the central point explaining history (the salvific Incarnation of the Son of God on earth), the Resurrection is not exactly a simple event, or a happening, inside the linear progression of a lot of other facts about Jesus: his height, his arrest and execution, for example. To say "Jesus died for the sins of the world" is a theological interpretation of a historical fact (Jesus was executed). One of the Jewish priests present at the Crucifixion, and hostile to what Jesus stood for, would surely be able to bear witness to the historicity of the death of Jesus but equally would surely not have confessed that this rather brutal execution was the core event of the covenant with the God of Israel. Only Christian believers would admit the latter. What divides them is the interpretation of the event. But evidently, neither friend nor foe can here avoid making an interpretation of the event of Jesus: the Christ event that stands at the very heart of what the church is too. Believers confess that their interpretation of the life of Jesus (making the Cross and Resurrection literally the *crux* of world history) is the correct interpretation (the Greek word for which is Orthodoxy, meaning "right opinion") and thus the essential truth of that moment in history. Nonbelievers will say that this is not the correct interpretation, and they might substitute a range of other possible ones.

One recent author expressed this issue starkly when he subtitled his study of the history of Jesus "The Life of a Mediterranean Jewish Peasant."[15] An Orthodox believer would find such an approach not only objectionable but also fundamentally misguided in the radical separation it makes between Jesus in his earthly, kenotic ministry up to his death, and Jesus in his heavenly glory after his Resurrection. Central to all Orthodox thought about Jesus (Christology as it has come to be called today) is the insistence on the hypostatic unity of the person of Jesus: at once Lord of the Ages and Suffering Servant of God; the same person simultaneously One of the Trinity and a suffering human teacher.[16]

Writers who like to dismiss all theological notions, or banish them from the field of history proper, of course like to believe that only they can get to the "real history" of events or people whom religious sentiment has smothered under layers of pious fancies. Cut away the theology and get back to real history is the order of their day. But in making this presupposition the dismissers too have already supplied their predetermined interpretation of Jesus while pretending this is a balanced or neutral analysis: in their case a heavily secularized non-theology. And they too, proceeding from such presuppositions, have then to excise all (and it is a great deal, most in fact) that is theological from the New Testament narratives (our primary sources of knowledge about the history of Jesus). Their method, of excising from the account all that has any appearance of the transcendent about it, leads the dismissers not to the simple evidential core of the narratives they pretend to expose as objective historians but rather to the heavily bowdlerized version of the events they are willing to read out of the partialized whole cloth of the material. At worst, they decide what they will find (according to set-out prescripts) and then they put it out on display with the panache of a magician pulling a bunch of flowers from a hat. But all the while the flowers were here, prepared in advance, as it were. The method is circular, and this is exactly why the so-called quest for the historical Jesus has, over two centuries of pursuit, with each generation of scholars claiming at last to be free from prejudice and presupposition, turned up so very different, and such thin, pictures of the alleged real Jesus of Nazareth.[17]

And so it is necessary from the beginning to admit that the Orthodox insist that church history is quintessentially a theological reading of historical events. It begins (as do the foundational sources) with Jesus of Nazareth, who is not taken as a Mediterranean peasant but rather taken as the Son of God. It focuses on his birth, which it reads as the Incarnation of the divine in history, it studies his Cross and Resurrection as one event of sacrificial death and glorious exaltation, and likewise it reviews the ongoing life of his church as the unfolding manifestation of a supreme eschatological action within the vehicle of linear history: that tension of the *ekklesia*, the church, acting within history and yet called to transcend it. In short, an Orthodox approach to the church works off the presupposition that God is Lord of world history; that Jesus is the divine Lord; that his Spirit continues his work of grace among humans; that his church represents the destiny of the human race—insofar as a particular material species of life—humanity—is called out of its natural limit (death and impermanence) to rise into immortality. These are absolute givens of any Orthodox theology, or of history for that matter. It amounts to what can be called a prophetic reading of history—and to this extent Orthodox church history is fundamentally shaped in its character by the selfsame motives and methods that created and developed the biblical narratives: that is, reading the world events as part of the teleotic acts of God within the cosmos.

All Christian Church historians in antiquity shared this biblicist view of history and seamlessly combined their historical statements with the interpretation of how this story of the church's life manifested its accord with God's plan. This was true among Christians from the first evangelists, of course, but applies clearly and explicitly from the writer of Acts onward (arguably the first church historian), who certainly designed his account as a sacred history. That commission then passed to the earliest writers of the Orthodox Church: historians such as Eusebius of Caesarea, Socrates Scholastikos, and Theodoret, and the great exegetes and philosophers such as Origen, Athanasius, and Augustine, who each saw the unfolding of the church's history as the manner in which God's plan of salvation was continually offered to the world, generation after generation, and who each recognized that this Jesus who came from the most humble origins in Nazareth was also the Chosen One, the Son of God, the Exalted Messiah, and the High Priest of Humanity. Like the very first disciples who knew Jesus personally, the Orthodox Church, in its writings and its confessions of prayer, maintains that this Son of Mary was also the Lord of Glory whom Peter spoke of at Pentecost (Acts 2.36): "Let all the house of Israel therefore know assuredly that God has made him both Lord and Christ, this Jesus whom you crucified."

But now that I have explained where I stand in terms of the philosophy of the history of the church, and how Orthodoxy sees the story of the church as simply, and straightforwardly, its own story, let us make a beginning with the actual narrative of events. As this will deal predominantly with New Testament evidences about the church (what the Orthodox see as their foundational charter), let us divide this next chapter into two parts: the first about proto-apostolic times, and the second about the immediate post-apostolic developments.

This material is embedded first in the evangelical traditions and then in the epistolary literature and the second-century Christian writings that show two different stages of the life of the church, one overlaying and absorbing the earlier. This pattern of adoption and development becomes constitutive of the ongoing experience of Christianity: it stores a vast amount of things, uses much of it but not all in every age, and adds to its store from new wisdoms learned in bitter troubles.

CHAPTER ONE

Ecclesial Foundations:
Proto- and Post-Apostolic Times

JESUS AND THE APOSTOLIC
CHARTER OF THE CHURCH

The past two centuries have seen massive and unprecedented levels of research on the history and teachings of Jesus. As a result, the texts composing the New Testament have received more, and closer, attention than at any previous time in the church's history. This is not to say that the scriptures were not attended to in former ages—far from it. There is not a single verse of the Bible that had not already received massive amounts of comment from the writers of antiquity, the Middle Ages, and early modernity; but the manner of approach followed the customs and prescripts of ancient literary criticism. Modern historical research, growing ever more sophisticated in its deductive methods, follows a very different set of prescripts and methods.

The ancient writers, to paint a picture in large brush strokes, tended to read the text symbolically: stories and things very often "stood for" something else. The escape of

Israel through the Red Sea, for example, was a macro symbol of salvation. The Promised Land became, for Christians, a stand-in for Paradise. The physical Temple building (in John's Gospel) becomes an overarching symbol of Christ's person as a center of life-giving divine presence. The tendency of certain things standing in for other realities (an aspect more of Hellenistic literary interpretation than of Aramaic storytelling) can be seen at its most acute in what is often seen as Mark's own interpretation (Mk. 4.10–20) of the Parable of the Sower, which has just preceded it (Mk. 4.3–9).[1]

Like the biblical writers of even earlier ages, the evangelists and the patristic exegetes also preferred to speak in symbolic forms, often through the medium of the story. Storytelling, of course, demands (or usually did before the plotless novel arrived) a few core images and events around which the tale could be folded, intimated, and developed. Certain symbolic episodes are given priority over more standardized fill-in narratives. The Gospel texts, for example, show a relatively simple literary structure: though it is different in each case for the four canonical writers: Mark, Matthew, Luke, and John. John builds his narrative around seven great "signs" (selected representative miracles) to encapsulate the ministry of Jesus and his theological significance, and also builds up a series of grand symbols and themes (such as Jesus and the Temple, and Israel's great cycle of festivals) to advance his teachings. Mark has a simple literary structure where he bookends the narratives about Jesus into five sections, each begun with an episode that either is repeated shortly afterward or starts with half the narrative and completes that same story shortly afterward. The five chosen bookends are symbolic summations of the teaching and status of Jesus and set the tone of the material that he assembles within each section, moving from his parables and miracles toward a deepening sense of foreboding as the meaning of his death is adumbrated. In this way Mark cuts up his entire Gospel into five *teuchoi*, or books.[2] These are immediately obvious (and necessary) to a reader of a scroll.[3] Mark's subliminal message is that just as Moses offered five volumes to the Jews (*Penta-Teuchoi* in Greek), so Jesus is now offering a new covenant to Gentiles, in his five Greek volumes (the new Pentateuch) of the Gospel.[4] In his Gospel Luke structures his text around a great Journey of Jesus, making it that all of Jesus's life was set on reaching its Exodus at Jerusalem.[5] He also has sophisticated ideas of Jesus as the midpoint of time, helping him to assemble the teachings of Jesus with a particular slant.[6] Like Mark, but in a more overtly traditional way, Matthew also sets Jesus's teaching in forms that parallel it with the teachings of Moses, but with a heavy stress on new fulfillments: "You have heard it said . . . but I say to you" (e.g., Mt. 5.21–22).

Because of this great labor expended on patterns of biblical interpretation over the past century in particular, today's generation of interpreters have gained greater confidence in being able to distinguish between, on the one hand, the forms of the Aramaic preaching of Jesus and his apostles in the first generation and, on the other, that of the more overtly Greek disciples of the second apostolic age, which we might, for brevity's sake, classify as (a) the era of Paul and the first Greek evangelists,[7] (b) the time of the New Testament Epistles other than Paul, and (c) that of the apostolic fathers of the late first century.[8] It is to be understood, of course, that one has access only to the preaching of Jesus and the very first disciples through the medium of (a) onward, there being no direct, unmediated, testimony from the hand or voice of Jesus. While some commentators seem to lament this fact, what the Orthodox would deduce from this is that Jesus comes to the world only from the Spirit through the church. The experience of the disciple's illumined faith is the seed bed from which all testimony, beginning with the written Gospels themselves, arises as an act of confession. As the Word is incarnated in the flesh of Jesus, just so is the Spirit articulated in the illumined medium of the church: that body of believers whom the Spirit lifts to confess Jesus as Lord (1 Cor. 12.3b). For Orthodoxy, there is no great chasm to be found between the teachings of Jesus and the manner in which his first disciples, the apostles, and the evangelists passed on those teachings. They may well have nuanced them for their various audiences; they did not make them up out of thin air. Just so, for the Orthodox, therefore, the fidelity of the later believers, in matters of the transmission of the teachings, needs to match the fidelity and carefulness of the first. There is, then, not a decisive differentiation in the Orthodox Church's understanding between scripture and tradition in the theology of revelation—a much controverted point of dispute between the Roman Catholic and Reformed theologians—there is only the single sense of the Sacred Tradition of Revelation given in the formation of the church.[9] Although that sacred tradition (*Paradosis*) is first manifested, and given its most authoritative and governing expression, in the New Testament itself, it is not restricted to it, insofar as it is ever continued in the ongoing life of the church, in its saints' lives and teachings, and in its sacramental mysteries, even to the ages to come.[10]

THE APOSTLES' RECEPTION OF THE
TEACHING OF JESUS

The recent scholarly distinctions of the first levels of the history of the church have made it possible now to consider how the message of Jesus himself was transmitted in the very first generation of the church. They have also, because the detail is very sparse and highly controvertible in its interpretation, given rise to a flourishing of speculation passing off as history. But it is important to know that the record is very patchy and one can only make deductions, from the reports that do survive, about the conditions that "might have" applied elsewhere. In relation to the life and teachings of Jesus, however, it is generally agreed that the burden of the Lord's own preaching was the message of the proximity of the Kingdom of God, and the need for a readjustment of attitude among the men and women of Israel in the light of that news.[11] This can be classed as an eschatological message in the sense that the late prophetic idiom of eschatology chose a dramatic incident of the advent of God's power felt in the world to focus the issue of repentance for Israel.[12]

This was a sharpened form of the traditional prophetic call for the people to renew their covenant fidelity. Many modern German- and English-speaking commentators had been led astray by Albert Schweitzer, writing in the early decades of the twentieth century, to overstate Jesus's messianic apocalypticism.[13] But that influence has fast been waning, and rightly so, for it is equally clear from abundant evangelical evidence that Jesus was more than a preacher of end times, and very much a teacher of repentance as the way to covenant restoration, as well as an interpreter of the Torah in the Wisdom (sophianic) tradition of the Old Testament. Repentance (*metanoia*) was the first recorded word spoken by Jesus (Mk. 1.15) and reappears throughout all his teachings in a variety of images and stories.[14] It is characterized, perhaps, most of all by that change of heart witnessed in the famed Parable of the Prodigal Son (Lk. 115.11–32).

Mid-twentieth-century approaches massively overstressed the identity of Jesus as an apocalyptic prophet, but it is clear from the whole cloth of his recorded life and teachings that moral exhortation, exorcism, healings and other great prophetic signs, and a good deal of sophianic material, were equally a constitutive part of Jesus's deliberate ministry.[15] Recent studies have also drawn attention to the manner in which the Greek Gospel writers highlight Jesus's role as moral teacher, comparable to the Greek sages of old.[16] What looms over it all, of course, in the way the evangelists received and re-presented the Jesus story in their various Gospels, is the great Passion and Resurrection account. In Mark it casts its shadow over the entire narrative. Twenty percent of the whole story of the life of Jesus is given over to his last week on earth, and in all the other Gospels the Passion story looms almost as large.

The message Jesus preached of the advent of the Kingdom called on his contemporary Jewish listeners to return (Hebrew *shub*) to the God of the covenant in a renewed dedication. He offered signs of his authority to be the one who called Israel back to God's favor, in the style of the great prophet Elijah. In his day illness was seen as a demonic assault on the well-being of a trapped soul. So it was not healings and exorcisms Jesus offered as signs of his theology; it was rather a consistent set of exorcisms (the healings to be included within that category) acting out the overall message that as God had once more, and wondrously, drawn near to Israel to call out to it, just so Israel needed to soften its heart and find forgiveness. This return to God would be like a return to life, a recovery from paralysis, a gaining of sight from former blindness. The powerful acts of Jesus (*pace* Morton Smith) were not done in the mode of a Hellenistic *Magus*, a magician who wanted to dazzle and impress an audience by superhuman power, but rather in the manner of a teacher of virtue showing how much a life turned away from God was a living death.[17] There is a great and humble understatement in the works of Jesus that is wholly missing in the (vast) surviving records of Hellenistic magic, and always an underlying theological pointing to the way the deeds reminisce the presence of God as felt in the earlier prophets (especially Elijah). The deeds support the message. The message is encapsulated in the healing and liberation that are effected in the deed.

The parables of the Kingdom show this message more expansively in narrative form. All turn on the surprise of God's advent: that it is so close, and that it is so generously abundant in its promise. Many of the stories Jesus tells revolve around the theme of the wedding banquet, one of the few times in a year, in a typical Galilean village, when most of his first hearers would ever have more than enough to eat and drink. Core to Christ's own theology of the Kingdom was the idea of the great joy one found in discovering God's reconciliation. It was like finding out to one's great surprise that God was a prodigally generous father, ready to throw a rich robe over the wastrel son, or a giver of harvests that offered a hundredfold return for the small capital expended.

Clearly, toward the end of what was possibly only his second year of preaching this *kerygma* (or proclamation) of joyful repentance that was the "one thing that mattered," Jesus learned that many of the leaders of the people (especially the Temple priesthood) rejected his view of God's benevolently merciful fatherhood (and a need to establish reconciliation that went above and beyond any sacrificial cult) and instead insisted that the only way to God's favor was the established path of the Torah regulations, in particular the expensive Temple sacrifices. These legal regulations had accumulated over centuries to become increasingly burdensome for an observant Jew in Jesus's day, but this path was represented by the Pharisees, who generally found the doctrines of Jesus, and his attitude to God's merciful benevolence, to be dangerously lax and disrespectful of the Law.

As Jesus moved toward Jerusalem for his final Passover there, his sensibility that he was risking his life for his teaching grew ever stronger.[18] Even so he was driven onward by his sense that he was God's chosen agent, or *Shaliach*, the Apostle of the Father, sent directly by him just as he himself had selected the disciples to be his own apostles (shaliachim).[19] For Jesus, this sending contained within it the authority (*exousia*) of God himself. His sense of being the messenger of God was distinctly different from a sense of hired servant (although his obedience to the Father was profoundly marked): it was colored through and through by his awareness that he was the Beloved Son of the Merciful Father, and the essence of the faith the disciples had in him from the very outset (and have retained through all subsequent history) is that this insight was not only true but truer in a fuller sense than they had realized before his death, and it was shown, in his resurrection glory, to be the quintessential summing up of his doctrine of the reconciling Kingdom. In short, Jesus glorified was proven to be the message itself: his death and glorification were the deeds that made the new covenant of reconciliation. His Cross opened the gate of Paradise.

The symbolic sign that Jesus decided on when he arrived in Jerusalem was the turning over of the tables in the underground passages of the Temple (the *Hoddayot*, where the animals were sold for sacrifice). It underscored his radical doctrine that God's forgiveness did not need to be bought ("What I want is mercy not sacrifice," Mt. 9.13), but it was a direct challenge to the Temple priests and their theology that the sacrifices were the essential sustenance of the covenant. It was the priesthood that very quickly afterward, using the Roman authorities, arranged Jesus's execution.

This brief discussion hardly does justice to the whole doctrine of Jesus as recounted in the New Testament, but it is important at least to try to give a synopsis of the baseline teachings. Now, before we turn our attention momentarily from what the Lord himself was saying and enacting, and move on to how the first apostles heard and interpreted him in their oral preaching that founded the apostolic church, it will be useful to pause for a moment and ask what this core proclamation of Jesus serves to do in defining that church that is born from it. And here I would suggest that this nexus of his own theology sets the charter for his church, under his aegis, to be essentially: the locus of the encounter with God; the arena of finding forgiveness and grace; the company entrusted with repeating the message that there is a great joy of salvation near at hand; the body of those who have believed that there is one thing that matters in reference to God—and that is the rightness of the heart, against which all other things fade in significance, since God "looks at the heart"; the family of those who venerate the Son in his glory, knowing that this is the gift of sonship given out as a new inheritance; the communion of those who wish to bring God's just mercy into play in the immediacy of their society.[20] These things, then, devolve directly from Jesus's own preaching of the Kingdom. Together with his ever-implicit profession that he himself is the Chosen Son of God, they served as that doctrine and presence first delivered to the apostles as their basic *paideia*, or instructional formation, to be passed on to the church as its first apostolic foundation.

The church, if it is to remain faithful to its evangelical charter, must always check itself against such foundational principles. This is the earliest and classic formulation of what Orthodoxy is. The meaning of "correct opinion" is the definition of the word "Orthodoxy," and it is this theology sketched out above that is the core system that all other Orthodox teachings—those about the church itself, or about a canon of scripture, or any other dogmatic matter—must defer to. It can be summed up in four simple words that can hardly be exegeted: the Mystery of Christ.

One important thing still needs to be mentioned in relation to the ministry of Jesus. For, "on the night before he died," as the liturgical tradition of the Orthodox Church never tires of repeating at its eucharists, Jesus knew that the whole topography of his ministry was turning on a new axis. His bold claim that God was renewing the covenant with Israel gave way to a sense that somehow in his own death and suffering (for in that last week in Jerusalem he now saw his arrest as imminently forthcoming) was the sacrificial event to

end all sacrifice: to make a new covenant with God and his
followers on the basis of his fidelity to the Father. Seeing the
Passover meal set before him, he thinks no longer of the bread
and wine of joyous feasting but now of the bread that has to
be broken apart in order to be of use; and the wine that is the
ominous color of blood. The New Passover meal now becomes a commemoration of his death and his hopes for the
continuing overshadowing of the hand of God: "He took
some bread and when he had said the blessing he broke it and
gave it to them. Take this, he said, It is my body. Then he took
a cup and when he had returned thanks he gave it to them. . . .
This is my blood, the blood of the Covenant, which is to be
poured out for many" (Mk. 14.22–25).

THE FIRST-GENERATION
APOSTOLIC TRADITION

It was this moment (underscored by the subsequent reflection
that they had all abandoned him in his hour of need in Gethsemane) that sobered the theologies of the apostles in the
time after the death of Jesus, that time when they first began
to muse on his teachings, the import of his miracles—but
most of all, the significance and meaning of his death and its
aftermath. This Last Supper, which is called in the Orthodox
world the Mystical Supper, was the pristine lens through
which all of Jesus's life, acts and teachings were now to be
focused for the apostolic generation. It is this apostolic tradition that is eventually crystallized in the New Testament texts
by the time the next generation comes. Then it moves from
Aramaic to Greek. But more essentially than that, it has
moved from being a simple record of what Jesus said and did

(as if he were just an example of moral sage or rabbinic Torah interpreter) and has become a matter of how his death and resurrection informed and synopsized everything the Lord meant about the coming Kingdom of God. If Jesus preached the Kingdom, then the apostles clearly preached Jesus as the potent sacrament of that Kingdom.

This first level of apostolic doctrine, then, shifts Christologically: toward the fuller meditation on the significance of the status of Jesus as redeeming Son of God; bringer of salvation to the world. This constant pushing of the Christological question, first elicited from the apostles by Jesus himself (Mk. 8.27–29), becomes the leitmotif of the first-generational apostolic teachings that become enshrined, subsequently, in the form of the Greek text of the New Testament. It is given a synoptic account in the Acts of the Apostles, in the style of an ancient historian (Luke) making a great leader (Peter) give voice to the essential philosophy at stake in a decisive moment of the historical narrative. Though Luke has, as it were, rhetorically shaped the Petrine sermon on Pentecost Day, we have no reason to think he has substantially misrepresented the generic character of Peter's preaching of Jesus's Kingdom, since this is also abundantly witnessed in the Gospels of Mark and Matthew. In that classic Petrine sermon in Acts 2.14–40 we see the shape of the earliest Christian sermons of the late first century, much illustrated by biblical proof-texts, and we note how the Christology of glorification is the axis around which the understanding of salvation turns: "This Jesus you crucified ... but God raised him up, undoing the punishments of death." "Repent and be baptized ... in the Name of Jesus Christ for the forgiveness of sins, and you shall receive the Holy Spirit."

THE SECOND-GENERATION
APOSTOLIC TRADITION

By the time of the transition from the first to the second century, and increasingly enriched by Saint Paul's teachings on the implications of the glorification of Christ, the apostolic kerygma begins to reflect more and more on the cosmic significance of the Glorified Christ. The pressure for this is most likely the manner in which that kerygma is being more and more picked up by Gentiles who are not as bound up in the chains of biblical proof-citations that were familiar to the first Hebrew and Aramaic speakers who had grown up in the synagogues. The Greek culture is not as alien to the generation of Jesus's first disciples as was customarily thought up to the middle of the twentieth century; but it is clear that the Christian movement, with Saint Paul as its great advocate, moves more and more toward a Gentile audience in the late first century: so much so that even by the time of Mark's Gospel in the seventies the evangelist has to explain basic Jewish customs (Mk. 7.3–4). The Epistles to the Ephesians and the Colossians, two closely related letters, represent the fruit of this second-stage apostolic reflection on the glory of Christ and the nature of his church. Their theology, summing up all of Paul's mystical doctrine of redemption, is conveyed in a spirit of liturgical hymnody, the crucible in which all authentic Orthodox theology has developed ever since; for if one wishes to find what Orthodoxy really represents, one needs to immerse oneself in its worship before studying its theology manuals. The election of the church is stated in Ephesians to predate history, since it is vested in that eternal love which co-inheres in the divine Trinity: "Blessed be the God and

Father of Our Lord Jesus Christ who blessed us with all the spiritual blessings of heaven in Christ. Before the world was made he chose us, chose us in Christ, to be holy and spotless and to live through love in his presence" (Eph. 1.3–4). The church is a profound mystery of Christ's own being: it is life "in Christ." The glorified Christ, through his church, is manifested as the axis of cosmic reconciliation: an *anakephalaiosis* of all things: "The mystery of his purpose . . . to bring all things together under Christ as the Head" (Eph. 1.9–10).[21]

This glorification in Christ is now seen as part of the divine glory that shines out in the person of Christ: "This you can tell from the strength of [the Father's] power at work in Christ, when he used it to raise him from the dead and to make him sit at his right hand in heaven: far above every Sovereignty, Power, or Domination, or any other name that can be named; not only in this age but also in the age to come" (Eph. 1.19–22).[22] The glory in which God has manifested the fulfillment (teleiosis) of Christ's work is that he is exalted as head of the church: "He has put all things under his feet, and made him, as the Ruler of Everything, the Head of the Church, which is his body, the fullness of him who fulfills the whole creation" (Eph. 1.22–23). In Colossians, which contains a shorter, more creed-like version of the Ephesians' hymn to Christ, the apostolic reflection elaborates how, if this cosmic fulfillment is perfected in history, it must echo the intent of God's plan prepared from before time (as in Eph. 1.9); and so Christ's primary role in fashioning the very structures of creation is affirmed, just as it is in the Johannine Gospel (Jn. 8.58): "He is the Icon of the Unseen God, the firstborn of all creation; for in him were created all things in heaven and on earth . . . all things were created through him and for him.

And before anything was created He existed, and he holds all things in unity. And the Church is his body, and he is its head" (Col. 1.15–18).

From this point onward, we have more or less all the fundamental statements of the Nicene Creed; for almost every line of that fourth-century liturgical song is collated from New Testament citations. The church, therefore, if not the selfsame mystery as the Kingdom that is to come (when God's times are fulfilled) is at least the present radiance of the Kingdom promised, and a sign of its continued working within history. Over the church, Christ presides in glory, continuing the task of reconciliation, which is what binds the cosmos in unity. For the Orthodox this is fundamentally what the term "church" signifies, before it means any sociological phenomenon: the mystery of salvation that shines out in the power of the Spirit.

These are lofty and difficult reflections to state, let alone to grasp. They give evidence of the high spiritual insight of the first apostolic generation. Theologians that came after it were not always so skilled, and certainly in the second century we see something of a dip in the vigor and profundity of Christian literature after the age of apostles. It is a slight depression, as it were, that lasts for a century and a half before the quality of Christian literature begins once more to pick up in the writings of the great fathers. In that transitional time we see certain things happening in the ongoing formation of the church. The first is that a fair deal of flimsy and fanciful literature starts being produced. Eager for more stories about Jesus—his childhood and alleged secret sayings—writers start inventing very Hellenized accounts. Jesus begins to be drawn in the style of a Hellenistic magician. His miracles become mere show-off feats. He is easily angered by those who do not show him respect. It is all a world away from what clearly was becoming a difficult idea to accept for the wider Greek world: that the real Jesus of the Gospel picture was profoundly humble and non-self-referential.

In the face of this rise of extraneous materials, the church leaders were called on to make quality-control judgments. Eventually this is why the so-called Gnostic literature and the apocryphal Gospels, almost all postdating the New Testament by at least a century, were soon set aside as noncanonical. This means that the early church leaders of worship generally did not want them read out at the Eucharist. This process of what should and should not be read out at common worship is fundamentally what now determines a "canon," a Greek word for the accepted standard list of scripture texts. We see in this the formation of the larger New Testament considered as a collection of authoritative apostolic instructions. The completion of this canon of scripture is a process that would continue more slowly from this point onward, in one form or another, until the internationally spread communities that now constituted the early church began to work on the principle of mutual acceptance of good practice and settled on an agreed canon of scripture.[23] This would not be until the middle of the fourth century. The noncanonical literature, however, was not proscribed by some form of oppressive censorship. There was no one in the church at this period who held such coercive power. The failure of the apocryphal literature to gain hold was more the death process of a remaindered literature. And, unlike the Gospels, this never was a literature for the people. It was obscure and elitist and demanded a high reliance on skilled interpreters to access its hidden meanings. It has little in it that smacks of common sense. It was not so much proscribed out of existence as not wanted. And literature that is not particularly wanted (not particularly good) does not travel. The four Gospels traveled to the ends of the earth because they were fresh and alive by comparison.

But although the agreement over the canon was a highly important aspect of church life, it was not the only thing that was being shaped and developed so as to give the historical experience of the church some concrete forms and structures. Much that went on in this respect can be said to be hidden: the quality of the faith and holiness of believers, for example. We know of the likes of the martyrs, but rare is any outward expression, at this period, of the inner life of believers. How could it be expressed except through literary form—and at this stage the genres of Christian hagiography had not been fully explored.[24] What does become more settled is the style of Christian worship. The Psalms are soon adopted as the prayer book of the church, and several early treatises begin to invite the Christians to read them as the living voice of Christ himself, not simply the prayers of ancient Israelite priests and Levites. The ritual of the Eucharist also becomes the central act of worship in the church. Around the central affirmation of what the Lord did "on the night before he died" the church gathers Old Testament texts of prophecy that show how these things were foretold in symbols. And equally, against the Old Testament symbols, evangelical passages are selected out from the whole narratives and set against the old stories in patterns of prediction and fulfillment. So, even as early as the Greek Gospels we can see Old Testament motifs juxtaposing things like Isaiah's Suffering Servant with the

Passion narratives; and symbols like Jonah in the Whale with Christ's burial; or the Crossing of the Red Sea with baptismal and paschal rituals in the church. The surviving homily of Bishop Melito of Sardis entitled *On the Passover*, which was his speech during the Eucharist of Easter Night sometime around the middle of the second century, is a fine example of this style of approach; and it shows how the church's understanding of scripture went hand in hand with ongoing formation of worship structures. Liturgy is the engine of development in all this.

THE AGE OF THE APOSTOLIC FATHERS

This is certainly why the leadership of the Christian congregations soon settles down after the apostolic age to be represented by the persons who led worship: the presiders over the Eucharist. It was their function, rarely shared out in any democratic sense until the modern age, to deliver the interpretation of the sacred texts that had been read out before the bread and wine were consecrated. Their homily was an integral part of the Eucharist: a way of showing how the Passion and Resurrection of Jesus (summated in the bread and wine now being offered) stood as the fulfillment of the salvation narratives that were being read aloud. The president of the worship was thus the one who had to link Word and Sacrament. Such a leader required not only a rhetorical gift (in an age that held rhetoric in high esteem) but also some degree of character, for the one who offered the great eucharist prayer to God, in Christ, was expected to demonstrate high spiritual acumen too. Such preachers, exegetes, public speakers, and ceremonial prayer presiders, all rolled into one, lived in an age where we know there were, as yet, no formal books of Christian prayers. These were made up, composed in a free spirit, as the leader presided, which, being repeated week after week, called for some degree of creativity. Accordingly, these liturgical officers, expected to be multitaskers from the outset, quickly acquired the role of supervisors over the general conduct of the community. Evidence from the earliest centuries of the churches in cities tends to suggest that they were drawn from the more wealthy and educated members of the church. This would mean they already had some rhetorical and leadership training, and also had property in which the community might gather. Very rarely surviving church buildings from this era, such as the second-century church at Dura Europos and the fourth-century shrine of Santi Giovanni e Paolo on Rome's Caelian Hill, show that these large houses were probably bequeathed to the community as permanent places of worship. Of course, in smaller villages a more modest "house church" arrangement might be expected; but one should not underestimate how quickly a community would want a building of its own. At this time there was no overarching authority structure to compel uniformity. It seems to have been generally agreed that those who knew the apostles, or could trace their lineage back to them, were held in very high esteem. Wandering ascetics, lifelong celibates, and inspired Christian prophets were also given high standing in the communities. A very early liturgical treatise called *The Didache* says that the local eucharistic presider should give way to one of these when they come through the town; but it also adds a cautionary note that the wandering prophets should never stay more than a few days in any one place. Their function is to move around and serve as missionaries of renewal.

As there was no single source of compulsive power in the early church, how was it that by the third century a fair degree of uniform conformity starts being witnessed in the various churches across a wide remit of the Roman Empire? It was surely that principle at work once more that determines the progress of most human groups: the innate instinct to watch over the garden fence and to copy the successful practice of others. So it was that the Letters of Saint Paul, first read in the churches to which they were addressed by that now legendary hero, came to be bundled together and read in many more churches, and eventually in all the churches. So too letters from famous martyrs such as Ignatius of Antioch started to be read in more churches than just those of Asia Minor; and so his teachings gained in international stature. Forms of worship—how psalms were assigned, or what poems were useful in liturgical intervals; what was a "really good" eucharistic prayer to use if one really did not feel up to making up a new one week by week—all these things started to spread throughout the second century, so as to become an established international practice by the third.

One of the offices most instrumental in all this was the church liturgical president, the *episcopos*, or overseer/superintendent. His office began to reach out over and across a range of other spiritual and institutional offices that we find witnessed in the very early Church (prophets, exorcists, healers, virgins, widows, deacons, gatekeepers, grave-keepers) and served to coordinate them. This very soon meant the episcopos had authority to exercise over them. The first instance of this is that the overseer of the Eucharist begins to emerge in the second and third centuries from the congregation of elders (*presbyteroi*) who formerly had all concelebrated together.

The elders, or presbyters, retained their spiritual standing but gave way when it came to preaching scripture. This was reserved as the function of the episcopos. Old English gives us a mutated form of this word: bishop. In the earliest city churches the three leading offices were bishop, presbyter, and deacon. The deacon took charge of the social outreach of the church and its finances, and thus had the potential to be a powerful agent in the church. But as the number of Christians extended, it was no longer possible to retain the simpler pattern of one town, one church, one bishop with his presbyters around one altar. Other suburban churches had to be built, and to these outlying edifices a presbyter was sent. So it was that it eventually became standard for the bishop to preside in the main city church with his deacons, while the presbyters went out independently to sanctuaries farther afield in suburbs and villages. The deacon retained an influential position but was now heavily subordinated to the bishop, who was so close at hand. When a bishop died and needed to be replaced, it was often the senior deacon who succeeded. But the presbyters retained their established rights, that only they and the bishop could preside over the Eucharist.

At first, as their very title suggests, the elders were probably the senior members of the Christian community whose quality of spirituality had recommended itself to the larger body of faithful. Confessors, those who had shown bravery and had survived persecution times, were also regarded as highly authoritative in the earliest communities. What was happening more and more across the international church in the second century was that the earliest traveling charismatic offices were giving way to a more locally established institution of offices. Because so many of the largest Christian communities were to be found in the maritime cities of the Roman Empire, where trade entailed regular passage of personnel from one zone to the other, what worked institutionally in one Christian church was soon found to be passed on to another. Establishment of structure and order grew by the spread of good, observed practice. By the end of the second century that establishment of an international pattern spread into the inland hinterlands too, a process that continued into the early fourth century and was fixed by the clear and widespread rise of the monarchical episcopate by the end of the third century. By the fourth century, in the Constantinian establishment of the church, bishops (at least those of the larger cities) were elevated to a status equivalent to that of imperial magistrates, and this sealed their position as the most notable persons of the region. By the end of the fourth century the rule of the bishop in his local diocese, subject more regionally to the supervision of the province's synod of other bishops (who submitted themselves to a collegial responsibility), served to set the local charters of the Christian communities across large zones of the empire. When truly international disputes and crises began to arise after the end of the third century the favor of the newly Christianized emperors brought in a system of super-synods, meetings of bishops greater than those of a particular province, which were accordingly called "ecumenical."[25]

By the third century bishops and presbyters, at least in the cities, were increasingly drawn from the more educated classes, and so we then see the rise of a theologically literate leadership. It is an age of more rapid developments, for once text was used as a medium of transmission of ideas, change happened more quickly than when one community looked over the shoulder of another to see what was best practice. The style of the development of the church in the third-century patristic age is the subject of a later chapter. For the moment let us return briefly to looking in at the window of the late first century, with a short review of a very remarkable set of letters that have survived from this time, the so-called Ignatian dossier.

This series of epistles tells us much about how this episcopal system of establishing an international order in Christian affairs gelled into place from the end of the first century onward. Ignatius was the eucharistic president, the episcopos, of the great city of Antioch. In the year 105 he was denounced to the authorities as a Christian leader, arrested, and taken under a guard of ten soldiers to Trajan's Rome. His guards disliked the whole idea of the journey, and they often bullied him. It was also Ignatius's responsibility to pay all the expenses as they journeyed from one city to another on the way to Rome. Trying to facilitate his passage as best he could, Ignatius wrote to the other bishop-episcopoi of the Asia Minor cities that lay along his path, asking them for food and accommodation. The bishop of Smyrna (Izmir), named Polycarp, became a champion of Ignatius, whom he saw as a martyr and confessor, and he not only arranged his reception by the other bishops of Asia Minor but also collected all the letters he wrote and circulated them. These writings of Ignatius and the late letters of Paul that speak of the establishment of the bishop-successor to the apostles are major factors in both witnessing the rise of the monarchical episcopate and ensuring its widespread adoption in the churches.

Ignatius projects the bishop as the source of unity in the local church insofar as he presides over the council of presbyters and the deacons, holding together in unity the celebration of the whole church's Eucharist. For Ignatius, the bishop stands as the iconic image of Jesus himself. His role as teacher of doctrine is underlined. In this respect Ignatius's letters witness how these earliest bishops often wrote to one another to give reports of what was happening in their churches. We have instances of other bishops sending one another letters to keep one another up to date. They are collectively known as *Eirenika*, or letters of peace. It seems to have been a primary way by which bishops tried to maintain lines of contact, creating a commonality between the city churches on the basis of the communion they established with brother bishops in the surrounding region. This would grow in later ages to become the principle of the synodical governance of all the ancient Eastern and Western Churches.

Ignatius writes conscious that he is the leader of the great church of Antioch. He warns his brother bishops in Asia Minor of alarming developments there: namely, that some believers had so glorified the spiritual stature of Christ that they had felt it necessary to deny that he was a fleshly being too.[26] In his letters we see certain characteristics that recur in the later principle of the episcopal governance of the Great Church: that the bishop is the successor of the apostles' authority; that he has this authority as a senior and spirit-filled Christian who continues the apostolic tradition of teachings (the scriptural consensus) and does not deflect from it; that he has the right to warn as well as teach; that he governs and keeps good order in the public worship of the church (by including or excluding extraneous texts or dissident teachers); that he ensures the connectivity of the churches and their staying in harmony with one another in terms of faith and order.

The presbyters and deacons become his eucharistic collaborators. This hierarchy, a Greek word that means "sacred order of leadership" is appointed by God to stabilize the church after the age of the apostles has passed. Together with the writings of the second-century bishop Irenaeus of Lyons, this notion of the episcopal order representing the apostolic succession in the church is a foundational element of the age of transition from the New Testament era to that of the formative ages of the second and third centuries when many other aspects of common governance and structure were then set in place. These centuries are in many ways the embryonic age when the recognizable practices that make up much of the Orthodox practice even today are brought into the light, commonly agreed across a wide range of the ancient churches, and refined in their development: things such as patterns of daily prayer, repeated styles that become the internationally accepted liturgical forms (with enduring variations in Eastern and Western customs), and orders for festivals and other sacraments, such as baptism, marriage, ordination, confession, and healing rituals.

Like young and vigorous seedlings, many of the structures laid down by the end of the first century (and designed to incardinate the apostolic teachings of the New Testament) were going to grow in stability and refinement over the next two centuries. In doing so they also become more visible to the historian. Contrary to what several European (mainly Protestant) commentators often used to say in the mid-twentieth century, there is next to no real evidence at all that there was some common form of culture shock among Christians of the late first century when Jesus's supposed imminent Second Coming did not materialize. This has increasingly come to be exposed as the invented hypothesis of the followers of Albert Schweitzer, an intellectual structure wholly superimposed on the earliest church evidences.[27] What is more fully witnessed everywhere is a strong and continuing development of the principles of the apostolic teaching in ever more settled urban environments of church communities clustered around the local celebrations of the Eucharist, each with a close eye on what neighboring brotherhoods were up to. The second and third centuries, if the first is an embryonic stage, are more and more recognizable in their classical lineaments.

CHAPTER TWO

Shaping Orthodoxy, Mapping Heresy

THE SECOND-CENTURY CHURCH THEOLOGIANS

It is the period of the second to third centuries where we first find individual Christian theologians standing out of the crowd.[1] It is the beginning of the age of theological treatises, and accordingly our knowledge of the life of the various churches of the Eastern and Western Roman Empire (what will eventually become the domains of the Greek Orthodox and Latin Churches) becomes more sharply clarified.[2] Most of the writers of these treatises are officeholders in the early communities: bishops or presbyters. Some, like Tertullian the North African lawyer (active circa 155–240), are moved to write in outrage against the unjust persecutions the church was facing. Under ancient Roman law a refusal to honor the gods of Rome was classed as not only a sacrilegious offense but also (on the grounds that the Roman pantheon assured the security of the empire) a treasonable affair of the highest order. In law, therefore, religious dissidence such as that ascribed to Christians was punishable by the most severe penalties without judges having to go through the full legal process. Tertullian became a vigorous defender of the church's institutions. He witnesses how Christianity was beginning to attract intellectuals to itself. He was the well-educated son of a pagan centurion and used his polished rhetorical skills in the service of the church. A very robust and able apologist against pagan cruelties, he also turned his fire on dissident elements that disrupted the unity of the churches in a sectarian way. In an influential treatise called *On the Prescription of Heretics*, written at the end of the second century, he developed the arguments against dissidence found in the late Johannine Letters and stood against the claims that anyone could speak for the church, insisting that one had to truly belong to it first, and to have absorbed its inner traditions.[3] In this work he systematically drew up arguments that clarified how apostolic tradition was to be recognized, not only by its content, but also by its widespread adoption among the great churches.[4] He mentioned with approval that already by the middle of the second century the bishops of the Eastern Church had agreed to meet regularly in synods, a word that means conventions, to regulate doctrine and practice. Several of his other works made a more detailed attack against specific dissident groups. His book *Against Marcion* argued that the eponymous Pontic theologian had falsified the Christian tradition by refusing to acknowledge the Old Testament as a legitimate and authoritative source of Christian theology.[5] In his work *On the Flesh of Christ* he argued that docetic believers who resisted the idea of Jesus truly inhabiting a fleshly body and earthly life had equally voided the idea of the redemptive incarnation of the Word of God. In early Greek philosophy *hairesis*, or heresy, had chiefly meant a divergent point of view within a philosophical school: whether one thought the world was round or flat, for example. Though often bitterly disputed, such divergent views were accepted as part of the intellectual process of questing after the truth. Tertullian marks a watershed moment in Christian affairs. Having reflected deeply on the antisecessionist views found in the late apostolic letters, he shows that if apostolic tradition is seriously compromised by any group, those who profess that position have lost the claim to belong to the church.[6] Reflecting the apostolic warnings, he gives a legal force to that argument: belonging to the church demands a consensus of agreement to the moral and doctrinal teachings passed on from the apostles. Beyond this is myth, and allegiance to myths does not carry the blessing of the Spirit of God. From this time onward the church adopts the view that heresy (now defined as a significant intellectual and affective departure from apostolic tradition) places one outside the church altogether. Hairesis has become a term no longer signifying a dissident opinion within a school but instead signifying a concept that denotes a cultural loss of membership.

This decision, whether to tolerate or exclude, was more and more given to the elders and bishops who presided over the eucharistic community. This is why such exclusion became known as excommunication: dissidents were no longer allowed to share communion with the main body of faithful. In modern times many Protestant Christians like to proclaim that their churches are open to all persuasions or none, and that their altars are free to all communicants. Not so the early church. The earliest rituals of Christian baptism show that the first communities stuck to a rigid code of morals and were always anxious about any dilution of the code, although they knew that human nature meant that there was a perennial temptation to drift. Before one was baptized there was a long period of instruction and close attention paid to lifestyle changes.

Justin, a philosopher from Nablus in Palestine (active circa 100–165), was also a pagan thinker, who converted to the Christian faith after, he tells us, having tried out a wide range of other philosophical lifestyles. His writings give us some of the earliest glimpses into the manner in which the earliest eucharists were being celebrated. He also engaged in a debate with a Jewish theologian named Trypho and records the results.[7] The debate largely centers on who has the right to interpret the Old Testament texts. The Christians now propose their most striking claim: that these texts can only be rightly understood, not in a historical, but in an eschatological sense. Jesus is the center to which the Old Testament runs, and back toward which the New Testament and lifestyle of the church always look. As Luke had already intimated in his Gospel: Christ is the "Midpoint of Time." From this period onward (and aided by the principles of Roman law) Christian thinking canonizes precedent in a strong way.[8] Justin in some ways symbolizes something that becomes a strong trend in this period: the first serious encounter of the Greek-speaking Christian world with Hellenistic philosophy. When Tertullian was in full voice against dissident teachers, whom he regarded as dangerously subversive to church order, since they preferred their own speculations to any check or balance the received tradition might impose on them, he uttered a famed warning against Christians becoming involved with secular philosophy:

Take heed lest any one beguile you through philosophy or vain deceit, according to the tradition of men, beyond the providence of the Holy Spirit. The Apostle had been at Athens and in his argumentative encounters there he became acquainted with that human wisdom which affects and corrupts the Truth, and is itself many times divided into its own heresies by the profusion of its mutually antagonistic sects. Accordingly, what has Athens in common with Jerusalem? What has the Academy in common with the Church? What have heretics in common with Christians? Our principles are derived from the Portico of Solomon, who himself handed down that the Lord must be sought in simplicity of heart.[9]

But this warning against worldly wisdom was, of course, couched in very learned rhetoric all the same. Justin has no such fear. He tells his readers that he quested long and hard through all the different schools of philosophy, always looking for the truth that would carry its own imprint of authority to command his life's direction. Nowhere could he find it, he says, until he found it in Christ, whose church gave him a living truth that satisfied all his mind's questions, all his heart's desires, and all his moral aspirations. Lactantius the philosopher makes the same case in a much more elegant and systematic fashion in his treatise *Divine Institutes*, two centuries later, where he says that the school of Christ uniquely combines all the aspirations of the ancient world for true religion, which is also pure wisdom, whereas all pagan religion proved to be brutal in its sacrificial instincts that were devoid of sense, and all its wisdom traditions fruitless in their divorce of reverence from understanding. Christ, Lactantius argues, was the Incarnate Wisdom who was also High Priest. His religion was the ultimate school of philosophy that society (Jewish and pagan) had been waiting for.

This much more positive view of philosophy, as a way to explain religious truth more coherently, continued to gain ground into the third-century church, partly because more of the Christian leaders were better educated and less afraid of looking at their biblical and apostolic traditions through the lens of philosophy. One thing noticeable about this time, however, is that the church never committed itself to any particular school of thought. It used elements of everything it could find that aided its quest for deeper understanding. It was profoundly eclectic in the use it made of secular learning. At every instance its choice of what to take or what to reject was dominated by its prior allegiance given to the biblical mind-set already established in the apostolic tradition it had received. One of the most renowned examples of this approach was the theologian Origen of Alexandria, who bridged the worlds of the second- and third-century church, and tried to harmonize philosophy and biblical revelation.

THE THIRD-CENTURY CHURCH THEOLOGIANS

Origen has rightly been described as the greatest theologian in the early church after Saint John the Evangelist. His readership has always been among the most intellectual of the church circles, and because he was so deeply versed in philosophical ways of expression and so consistently approached the scriptures as symbolic literature, he earned the enmity of many sections of church society. At three different periods (in his own lifetime in the mid-third century, then in the time of Theophilus of Alexandria in the fifth century, and finally in the time of the emperor Justinian in the sixth) his work came under hostile scrutiny each time he was crudely and carelessly read. It was an easy thing, in the later centuries, to hold up parts of an early writer and find fault with hindsight. So it was that the Orthodox Church set his works and his name aside as not being an author that the church would canonize. Even so, his teachings had by then been sifted, clarified, reordered, and heavily adapted by a series of the greatest saints of Orthodoxy, some of the leading fourth- and fifth-century fathers: Saint Gregory the Theologian, Saint Gregory of Nyssa, Saint Maximus the Confessor. Even Theophilus of Alexandria and Jerome, who both censured and anathematized Origen, continued to use his works and theories extensively—but simply unacknowledged. Saint John Chrysostom's exegetical writings used him so much that Origen's biblical achievements were never lost to the wider world of Orthodoxy. This is why Origen must be considered in this present section, for he is, in many ways, one of the great architects of the systematic theology of the church in the following, fourth, century, which emerges as classical Orthodoxy.

His real problem was his great fertility of thought. Origen set out so many different opinions (in his own era he taught and envisaged speaking to what we would now call a graduate seminar audience) that he could not foresee that this would not be a good idea in terms of the wider reception of his writings as they were simplified and reduced to propositions across a much larger, and often less educated, audience. What was suitable in a university seminar context was not often appropriate in the greater audience of the church congregations, or for the less educated desert monks who were often scandalized by his nonliteral readings of the Bible. The main tenor of his thought, however, is generally on target in terms of Orthodoxy. In terms of the divinity of Christ, Origen was a faithful and strong advocate of the Lord's eternal status; though his Christological statements often were so colored with subordinationism that he was significantly corrected by the later bishops who used him, such as Saint Athanasius and the Cappadocian fathers.[10] Origen's speculations on the preincarnate existence of souls and their lapse to this material cosmos as a penance for prior failures (a theory much exaggerated by later critics) were issues the church did not wish to pursue, feeling they had little biblical, and thus apostolic, sanction. But Origen's overall biblical theology set a tone that was extensively followed after the third century. We can now look at the solidifying character of the early standard of church Orthodoxy in this period in four different, but representative, areas: the self-definition of the church through the Bible; its approach to the understanding of the Person of Christ; its growing articulation of the mystery of God as Trinity; and its understanding of its own role in the world. These are the cardinal foundation stones of ancient Orthodoxy.

THE CHURCH AND SCRIPTURE

Wherever Origen was taken up in the subsequent generation, and reexpressed by the great fathers, his thought provided a major structure for the later church, for approaching the issue of how the biblical material might be read in the light of modern questions. To this day the Orthodox Church follows his principles of spiritual interpretation of the scripture: that there are levels of meaning contained in the sacred text(s) and that they all relate back to the centrality of the Christ event. This means, of course, a fairly deep-seated departure in the church's approach to sacred scripture from that of the academy or the disinterested reader who approaches it from a literal-historical angle. It means that the church, from earliest times, was committed to reading the texts (both those of the New and those of the Old Testaments) Christologically. It read the Psalter as if it were the direct teaching of the Word of God himself, the preincarnate Savior, Logos of the Father, Second Person of the Trinity, and not the historically grounded sayings of this or that Levite or Temple servant composing hymns for use in Israelite worship—though of course the latter reality is not denied at another level either. So there are different levels of meaning. When the psalmist cries out "My God, my God, why have you forsaken me?" (Ps. 21.1), the church in its prayerful reflection on the text refers it to the mystery of the Passion (as the evangelists have already suggested in Mk. 15.34 and Mt. 27.46).[11] This Christocentric reading of the Psalms, Origen argued, made the Psalter one of the most valuable books of scripture, ranked alongside the Johannine Gospel and Pauline theology for its richness of insight. Saint Athanasius of Alexandria, in his short treatise *To Marcellinus on the Psalms*, made this approach classically standard for the Orthodox Church. Modern so-called critical approaches to biblical interpretation massively favor the historical or literal meaning of a text. This is the "pearl of price" that the exegete is trained to excavate, or deduce, from the reading. But in the church a different approach is taken. Historical study is honored and valued, but the text is first of all regarded sacramentally. Since it is the word of the Divine Word, the church senses it is not fully grasped when only exegeted historically. This is because it is possessed of transtemporal (metahistorical) significance. It is best approached within its own genre: eschatological message, having to be read eschatologically. The manner in which this is best facilitated is to recognize (as Origen first had argued and generations of later fathers of the church agreed) that one may deduce multiple layers of meaning in a given text of scripture: the historical or literal meaning of what it meant in its immediate context; the moral level it might have as an encouraging or corrective exhortation, the more secret meaning it might have to those souls who were spiritually purified and more acutely aware that through the prayerful reading of sacred scripture the Spirit of God often moved their minds and hearts to deep insights and understandings: the message, as it were, of divine love made new in every generation.[12] This inspired nature of the text, suffused in all ages by the living Spirit of God communicating with his church, made the scriptures ever fresh, ever relevant—not merely a dead letter. In this way the Orthodox Church's exegesis is always Christ-centered, meant to bring the resurrection presence of its Lord to immediate effect. And this applies equally to its preaching too. Indeed, the proper context for the church's preaching is the eucharistic liturgy. Other forms of preaching (such as evangelism, moral instruction, and apologetics) are not the celebration of the church's kerygmatic mystery as such but rather a preparation for it. The early church strongly held to the view that the mystery is reserved for those who are already initiated, and this runs on into contemporary Orthodoxy too. Orthodoxy never endorsed a hard doctrine of predestination as did some parts of Western Christianity, but it held, and still holds, to a strong sense of the mystery and grace of divine election, which makes the church never reducible to a simple matter of sociological analysis.

It was this deeply sacramental approach to scripture that brought the third-century theologians of the church into sharp conflict with two predominant sets of religious thinkers around them. On the one hand it made the church clash with Jewish exegetes who resisted the Jesus-centered reading of what it saw as its own bible. The synagogue resisted the way the Orthodox Church insisted the Old Testament had to be read in the light of the New, which illumined it. Accordingly, it tended to resist the practice of attributing symbolic meanings to passages and preferred a literal and moral reading, a movement that was deepened by the Rabbinic schools after the third century.[13] On the other hand, the church also resisted the various Gnostic teachers (*didaskaloi*), or philosophically inclined rhetoricians with private schools in the larger cities, who wished to approach and exegete the scriptural texts (and other mystical texts of their own composing set alongside them) as a set of ciphers of deeper truths that had to be interpreted by the specialist professor. The third-century church theologians set the Orthodox tradition firmly on the path of reading between these two extreme polcs. They described the preference for the literal-moral reading alone as a very limited scope but also saw that the highly symbolic reading veered too often into a mythical approach. By the end of the third century the Orthodox Church had adopted a complex set of values that used the scriptural library of texts as its own moderating safety net. It read one text in the light of several others, on the grounds that the entirety of scripture emanated from a single source: the merciful mind of the Savior-Logos, now incarnate, who mediated his message of joy to the world through his living Spirit. This was the principle of consonance.[14] If one text seemed, on its own, to be rather unpalatable in a literal sense, it ought to be read in a higher symbolic sense.[15] As Origen had summed it up succinctly: interpretation must be guided by one supreme principle:

"Nothing unworthy of God's majesty."[16] Above all it applied the concept of seeking the mind-set of Christ (*phronema*: Phil. 2.5) in all things; seeing as the *skopos*, or overarching "intentionality," of the scripture principle, the offer of merciful redemption to the world in Christ. The scriptures were approached as a tool of spiritual ascent. But for their right understanding a certain level of maturity of soul was required. The dim-witted and the soul-starved could certainly make a disaster out of them. This catastrophic (mis)use of scriptural texts, aphorisms, and injunctions has often been the bane of the church in later ages. Saint Athanasius of Alexandria would sum this up very neatly in the fourth century when he said: "But for the searching of the Scriptures and for true knowledge of them, an honourable life and a pure soul are necessary, along with fitting Christian virtue. Only then, when the mind guides its path this way, can it attain what it desires, and comprehend [scripture], in so far as it is permitted to human nature to learn the things of the Divine Word. But without a pure mind and a modeling of one's life after the saints, a person cannot possibly comprehend the words of those saints."[17]

In short, the Orthodox Church from the third century onward, and into the present, has produced, from the writings of its saints, a massive amount of biblical commentary. It has shaped all its preaching around sacred scripture, and its mind-set and doctrines are formed in this crucible. Its monastics and lay people use the Psalter as their daily prayer book. The monks recite the entirety of the Psalter each week before beginning over once again; and they have done so since the earliest centuries. A massive amount of scripture is found in active use in all of the church's liturgical and prayer services.

Someone regularly attending Orthodox Church services will be exposed to the Bible in a profoundly deep and broad immersion experience but will also find that this is one that is poetically shaped, not syllogistically; mystically suggested, not apologetically argued.

The third-century theologians provided many other foundations for what would later be more systematically elaborated in the following patristic centuries. For brevity's sake I would like to summarize this aspect of foundations in the form of three major positions or inheritances that the third century left as a legacy. In all three instances (I offer them as representative) the church leaders were faced with a particular controversy that led them to formulate a much larger point out of the argument. Typically a dissident opinion had been aired that caused the faithful at large some anxiety as they sensed that it challenged or contradicted the received tradition in some deep sense. In these cases the church leadership typically reacted with a (paradoxically) progressive conservatism so as to offer the faithful guidance as to what the church's main doctrine was, as distinct from hairesis. They offered solutions that were in the spirit of the tradition: demonstrating the principle in each case that the Orthodox tradition was not a dead letter but a living sense of how the Gospel reasserted itself in new environments.[18] Our remaining three demonstrations of the cardinal foundations of Orthodoxy lead us now to look at how the third century dealt with discussions on the nature and person of Jesus: namely, its *Christology*; how it articulated its metaphysical and soteriological doctrine of God, in other words, its sense of *Trinity*; and finally how it reflected on itself and its own role in society, that is, its *ecclesiology*.[19]

THE PRE-NICENE CHURCH ON THE
PERSON OF JESUS

The Orthodox Church was faced with many contesting views about Jesus in the earliest centuries. Its core tradition was clear enough. He was not just another prophet.[20] He was the subject of the prophets' hopes.[21] He was higher than the angels.[22] He was the Lord and the Son of God.[23] He suffered for a while but was exalted to the side of God the Father.[24] He was the High Priest and mediator of all creation with God.[25] He had been chosen as God's agent of creation before the world was made.[26] This was so clear that it was abridged as a "biblical confession," a kind of synopsis of the whole scriptural attestation of Jesus's exalted status, so as to serve as a hymn that baptismal candidates could recite as their statement of faith and repentance. This by the mid-fourth century would become known the world over as the "Creed"; but at first it was a liturgical hymn that simply synopsized the scriptural affirmations about the Lord Jesus: born of the Father before time, born of a virgin within time, so as to call the world to salvation and glorify it within his own exalted glory, thus restoring it, in himself, to communion with the Father, and manifesting this at his Second Coming. This is the very essence of the apostolic tradition. To preface it the church added its faith in the One Father as Lord and Maker of all things, visible and invisible, in order to refute the teachings of the Gnostics, who regarded the God and Father of Jesus as a different deity to the "God of this world," the Demiurgic god of the Old Testament. And to complete it, the church later added other phrases it felt necessary to amplify the apostolic tradition beyond the central core affirmation of the soteriological Christology: in other words, it added its belief in "the Holy Spirit who has spoken through the prophets" (a bare statement that would be expanded in the fourth century with more explicitly divine titles for the Spirit) and its belief in the unity of the church which that Spirit inspired.

This is the fundamental structure of the Creed which the Nicene fathers turned to in the next century to give a clear statement of the apostolic faith when tested by the Arian heresy. So, the Christology is relatively simple and hardly difficult to find, being imprinted consistently throughout the New Testament. Even so, the third-century church was faced with difficulties. Because if Jesus was exalted as eternal Lord alongside the Father, who was the one and only God: how could the Christians explain their sense of the unicity of God to outsiders—let alone themselves? One way would have been to insist strongly on the subordination of the Son to the Father: their distinct difference and separation from one another. One as Lord and one as Servant. The confessions of the early Church, however, are all concerned with Jesus being a servant in his humble and suffering ministry but being exalted alongside God as his most intimate Son and companion. In the apostolic statements there is a high insistence on Jesus being one in the glory of the Father: not being merely a creature and servant alongside the unapproachability of the Divine Oneness. The church's earliest Christology sustained this in praise and prayers. And yet the church retained, equally strongly, its confession of the total unity of God. There is one and there is no other. So how could the position of Jesus "within the deity" be reconciled with the absolute unity of God if one side-stepped a strong confession of Jesus's, or the Son's, subordinate status? For a time the second-century

Roman church leaders suggested that one way would be to stress that the Son was different from the Father in terms of Person but not in terms of Monarchy. There would be one single active "power" in God: and this must be seen as shared between the Father and his Plenipotentiary Son. This had some mileage in the preaching of the church leaders, such as Pope Callixtus, but certain lay teachers approached the same idea from a different, more metaphysical, angle and argued that either the Son and Father and Spirit were interchangeable names of the same reality or Jesus was a simple Man who had been supremely lifted up into communion with God the Father in order to accomplish a salvific mission (but at the end of the day was no more than a God-filled man).

The more reflective theologians of the church found these positions deeply out of harmony with the apostolic tradition and launched a massive attack on Monarchianism's imaginations. To do so they elevated the testimony of the Fourth Gospel to a high place and approached the issue of divine unity from the perspective of the title the evangelist used in his Prologue: "In the beginning was the Word and the Word was with God and the Word was God." The term *logos*, or Word had a pre-history in Greek religious philosophy, and had already been identified, by John, with the Wisdom (*Sophia*) tradition of the Old Testament, which saw the Word and Wisdom (Heb. *Dabar* and *Hokhma*) as a single creative divine power. Accordingly, not least because the approach had apostolic sanction, Logos theology began to dominate the Church's preaching from the late second century onward. Christ Jesus was described, in this image, as the eternal Word who existed from all time with the Father, and was spoken out from the Father's own being in the expressive act of the creation. The word of creation was the Logos himself. This was why the Logos also assumed the task of repairing the creation once it had fallen away from the knowledge of God. On the terms of the Logos theology, the "Word became flesh" to accomplish the mission in time, but this lowliness masked the metaphysical unity of the Word and the Father, which was composed of oneness of being: an ontological oneness. Searching around for a clear enough semantic that could get their point across, the early Logos theologians insisted that the Word was one in being, and one in power with the Father, but differentiated in person and mission. They believed that this manner of speaking alone could reconcile the metaphysical problems they had encountered as to the unicity of God with the apostolic deposit of the scriptural faith they had received. Their solution remains to this day the basis of the Orthodox Church's faith in Christ's divine person. But it clearly put further pressure on the theologians to explain more about the differentiated unity of God it thus professed.

THE ANCIENT CHURCH ON THE TRINITY

This was why the third and fourth centuries become the arena for a great deal of affirmation about God as Trinity.[27] It is a Christian neologism meaning a three-oneness. It would take more than a great book to extrapolate all this; but suffice it so say here that the early church theologians, again looking back to the inspiration of the apostolic biblical evidence, affirmed that the unity of God was not a bare and undifferentiated monolithism but rather a complex unity; not a mathematical singularity but rather a notion of oneness that derives from the idea of absolute communion; and in its ideal of communion offers to the cosmos its hope for salvific union with God. In other words, the union-communion that is God reaches out to the world to draw the believers into its scope. The trinitarian communion of God's energy creates the world in a foundational pattern that both seeks ever to be reunited with its Maker and senses always that in loving communion it comes closest to that realization, since that was the creative energy that first fashioned it. The Trinity, therefore, is no less than God's outreach of being: from the Father, through the Son-Word, in the Holy Spirit, to the world. Then from the inspiration of the Holy Spirit in the heart of the believer to the ever-increasing divine reality of the Son, and through him (as light passes directly through limpid clarity) back to the Unapproachable Father. He who is unapproachable in himself becomes accessible through the Son in the gift of the Spirit. The doctrine of Trinity is no abstract or idle speculation, therefore; it is simply the shorthand for the entire apostolic doctrine of salvation in Christ. The Trinity is the power of God's own outreach, his *synkatabasis*, or loving condescension.[28] Just as the divine outreach to humanity is triadic, so too is the same energy returned as humanity's movement back to God. The Trinity is thus an explanation of the apostolic teaching that in Christ, God is our salvation.

This notion of complex and living unity was a stunning and new insight into God, an idea of Divine Oneness unique to Christianity, and one that is faithful to Jesus's tradition that God was closer to us than we are to ourselves. The unity of the Son and Father thus becomes more than a moral notion: it is a metaphysical reality. We can see later how the fourth-century fathers finally clarified what they meant by this onto-logical unity in essence (*ousia*) and differentiation in person (*hypostasis*); but for the moment, so as to follow on the line of inquiry as to what constituted the apostolic tradition in the mind-set of the early church, it is worth noting how, over and against the Monarchians who wanted to follow the logical line of their own linear deductions (about mathematical unity, or the supremacy of the monist Yahwism of the Torah), the church's larger tradition of worship held fast to its instinct of divine acclamation of Jesus even before it had a technical theological vocabulary to express it. Once it was assured that this form of words (and not a range of other forms of words) caught the essence of its scriptural creeds, then it affirmed the doctrine universally in its episcopal preaching. Much the same thing can be seen time after time afterward; especially in the fourth century, when many more doctrinal controversies sprang up and the broader church tradition applied the same principles to refining its teaching and setting aside as heresy those formulations that did not conform to it.

Some scholars today write as if any Christian teacher of the early centuries has just as much right as any other to speak for the early church. They often argue this point to make a further claim that the notions of heresy and orthodoxy are themselves anachronistic (inapplicable in the early centuries) or even irrelevant. Many of the ancient Gnostics held the same opinion. But the apostolic tradition of the church did not have such a postmodern view. It knew what it was and it affirmed itself, even through changing conditions and new controversies, because it was able to apply the *canon* (yard-stick) of apostolicity with almost a systematic rationale. Just as it knew who and what it was, it was able to state very clearly who and what were *not* it. By the end of the second century this had already been elaborated in the work of the great anti-Gnostic theologian Irenaeus of Lyons into a fourfold principle of determining the apostolicity of the church. For him (and for the greater Orthodox catholic tradition following after him), the four testing points of anything claiming to be authentically Christian Orthodoxy were: first, correspondence with the apostolic tradition set out in the New Testament and through it to the Old.[29] Second, that this should be recognized in shorthand in the baptismal creed each one had professed at baptism—that received "rule of faith" which was clear to the simple-hearted as well as the sophisticated.[30] Third, that a given set of teachings should confirm to the preaching established in the church by the collective of bishops, whose conformity with the tradition and with each other demonstrated their "apostolic succession."[31] And fourth, Irenaeus adds, that the entire Christian tradition of Orthodoxy should demonstrate a fundamental skopos, or tendency (what we might call a giveaway character or genetic imprint), and that was how it all coinhered in Christ—ran to Christ from every point. This Christocentricity (of salvation, of the knowledge of God, of creation, of anthropology, or whatever else) was the hallmark of the Orthodox Church's mind-set. The application of these four testers (*canons*) has always been the foundation of the claim to apostolic catholicity. They are thus the quintessential definition or proof of what Christian Orthodoxy is; and the Orthodox Church still holds to these foundational principles as the litmus paper of its identity. It was the Greek theologians of the early church who first clarified this after their many encounters with versions of the Gospel they considered to be deeply flawed or simply fake: the many heresies the church labeled in its early centuries, most of which are still alive and kicking in today's world. It was the Greek theologians, in the main, who showed how such a system of authenticating church identity might work in the practical diocesan structure of the local churches.[32] To this day Orthodoxy still adheres to these principles, which it first outlined in the early centuries.

THE CHURCH ON ITS SOCIETAL ROLE

Our third representative example of how the Orthodox Church clarified its identity in these early centuries is taken from its reflection on its own social-moral role. From the very outset, not least because Jesus himself insisted on it, Christianity understood that the Good News was not merely a message but a plan of action—and one that required commitment and life-changing decisions from its adherents.[33] Soon after this period, many of the church fathers would customarily call Christianity "Our Philosophy"; though that, of course, was in an era when philosophy itself was seen as a life orientation, not simply a set of intellectual presuppositions.[34] Knowing that it was the witness of the Kingdom of God on earth, the early church strongly felt its duty to represent a high standard of ethics. Had not Jesus challenged them from the outset? "For I tell you, unless your righteousness exceeds that of the Scribes and Pharisees, you will never enter the kingdom of heaven" (Mt. 5.20). And though today centuries of reading the Gospel accounts have presented to us the Scribes and Pharisees as rather carping critics, and even hypocrites, in Jesus's time they were widely regarded as the most reverent and morally observant class of society. This is the whole point of Jesus's aphorism. The earliest apostolic teachings on Christian morals are found in the New Testament, sources that are

69

replete with moral injunctions from the time of Jesus himself, to that of the first and second generations of the apostles.[35] The writings of the apostolic fathers of the church dating to the first and early second centuries continue this style of moral injunction; often using genres of Stoic moral exhortation (*encomia*) to encourage the believers to persevere in an exemplary lifestyle. The powerful sense also given to members of the early church that they had been redeemed in Christ, and given redemption in his blood, seems to have led some communities to think that they were "the saints" of God (a title that is conferred on them in the Pauline literature).[36] Paul had even suggested that because they were the redeemed saints the Christians would serve as Judges of the World when the Final Days came (1 Cor. 6.2). This sense of self-importance seems to have clashed with Jesus's own command for the heart to be always ready to repent its tendency to wickedness; and in parts of Asia Minor, as we might deduce from the Johannine Letters, the apostolic author writes to rebuke congregations who had convinced themselves that the church was now beyond sin (1 Jn. 1.8–2.6). The apostle John reasserts realism: the destiny to holiness is a real Christian experience, sensed in the Spirit and already to be touched, and yet, even so, the individual believer is never exempt from the need for personal repentance.

This paradoxical tension (between the perfection of grace Christ had conferred on his church and the moral failings that were still manifested in individual lives) was something the church could never quite resolve. To this day it still cannot. News of deep moral failings within the church comes always as a shock and with a sense of disorientation. Christ's command was: "Be perfect as your heavenly Father is perfect"

(Mt. 5.48), not just "fairly good," and certainly not be worse than the worst. Some movements in the early communities tried to resolve the tension by defining the church as the society of the morally pure. In this understanding, those whose lives did not measure up had ceased to be members of the church. They were no longer held to be "in communion" with the saints. Soon this lack of spiritual communion manifested itself quite physically: such people were prevented from attending the Eucharist; they were not given Communion—hence excommunicated by the leadership. This pattern of exclusivity in the face of recalcitrant members of the church was given a precedent as early as Saint Paul, who had cut off the (presumably Gentile) believer who had not observed the marriage degrees of consanguinity and had, in Jewish eyes, committed incest by marrying his late father's wife, who was not his mother (1 Cor. 5.1–5).

There is a severity of tone in these earliest moral injunctions that needs to be set in the context of what we may surmise "really happened" in the ongoing life of the churches, where pastoral discretion is usually not recorded at all, precisely because it is discretional. Anyone who has had the governance of a congregation, however, knows that there is often a considerable shortfall between expectation and performance; and the pastoral leader has to deal with it; be seen to deal with it; as well as be seen to have an overarching compassion for all the people. Some of the earliest rules (now called canons) that were instituted by the bishops were concerned with this keeping of moral standards. To us moderns they seem quite harsh; again because the rules presume discretion on the part of the bishop but do not state how this is to be exercised. Sexual morality was high on these agendas.

Although baptism was the sacrament of repentance par excellence, the earliest rules prohibited actresses, soldiers, magicians, soothsayers, and prostitutes from even applying for admission to the church. These rules did not even start to be relaxed until late into the fourth century. Baptism was, at first, regarded as a once-for-all remission of sin; a rebirth into a totally new life. As the century wore on, however, the reality of baptized Christians falling once more into their old sinful pagan ways became more and more an issue. At first this issue was resolved by admitting the power of repentance and spiritual cleansing through almsgiving, fasting, and redoubled prayer; but it was affirmed that there were three sins that, if committed, were unforgivable. The church had no power to remit them, and the guilty person no longer had any place in the church. These were the sins of murder, adultery, and apostasy. Again it would not be until much later that the church's sense of its powers of granting forgiveness would be stretched to cover these offenses too.

What really focused the mind of the early communities, however, was the crisis of the persecutions. Our image today is that these early centuries were the age of the martyrs. And this is true of course, insofar as the early church made it its business to record those unjust deaths and place them before the eyes of believers ever afterward as high examples of fidelity and courage. What is equally true, judging from the episcopal canons that have survived from this period, is that the persecutions produced more than a sheaf of martyrs: they also created a tidal wave of believers who had either run away from the test of martyrdom, denied Christ before the authorities, or willingly sacrificed to the old gods while holding their fingers crossed behind their backs, as it were. How to deal with these lapsed believers became a lively issue for the bishops once peace was reestablished in the communities. Even those who had only handed over the sacred vessels and scriptural books to the demanding secular authorities were regarded as "handers-over." The word in Latin is *traditor*, and it gave us our word for traitor.

What emerged up to the end of the third century was a system of penance that was very strict in relation to the conduct of the clergy. If members of the clergy had lapsed, they were never to offer the eucharistic oblation again. If they had been tortured beyond endurance and had lapsed in their weakness, then they could retain some standing in the church but were still never to offer the oblation. If clergy exhibited shameful sexual or other moral lapses, they were to be deposed from office on account of them. Lay people could be treated more leniently. But if they exhibited serious moral lapses, especially sexual, or if they had denied Christ in time of persecution and wanted readmission in time of peace, then they were to be made to undergo public humility (not to say humiliation) in the lobbies of the church buildings: to kneel down as sinners while the rest of the community stood in prayer and not allowed to take Communion until many years had passed. Sometimes they were only to be allowed to take Communion once more on their deathbeds. It was the bishops and presbyters who had the charge of administering this system. It seems to have had some force in the early post-persecution years but to have increasingly fallen out of use (doubtless because of its severity), until it was more or less abolished as a redundant relic in the late fourth century.

One other thing the age of persecutions produced, however, was the sense of betrayal when one set of believers lapsed and abandoned those who had to suffer. Often, of course, the lapsed were only too ready to show their willingness to the persecuting authorities to supply names and addresses of those they should arrest. Deep feelings resulted from this—as has been the case in every age of persecution since then. It takes more than one generation for a community to get over such bloody betrayals, as the post-Communist Russian Church has shown. Two African groups who came through the persecutions with a kind of fiery spirit of resistance were the Novatians and the Donatists.[37] Both regarded the issue of the lapsed and the faithful as a kind of apocalyptic challenge to the identity of the church. As the New Testament had prophesied, persecution would be the destiny of the true church in history.[38] The spirit of resistance it required marked it essentially as a community of resistance. Compromise with the secular and corrupt world, they went on to argue, could only defile the nature of the church.

This hardline and exclusionist approach to the nature of the church—the congregation of the pure who must distance themselves from the sinful mass—picked up and exacerbated one strand of the late New Testament apocalyptic message. The era of persecutions seemed to underline that this view of the world was true: that there could be no safety in the larger pagan society that surrounded the church, and was so ready, with so little excuse, to condemn the innocent to such bitter tortures. In the peaceful aftermath of the African and Roman persecutions there grew up immense problems within the churches' day-to-day life. The Novatianists demanded that those who had lapsed from the confession of Christ in the persecutions had utterly lost the ability to number themselves among the faithful and had to be excluded from the church's worship. Bishops who tried to reconcile the fallen and readmit them in various forms had to be denounced as laxists. The Donatists insisted that any cleric who had collaborated in any way—even to the extent of handing over the books or vessels— had automatically lost the right to be a minister of the church. The sacraments that they celebrated afterward were null and void. This specifically meant that the ordinations they conducted were invalid, of course. And with a welter of cross-recriminations among the African churches as to who had collaborated or not, the whole issue of which community represented the "real church" and which was a pseudo-community with false sacraments tore the congregations apart, despite Rome's attempt to offer a message of reconciliation. The schisms caused by these recriminations lasted until the collapse of Christianity in Africa before the advent of Islam in the eighth century.

The core issue in both these movements threw light on the very nature of the church. Was it by definition a congregation of the pure that could not stand the admixture of any defiled elements? Or was it a family that was made up of many elements: some zealous, others less so; some serving as examples, and others needing to be encouraged to reform? In the end the larger Orthodox tradition, while never losing sight of the church's destiny and definition to be the sacrament of God's pure elect, the icon of the Kingdom of God on earth, fell decidedly in favor of the concept of the family that had many elements. It retained the concept of the pure elect not only in an abstract, metaphysical sense (the ideal identity of Christians as saints) but also in the very practical local sense: for it determined that if a schismatic group resisted the apostolic consensus and significantly departed from the tradition, then its sacramental worship was rendered devoid of power. The loss of power was proportionate to the degree of departure: a factor that has made modern-day ecumenism a difficult matter to adjudicate for contemporary Orthodoxy. In lapsing from the communion of the church a dissident group was felt to have fallen away from the full vigor of the Spirit's energy operative within the church.

To keep the family morally alert, the church of this era placed a great stress, therefore, on the necessary holiness of the clergy. They were to be expected to manifest a specially dedicated and pure lifestyle. If they did not, they deserved to be sidelined: suspended for correction or deposed permanently. Many of the synodical canons of this time turned their focus to the reform of clergy. But laity who faltered in the moral life were to be encouraged toward repentance, not cast out from the church, unless the fault was so heinous that some form of public statement of exclusion was felt necessary—an exclusion, however, that should never be absolutized. In this way Orthodoxy felt a balance had been achieved that was listing toward mercy and the principles of reconciliation in a fallible family of people trying to live the Christ life. Accordingly, the principles of mercy and reconciliation can, to this day, stand as genuine and accurate adjudicators of how well the church continues to be itself, by measuring how it performs its quintessential ministry of reconciliation.

THE CHARACTER OF THE CHURCH AT THE END OF THE THIRD CENTURY

Our attention so far has been on the Orthodox Church in the period of its gestation, as it were. We have seen how it absorbed the teaching of Jesus and the first apostles and out of them wove together the fabrics of what we now know as the New Testament. It learned, over the course of the late first and early second centuries, despite temptations offered by Marcion and his like, not to cast aside the Old Testament or to exalt it literalistically, but to read the Old through the lens of the New. It faced many examples of individuals claiming to speak for it collectively, especially leaders of elite philosophical schools who heavily allegorized New Testament ideas, sometimes to the point of obscure mythology. In these cases it fell back on the traditional creeds it had used in its baptismal rituals, the simple enunciation of the Gospel history as being paradigmatic for every age. It exalted the apostolic tradition, which it distilled from the totality of the New Testament ethos, and it brought forward its system of local governance: the men it had selected to lead it in prayer, to be the guardians of that principle of apostolic tradition. At first the churches were governed by a council of elders, but very soon (and undoubtedly on the basis of best practice and common wisdom) the collective pattern gave way widely toward the principle of single governance of the college of presbyters by one leader. He was to be known as the episcopos, or bishop, and by the third century the burden of representing and defending the apostolic tradition fell to him primarily, though never exclusively. The vagaries of whether the local bishop was up to it or not was settled by the principle of synodical governance of the bishops collectively, each one helping, informing, and maintaining consensus with the others and with other provinces of bishops. So it was that by the end of the third century the whole system of how the church recognized and maintained itself was in place. There were numerous examples of the refusal of this system: largely individuals who knew better, who propagated a tendentious doctrine, seized on an aspect of the wider tradition, and bent the whole out of shape to prioritize it. These the Orthodox Church classed as hairesis: a belief system that departed from the church and could no longer claim its identity or its powers. What also grew as the church of the fourth century began to dawn, in an era of social peace and acceptance, was an ability to look back on two great periods of theological creativity that were behind it: the New Testament library and the writings of the theologians stretching over three centuries. The church now had a significant library, and Christian intellectuals were reflecting on it more and more deeply, producing commentaries and refinements on its basis. What emerged from this was an international drawing up of a short list of great figures from the Christian past. Some of the names on it were controversial: such as that of Origen of Alexandria, whose writings in any case set examples that were to become classical; but others, especially episcopal martyr theologians, were given a high status; and their decisions were referred to as solid precedents. Such names show already the evolving notion of the "father of the church." The age of the fathers, however, was especially that golden age, for the Orthodox world, of the fourth and fifth centuries when Christian emperors not only established peace for the church but also gave it assistance in bringing its philosophy of mercy to apply to a new social order. To this age we shall now turn.

CHAPTER THREE

The Classical Patristic Period

ORTHODOX ECUMENE

The fourth century saw a sea change in the affairs of the Christian Church. If the second and third centuries were its adolescence (learning to react to changes, intellectual challenge, and bitter political oppression), then the fourth century was, in many ways, its coming of age: the period when the Orthodox Church (its foundational constitution now internationally established on the basis of the apostolic tradition founded on scripture) emerges in most of its classical and enduring lineaments.[1] This time of peace and rich intellectual life has often been called the *Pax Constantiniana:* Constantine's peace. It is useful, then, to record Constantine's story very briefly. The dawn of the fourth century coincides with the growing visibility of the Christians in all walks of life, now including the army. At first, belonging to the military profession was a cause of exclusion from baptism. But by the beginning of the third century Christians were obviously serving in the military and still seemed at home in the church. There were moments of crisis (each time a serving soldier collected his wages he was supposed to offer incense to the *genius* of the emperor), but already many were regarding such things as examples of civic respect rather than religious affiliation. They had the authority of Saint Paul behind them when he dealt liberally with the crisis of whether it was legitimate to eat sanctified meat that had been offered to the idols in pagan temples (1 Cor. 8.1–3).[2]

This growing spread of Christians into state structures was to suffer a shock. A new upsurge of anti-Christian persecution of the early fourth century, in the time of the emperor Diocletian and his caesar Galerius, marked a new element in the state's awareness of the church. Previously the existence of Christians had been a cause of distaste because of their exclusionist attitudes. But now, it seems, they were marked out because they were feared as a threat to the security of the political system. The story, as Christian historians recorded it, was that Diocletian was engaged in the official imperial ritual of the performing of auspices, and the assistant priests with him claimed that the rite had been frustrated by evil powers.[3] What seems to have happened was that Christians among the high courtiers present for the occasion made the sign of the cross during the rites to avert the presence of the old gods from themselves. These old gods were already widely classified among the Christians as "demons."[4] In the aftermath of this a serious purge was conducted, removing Christian officials from the imperial household. Under the stimulus of Galerius, this soon expanded into a wider purge of Christians from the capital at Nicomedia. The great church there was set on fire by the troops, and it inaugurated a wave of denunciations of believers.[5] The purge has gone down in history as the

Great Persecution (303–313). Living in Nicomedia at the time, and held hostage there because his father, Constantius Chlorus, was the caesar of the western provinces, was the young noble Constantine.[6] He was being educated in rhetoric and political theory by the renowned Christian theologian Lactantius, and many of his later ideas about the golden age of Roman justice reflect the Christian philosophy that Lactantius demonstrates in his masterwork *The Divine Institutes*. It is possible that Constantine already had a much earlier immersion in Christian culture, from his Christian mother, Helena, whom Constantius was commanded to set aside on his elevation to the purple, but whom Constantine brought back to high eminence on his own accession: a time when she acted as an extremely generous patron of the churches.

Although in 303 Constantius's son had been envisaged as likely to be promoted to the role of caesar, by 304 Diocletian seems to have followed Galerius's advice and to have barred Constantine from accession to the throne. It is possible this was related to the issue of the Christian purges, which Galerius was continuing with ferocity. On Diocletian's retirement in 305, Constantius and Galerius were both elevated to the rank of supreme emperor. Constantine's father assumed the rule of the Western Empire at Milan. At this time Constantine and Lactantius fled from the hostile environment of Nicomedia and made their way westward. Constantius, becoming seriously ill in Britain in 306, proclaimed to his troops that his son would be a worthy successor and, with enthusiasm, the garrison at York raised Constantine on the shield and acclaimed him as the new augustus of the West.[7] This canceled all the legal plans for a process of accession made by Diocletian and agreed by the other senior emperors, and was effectively the inauguration of the long Roman Civil War (306–324) that would finally see Constantine emerge as the supreme monarchical emperor of both East and West. His first major act as politician was to force his eastern ally Licinius to legislate for a toleration of Christianity, with the Edict of Milan, issued in 313.[8]

This decisive abjection of Galerius's religious policy of oppression followed soon after one of Constantine's major military successes in Italy: the battle of the Milvian Bridge. This was the moment when the forces of Constantine took command of Rome from the legions of his western imperial rival Maxentius, and when he secured his power as single ruler of the West. The event has assumed monumental significance in the annals of the Orthodox Church. Lactantius and Bishop Eusebius of Caesarea give varying accounts of it (one as a dream, one as a vision), but the core of the account is that, on the eve of his battle with Maxentius, Constantine, claiming a divine intervention, commanded his troops to inscribe a mystical sign, a *labarum*, on their shields, which would secure them victory.[9] This was a cross-shaped figure with a looped upper part. It spread like wildfire through the Christian sections of the army (and there must have been quite a few of them already allied to Constantine) that this was either the Cross itself or the Christian cipher of the Chi-Rho (a cross intersected by an elongated letter *rho* standing for the name of Christ), and so the god that had appeared to Constantine must have been Jesus.[10] The dramatic and decisive victory that followed, on October 28, 312, ousting Maxentius from a city that had seemed all but impregnable the day before, and on the supposedly auspicious occasion of his own anniversary of accession, seemed to the Christians a decisive intervention on their behalf by Christ. It is an aspect of history that has long been argued over, but it is not at all improbable that the Christians' conviction also impressed itself on the consciousness of Constantine himself. Forever afterward he definitely favored the church above all other forms of religiosity in the empire, even though for a long time he continued to serve as a *president for all religions* or, in his preferred terms, *bishop of those outside the church.* When the reluctant, and wholly pagan, Senate of Rome ordered him a triumphal arch to celebrate this victory, it is of note that the emperor seems to have ordered a change in the traditional religious terminology inscribed on it. Instead of attributing Constantine's victory to the Roman gods, the arch (still to this day) records rather that he was led to victory *instinctu divinitatis*: by the guidance of "a" divinity (unnamed and in the singular).[11]

When Constantine assumed sole power across the Roman Empire, after defeating Licinius in 324, who had instituted new purges against Christians, he began to develop his political administration with a decided favoring of Christians. He began by offering the church restitutions for much of what it had lost in the years of persecution and confiscation. He offered grand buildings as churches (the Lateran basilica and palace complex to raise the profile of the popes in Rome) as well as building many new prestigious Christian shrines (Saint Peter's in the Vatican, the Church of the Resurrection at Jerusalem, and others). He advanced Christian courtiers, taking learned bishops as his close advisers, chief among them the Roman and Alexandrian popes, Eusebius of Caesarea, Eusebius of Nicomedia, and Ossius of Cordoba. He abolished crucifixion as a legal penalty under Roman law and adopted other measures influenced by the church. What had the most impact internationally, however, was the way he elevated Christian bishops to the rank of a parallel magistracy. In this way he opened up the system of justice to the poorer classes of people. Now when a litigious matter arose Christians could opt to have the case heard in the episcopal court, rather than by the state magistrate. Bishops now became important legal personages, not simply leaders of the common worship. The legal system that directed their minds was primarily that of the ecclesiastical canons, highly moral in tone, that took evangelical justice as its direction rather than casuistry.

This manner in which Constantine had amplified episcopal power took the synodical principle we have already witnessed as being a chief factor in the international establishment of the apostolic tradition and gave it much greater prominence. Constantine, and soon others across the empire, began to see the larger gatherings of bishops to adjudicate matters of significance in terms of a parallel Senate. Like the Senate, the episcopal meetings issued laws (canons), and with the ascent of a Christian-leaning imperator those episcopal canons were soon to be given a status in law, just as the magisterial decisions of the bishops in their day courts held the power of law. But the church, in both western and eastern provinces, having just emerged from civil war with the added oppression of persecutions, was in a highly disrupted state. It had to deal with lapses, betrayals, requests for reconciliation, and demands for just punishments of traitors. Many deeply divided factions were seeking redress. Constantine applied pressure on the Christians (looking to the bishops of the great cities to take the lead) to organize themselves quickly and resolve their conflicts. Two of those deep divisions had already been brought to his notice. The first, the Donatist crisis in North Africa, was based upon the argument that if anyone had lapsed in the persecution he or she was no longer part of the church, and so if any cleric had fallen, his ordination was utterly voided and he could not appoint anyone else through ordination. This resulted in the African churches being split into two hierarchies of bishops who refused to recognize the legitimacy of the other. Constantine answered the plea for redress by transferring the case to the adjudication of the bishop of Rome.

The second crisis was a more intellectual matter. It too arose out of a context of schismatic factions in the aftermath of the persecutions in Egypt.[12] Clergy loyalties were divided in the great city of Alexandria. The school of Origen (died 253) had left unresolved questions among the intelligentsia about the eternity of the Word of God and the precise status of the doctrine of the divine Trinity. The bishop Alexander taught a clergy meeting that the Son being eternal had no time when he did not exist, and thus was coeternal with the Father. One of Bishop Alexander's clergy, the presbyter Arius, dissented from the teaching and claimed that if the Son was eternal as the Father is, the doctrine of monotheism was compromised, because to attribute the title "Son" implicitly implied a concept of subordination. When it became clear that this matter was too large a difference to be contained by the "let's agree to differ" principle applied in a university seminar, but rather touched the whole structure of Christian belief (was the Son truly divine or only notionally divine?), Bishop Alexander suspended Arius from his presbyteral duties. Arius appealed to high-ranking bishops he had known of old, whom he knew supported his teachings, and so it was that his appeal came to the ears of Bishop Eusebius of Nicomedia, an intimate adviser of the Constantinian court.

In previous times, such questions as this would be sure to call for a large-scale meeting of bishops of a particular province to hammer out what all sensed to be in accord with the apostolic traditions of the past. But now things had substantively changed. The emperor was in something of a hurry to get the church organized and peaceful so that it could function as a coherent vehicle of moral and eirenic governance in all the towns of the empire. In the eastern provinces where Licinius had so recently been oppressing it, it did not have the same stable structure it enjoyed in the western provinces. But Constantine needed the church to establish a new set of principles organized around monotheism, to offer a new vision for a new age. Accordingly, he found the dissensions over this issue Arius had raised highly irksome. And so began a new era, for Constantine planned to celebrate the twentieth year of his royal accession (325) with a series of great celebrations. One of those would be an international gathering of bishops; for the first time in Christian history a truly worldwide (*oecumene* in Greek) representative synod. Constantine himself would summon it, pay all expenses for it, and sit to listen to its adjudications, before accepting its results and seeing to it that they were enforced. This was the birth of the notion of the Ecumenical Council: a synod of bishops that was super-provincial in size and scope—and thus seen as a truly momentous gathering of the most senior pastors and intellectuals of the Christian world.

What had happened in this apparently logical extrapolation of the old principle of synodical governance was that the issues had been placed under a great magnifying glass. It may well have been the case that only bishops were allowed to sit and make the decisions (on the grounds that the high priests of the church would be guided to a unanimously correct decision on all matters).[13] Imperial officials were able to publish the decrees, and even enforce them to some extent, but not to formulate them. Even so, the public attention that this system was to give to the intellectual matters under debate opened up a wholly new window onto the scrutiny of Christian doctrine. A problem of a bishop and presbyter in Egypt now became a matter of concern for the entire Christian world. It was something like the church now having an amplified sound system. The squeaks and rustles of an earlier age suddenly become loudly broadcast. The result is that we have much clearer knowledge of, and much more extensive texts preserved from, this period. It has also, at least for the Orthodox and Roman Catholic worlds, become a classically constitutive period of formation for the church. It is the heritage, other than the New Testament itself, that the Western Latin and Eastern Orthodox worlds still have in common: the patristic age.

The massively increased status of these super-synods, and the difficulties that ensued when rival synods started to contradict others and claim a paradoxical ecumenical status for themselves, would eventually lead to the principle being enunciated that unless the wider church received (generally accepted) the conciliar doctrines, the council could not claim the status of ecumenicity, thus reserving a critical role for the larger body of faithful in recognizing and validating the teaching role of the bishops. But this was to follow later. What was in the process of arising now was the system of the Ecumenical Councils as the highest legislative authority in the Orthodox Church.[14] At each of these meetings there also seemed to be a great Christian hero (a father of the church) fighting for the truth that the council eventually confirmed. This system of securing doctrine served to extend the earlier concept of the apostolic tradition, with the respective refinements of conciliar and patristic theology as part of it. This is now constitutive of the particular way Orthodoxy sees how Christian doctrine is maintained and repristinated from age to age.[15] There are now seven of these great councils that the Orthodox Church recognizes and accepts as a quintessential summation of major aspects of its teaching. All of them in different ways turn around the axis of the understanding of the divine role of Christ, especially his saving dynamic as operative in the world.

In the remaining sections of this chapter I concentrate on four symbolic moments in that story; not giving a blow-by-blow account of all the individual councils (though in a sense that is a digested course in fundamental Orthodox theology) but rather choosing the great personalities, most of them bishops, who were responsible for the outcomes of four major moments in that ecumenical period: the bishops Athanasius of Alexandria, Gregory of Nazianzus, and Cyril of Alexandria and the monk Maximus the Confessor.[16] Because of the major role they each played, all of them have come to be acclaimed as major fathers of the church; saints, so the Orthodox world confesses, in whom the Spirit of God dwelt deeply, and who were each given the destiny of having their hand on the tiller of the ship in times of crisis, so as to keep it sailing in the way of truth. It is a consideration, in short, of four brilliant and illuminated minds and the ecumenical settlement their work led to, or defended. It is also an exercise in studying four theologians who stand at the very heart of the identity of the Eastern Orthodox Church.

FOUR BRILLIANT MINDS AND THEIR ECUMENICAL SETTLEMENT

Athanasius of Alexandria and the Council of Nicaea (325)

Soon after executing his imperial rival in the east, Licinius, Constantine set out to bring peaceful order into church affairs there. Knowing that the theological dispute in Alexandria between Bishop Alexander and Arius was a serious matter of bitter division, he summoned a trusted Latin theologian, Ossius of Cordoba, to research ways to resolve it. In 324 Ossius tested the waters at a large synod in Antioch, which met to resolve the ongoing disputes over the legitimate episcopal succession of that see, and the result of that sounding was an imperial summons for all the bishops to assemble at his temporary palace at Nikaia, or Nicaea (victory city), modern-day Iznik in Turkey. Constantine put the imperial transport system at the service of the traveling bishops, and he managed to get one of the largest assemblies of senior clergy the Christian world had ever known. The pope at Rome sent delegates but did not attend in person. Attendance was mainly from the eastern provinces, with even British bishops rumored to be present.

After days of public and open debates where rhetorician-philosophers expounded opinions, the sessions of episcopal deliberation commenced. The question was seen, even then, as fundamental to Christian faith. Was Arius right, and therefore should Bishop Alexander be censured for false teachings? Or was it the other way around? On a matter so basic, the question "Was the Logos of God fully divine or not?" was sensed to involve a whole array of subsidiaries: How to read the scriptural evidence? How to synopsize the apostolic tradition? What status did episcopal synods have in the doctrinal tradition of the church? The Council of Nicaea has been seen, almost from the moment it concluded, as the touchstone of Orthodoxy. This is why its creed, or at least a version of it, has become the archetypal symbol of what Christian catholicity is.[17] The Council of Nicaea is, as it were, the sharpest summative digest of the entire apostolic tradition—and this because every line is more or less entirely constructed out of the New Testament itself.[18] The difference between the Nicene Creed, however, and a purely New Testament recitative (lines pasted together) is twofold: first, in the creed it is now the New Testament that is used in a liturgical and doxological setting (the creed began life as a confessional hymn for baptismal candidates), and so the creed represents the scripture as interpreted through the lens of the broader church tradition (its life of prayer, mysticism, exegetical customs, and so on) as supervised by the presiding bishops; second, the creed is the New Testament with the addition of a single, but important, philosophical term added in as a clarification of what the Hebraic idiom of the scriptural poetry meant in a contemporary Greek setting. The word "homoousion" (or "of the same essence as") was added (to be understood in the light of the scriptures surrounding it) as a definitive answer to the particular philosophical question raised by the Arius controversy: namely, was the Divine Word of God, Son of the Father, really divine, or only honorifically divine? Was he God of God, truly God from true God, or was he a subordinate god? Or just a very exalted creature?

The Nicene Creed was agreed by the council largely because it was founded on the substrate of one of the old baptismal creeds that rehearsed the traditional apostolic confession demanded of baptismal candidates. In other words, the conciliar fathers were making a very conservative reaction to the issue of Arius's questions. They were stating the faith received, not trying to speculate on anything new. But Arius had posed the question in an acutely new way. Was the Word of God fully divine or was he a subordinate creature, albeit a highly exalted one like an angel? Arius and his school had already assembled a dossier of scripture texts that seemed to them to support that latter idea. The Alexandrian theologians, led by Alexander the bishop and his deacon Athanasius, had assembled a body of scripture texts that supported the opposite. Arius took his stand on logic and argued that the Son of God could not possibly be called Unoriginate (an essential attribute of God) if he originated from the Father and so must be a creature. Alexander and Athanasius countered that if the Son's origination was a divine act outside time (as it had to be, since all acts of the Eternal Father were timeless), then such an origination carried with it no implication of subordination or difference of stature and certainly did not imply any before or after, since such terms only worked within time and the created order. Outside time meant outside the created order, and thus the birth of the Son from the Father was a begetting of the Son of God, which was outside human comprehension though clearly a divine act: God from God, true God from true God.

One of Arius's main points of objection to the affirmation of the divine status of the Word and Son of God was that it seemed to compromise Christian monotheism. If the Son was God and the Father was God, were there not inevitably two gods? Again Alexander and Athanasius argued that mathematical enumeration, indicating separateness of things, was a concept that applied only to material—that is, created—realities. The conception of how the Father and the Son were related could not be reduced to a mathematical notion, since it was outside time and space. In the time of the council, Athanasius was satisfied that, with the assistance of Ossius of Cordoba, the creed was adopted that refuted Arian propositions, but as the years followed 325, many of the bishops increasingly found the Nicene statement difficult to accept because this matter of mathematical logic seemed to them very troubling. This was where Athanasius came into his own as a theologian. Bishop Alexander died in April 326, and Athanasius succeeded him in a troubled domestic situation. Between internal problems and external imperial pressures Athanasius would have to undergo no fewer than five political exiles for his defense of the Nicene faith in an era that often seemed to have a wish to bypass it. His faithfulness to Nicaea as the cardinal point of defending the apostolic tradition caused the great Saint Gregory of Nazianzus, in the next generation, to acclaim him as "the true pillar of the Church; for his life and conduct set a standard for bishops, and his doctrine set the standard of the Orthodox faith."[19]

Athanasius made several great contributions for the secure establishment of patristic theology and was afterward regarded by the Orthodox Church as one of the greatest of the authoritative fathers: theologians who were episcopal teachers, inspired saints, and defenders of the apostolic tradition in their own generation. First of all, he was schooled in the advanced theological traditions of Alexandria and was able to understand the issues raised all around him. He did not bury his head in the sands of antiquarianism or mere repetition of past utterances as many lesser churchmen and women have tended to do. But more important, he was also able to distinguish between the speculations of learned thinkers and the authentic expression of the apostolic tradition: that core of the evangelical faith that the Orthodox Church had corporately inherited and was duty bound to pass on to later generations. He was thus able to sift the theological inheritance of Origen of Alexandria (died 253), which was standing behind the current Arian dispute, and to resolve the matter by pointing out the assonances and dissonances of each school.

Though Athanasius's Christological thought tacitly admitted the profound weight of Origen's ideas, Athanasius struck out boldly to say that the inherent subordinationism he also found there had to be removed: for if the Son was of the essence of the Father, then that essence in which the Son personally subsisted was in ancient terms none other than the Father's own, and in this case everything that the Father was by essence (that is, by nature) was attributable to the Son.[20] Accordingly, Origen was wrong to suggest that the Son was "less than" the Father. Everything that was in the scriptures that suggested otherwise ("The Father is greater than I" [Jn. 14.28] and suchlike) was meant to refer to the state of the Son in his earthly incarnate state, where he had "emptied himself out" "in the form of a slave" (Phil. 2. 5–11) in order to work the salvific restoration of the human race, which he himself, as Divine Word, had first designed for divine glory.

The second great advance Athanasius achieved was, once again, to simplify the deep subtleties of the earlier Alexandrian and bring to a coherent and teachable form his doctrine that the Incarnation of God the Word was meant for the restoration of the human nature to divine communion. Athanasius brilliantly expounded the view that the Incarnation was not merely an isolated act that the Word undertook (the assumption of human flesh) for a limited time in history. On the contrary, it was no less than a second creation. The Incarnation was the major act of divine redemption of the cosmos. It was the decision by God himself, Second Person of the Trinity, to enter into the most profound communion with humanity as a whole, by becoming no less than the God-Man. This union (the exact terms of the conception would be refined over many years to come) was a most profound one that allowed the Immutable Word to be within history, and to suffer; but it also had a reciprocal effect, for it took what was mortal by condition (humanity) and rendered it immortal by its intimate association with the immortal deity. What Athanasius then stressed was that what thus happened in the case of the body of the Incarnate Word Jesus (the divine suffusion of his flesh to make it radiant and life-giving) also happened in the body of his believers, the church. Their own mortal bodies were lifted up into the mystery of the Incarnation, and even their flesh was rendered grace-filled by their union with Christ. As a pastoral archbishop, Athanasius was able to draw the practical connection here, between the deep theory of redemption and daily church life, for he said that this particularly took place in the encounter with Christ in the Eucharist. With a brilliant eye for succinctness in preaching, he expressed this in his most famous aphorism: "He [the Word] became Man that Man might become god." This was provocatively expressed. One needs to understand it in terms of "deification by grace," or what the Reformers would call "the sanctification of the righteous by grace"; but there is no doubt that the commentators were right in saying that Athanasius brought a robustly physical and transformative theory of atonement into play by this approach, and it is one that has informed and illumined much of Orthodox thinking ever since.

Toward the end of his life, the staunch defense Athanasius gave of the necessity for holding fast to the Nicene Creed, despite all the pressures of an increasingly Arianized court pushing in the opposite direction, allowed the Nicene faith not only to endure but also to shine in the eastern provinces. His fight at so many times appeared so hopeless (though the Latin Church was steadfast in its support of him) that he has attracted the descriptive phrase *Athanasius contra mundum:* Athanasius standing alone against the world—for the defense of Christianity. Again in his last years he set the tone for future theological development by seeing that his earlier works had so emphasized the "divine flesh" of Jesus that he had somewhat neglected the equally necessary truth that the humanity of Jesus was like ours in all respects other than sin, particularly that he was an ensouled being—a real human being, not simply a divinity appearing in a fleshly epiphany as some had suggested.

Again toward the end of his life Athanasius was faced with a question about something that had, until then, largely been unspoken in Christian tradition: the precise status of the Holy Spirit. One of his country suffragan bishops, Serapion of Thmuis, asked him about this specifically, and this occasioned his *Letters to Serapion*, which deal with pneumatology. It used to be thought that this was when he first turned his mind to the issue, but recent scholarly work has shown, to the contrary, that his late doctrine is simply an expression of what he had always taught as a bishop.[21] It was not as if the Holy Spirit had been an unknown factor in earlier Christian teaching and liturgical prayer. The Spirit was invoked and honored in so many avenues of life, not least the baptismal and eucharistic sanctifications that constituted the mainframe of Christian liturgy. Nevertheless, in early Christian practice there was a robust tradition of *arcana sacra:* sacred secrets, some things too holy to be spoken of in ordinary discourse. The tradition of keeping the sacred mysteries (liturgical prayers and services) hidden from pagan outsiders was extensive in the earliest communities. Bishops who were baptizing candidates delivered the Christian doctrine of the Holy Spirit's work and graces to them on the eve of, or during, their actual baptismal ceremony. This was something not ever to be shared with those who were not allowed to communicate at the Eucharist, and to have it was an essential prerequisite for anyone who wished to communicate. This custom of the early church meant that by the fourth century there was not an established body of texts and discussions about the Spirit comparable to what was available about God the Father's role in creation, and God the Son's role in redemption. It was generally understood that the Spirit was involved in both acts of the Godhead, but it was understood too that it was in the process of sanctification (the ongoing life of Christian ethics and prayer) and in inspiration (the revelations given in scripture and spiritual insight) that the Spirit was most intimately involved. In the Arian period, when Christology was being so radically scrutinized and energetically discussed, it was inevitable that the Christological question reopened the ancient confession of God as Trinity and thus put pressure on for a more extensively elaborated treatment of the nature and work of the Spirit.

This ran against the grain of many conservative churchmen, who preferred a pious obscurity, content to remain within the limits of the great discourse on the Spirit of God set out at the end of John's Gospel and in the Pauline Letters. But Athanasius once again had an eye to the need of the contemporary church and spoke up for greater clarity. Both in his early writings and in the more extensively argued *Letters to Serapion* he plainly taught that the Holy Spirit is: uncreated (that is, divine), eternal, intimately united to the Son and his salvific mission as its energy in the world, inspirer and heart of all scriptural revelation, and therefore worthy of all worship and essential for salvation in Christ.[22] In his monumental teachings on the significance of the Incarnation as the primary redemptive act of God in Christ, and in his teachings on the Holy Spirit as God's energization of holiness in the church, Athanasius set the agenda for the church's next generation of theologians to more clearly state the doctrine of the Holy Trinity. What is more, he set the example and standard of what a theologian was who stood for Orthodoxy. In this way he became an archetypal father of the church. The Orthodox Church ever afterward took to its heart that select group of theologians whom it acclaimed as specially and energetically defending the content of the apostolic tradition and how it could be renovated, more clearly expressed, and closely defended in passing generations with new issues. One of Athanasius's admirers in that next generation (who composed an acclamation of him as a great saint) was Gregory the Theologian, to whom we shall now turn.

Gregory the Theologian and the First Council
of Constantinople (381)

Saint Gregory (329–391) was born in the small Cappadocian town of Nazianzus, where his immensely wealthy father was both the local archon, or ruling squire, and the church's bishop.[23] Gregory received the most refined education money could then buy, studying philosophy for ten years at Athens before returning to Cappadocia and assuming the duties of a priest assisting his father, while also living out the studious and retired lifestyle of an ascetic. In 372 he was consecrated bishop to assist Saint Basil the Great in his struggle with the Arian court of the emperor Valens, but disgusted by the party politics at play among senior clerics, he retired back to Nazianzus. Saint Basil had been one of the leading pro-Nicene theologians and apologists in the generation after Athanasius. After Basil's death in 379 the leading Nicene theologians called upon Gregory to leave his life of seclusion and come in haste to Constantinople. The Arian emperor Valens had recently been killed, and the capital city (then fully occupied by Arian clergy in all the churches) was awaiting the appointment of a new emperor. Gregory was petitioned to go there and preach the Orthodox faith. He took up residence in a large villa in the heart of the capital and consecrated it as a small church. In this, known as the Resurrection Chapel, he gave a series of orations on God, Christ, and the Holy Spirit, which have since been accepted as the core theological teachings of the Orthodox Church on the Holy Trinity.[24]

Gregory offered this series of dogmatic sermons in order to preface, and prepare for, what he hoped would be a second great and ecumenical council that would definitively end fifty years of Arian ascendancy, during which the Council of Nicaea had been systematically disparaged by the court and its favored bishops. He starts his series of lectures with a discussion of what it is to do theology correctly and in accordance with the apostolic tradition. "Not to all men is it given to philosophize about the things of God," he argues, only to those whose hearts and minds have been purified by the Spirit of holiness, so that the eyes of their spirit are enabled to perceive the mysteries of the Spirit.[25] He sets out to censure "people whose ears and tongues itch for the delight of profane words and pseudo-scientific paradoxes."[26] If one's life is not illumined by the grace of the Spirit, then one cannot hope to approach the great mystery of the faith, he argues. As the apostle Paul was lifted up into heaven, in order to be able to receive the capacity for such great insights into the nature and work of God, so too the one who expounds the Orthodox faith must share in the intimate grace of the Spirit by a life that is both pure and seriously dedicated to the careful study of the church's life. Gregory has in his gunsights the leaders of the Arian movement who were, by and large, city bishops enjoying state patronage but who often displayed little theological refinement; and also a particular theologian called Eunomius, one of the most radical Arian theologians of the day, who had argued the *heterousiast* position: namely, that the Son of God was a being wholly different from God; that both the Son and the Holy Spirit were nothing other than creatures, angels if one liked, called into service by the single and monolithically separate God the Father.

Gregory's theology, therefore, goes back to the foundations, to restate the Nicene doctrine in a manner that takes cognizance of another generation of church controversies. This is why it stands as such a dense, magisterial, and succinct statement of Orthodoxy, and why the Eastern Church calls Gregory "the" theologian. Speaking of God, he says, is a great and mystical ascent, like that of Moses climbing Sinai to see a glimpse of God's power passing by.[27] Plato had famously said that to conceive of God was difficult, but to express him in words, impossible. Gregory cites the opinion and mockingly contradicts it. God's nature is so mystically beyond the powers of human cognition, he says, "that it is impossible to express him in words, but even more impossible to conceive of him in the mind."[28] From that time onward this approach— the very tentative ascent toward saying anything about the God who truly transcends all thought and perception—has dominated the ethos, theology, and spirituality of the Orthodox Church, giving it a mystical character that shows in all its formal and more personal aspects of life.[29]

Gregory defines God as the point of ascent to which all life, especially all consciousness, turns by an inward longing. Since God made us in his image, all humans have an innate affinity with the divine: all are mystical sacraments, not merely ignorant animals. The sense of God is native to us, and the destiny this gives to humanity is unique, for it calls to human nature to extend beyond itself, to transcend the limits of a mortal nature that is doomed to death and corruption within this time and order of reality. For Gregory, the Incarnation of the Divine Word was the major act (a second creation) of God reinviting his own people back to their true nature: a moral, intellectual and spiritual (noetic) ascent that will be completed (for those who have advanced along its path in this life) in the form of full communion with the Word in the afterlife.[30] As did Athanasius, Gregory saw the Christ as the Word-Enfleshed. God had assumed humanity into such a close union with himself that it had rendered the humanity of the Lord radiant with power: even in his Passion and death he worked divine transfiguration. His Passion was the universal forgiveness of sins, and his death was the gift of immortality to the human race, through the grace of resurrection given in place of mortality. Against those who were trying in his time to suggest Jesus was some form of divinity transiently passing through history, Gregory countered: "What he did not assume, he did not heal."[31] He went on to argue that in Christ the Divine Word took on himself every aspect of human life (its joys and sufferings and limitations) in order to suffuse everything with the divine grace of freedom and joy. His Incarnation, for Gregory, becomes the doorway to true human fulfillment: a fulfillment that eventually expresses itself in a fullness of life that will dawn on it in its divine transfiguration alongside the Word, but that truly begins here and now in the manner of life one lives on earth. The Incarnate Christ becomes, therefore, the paradigm of all discipleship and the vehicle of human transformation.

Some in Gregory's day were beginning to turn to biblical fundamentalism as a presumed safe haven in times of confusion. Gregory warns them consistently against such a false turn. They had argued that since scripture does not explicitly call the Holy Spirit "God," the church should not continue to speak of him in divine terms. In his *Oration 31* Gregory speaks boldly of how the Spirit is God from God, like the Word, consubstantial with the Father, as is the Son, and just as divine as he is, by virtue of having the same divine essence. The Spirit comes from the Father by procession (*ekporeusis*), as scripture says (Jn. 15.26), just as the Son comes from the Father by begetting (*gennesis*). This is why the person of the

One God is trinitarian. For Gregory this was not a peculiar conundrum that was to be rehearsed but not seriously considered: rather, he brings it to the center and forefront of the Christian confession. The Trinity is the unapproachable mystery of God's own being as a communion of love. It is known to us only in small part insofar as it is also God's energy of salvation outreach—God's stretching out to the world, first in creation, through the Logos, and then in that energy of the restoring of the original created design—redemption through the Logos's Incarnation. In his theology, Gregory insisted that the whole Orthodox world should confess that the Son was begotten of the Father, and that the Spirit proceeded from the Father; and this was effectively the profession of faith adopted at the First Council of Constantinople (381), where Gregory presided as archbishop of the capital city. This was the trinitarian faith of the early church, shared with the Western churches across most of the first millennium, until later popes inserted into the creed—which originally read: "And we believe in the Holy Spirit who proceeds from the Father"—the addendum that made it then read: "Who proceeds from the Father and from the Son (*filioque*)." Western Christian trinitarianism thus departed significantly (and some Orthodox would say substantively) from that of the Nicene fathers. The Orthodox world still maintains that the procession of the Spirit and the begetting of the Son, both from the single source of the Father's own being, as two hypostases of his single Ousia is the only way to ensure that Christian Trinitarianism sustains the Unity of the Godhead, and the proper order (*taxis*) of the divine outreach of salvation to the world.

Many people today seem to regard the Trinity as a dead letter and are apparently not so concerned about this: often

THE CLASSICAL PATRISTIC PERIOD

they cannot see why the Orthodox get bothered by it at all. But the filioque controversy reveals two things the Orthodox think are fundamentally damaging to Christian faith. In the first place, the insertion of this clause into the basic creed of Christendom on the authority of the pope alone (for the West) augured bad things to come in the perspective of the Orthodox. The Eastern Church never would allow any single bishop, however exalted his role or his city, to stand alone as the arbiter of Christian apostolic tradition. That role belonged to the collective mentality of the church articulated in the larger episcopal synods, whose results had then to be presented to the faithful for acceptance. Allowing a single bishop to adjudicate such matters on his own authority, so the Orthodox thought (and still think), would lead to problems. The Reformation-era fragmentation of Christendom in the West was one such example of this (still to be resolved). The second issue was more important. Several theologians in the early Western Church had suggested that God was one and three because he had one single essence (or nature) and three distinct persons all possessing that nature equally. Seizing on this model, the medieval theologians who taught the filioque clause did so as a way of teaching the "full divinity" of the Son and the Spirit and how all was shared within the life of the Trinity. As Gregory had pointed out, however, God does not have a nature in the sense of possessing one in the manner in which all creaturely things have a nature. A nature in this sense is a set of existential limits that border and thus define a quantifiable reality. God is not of the created order, and one cannot suggest that he has a nature that so limits him in the sense that he could be said to "possess" it. In short, this model was an unjustifiable diminution of the inexpressible and unapproachable essence of God. Gregory the Theologian taught, by contrast, that God the Father is (as the scripture first described him at Sinai) "I am who I am." He is. He does not exist in the manner of created beings. He simply self-subsists as himself, the All-Powerful Father. He alone has being: all things other have dependent existences out of that being.

So how did Gregory conceive of the Trinity? The Father, before all time and all created beings, begets the Son. This does not mean, as Gregory hastens to point out, that there is scission or any separation involved. God begets his own Son in order to reveal himself to the world; through the Son-Logos, the Father will create all existent things. What this begetting is, however, is beyond our conception, though we know scripture uses the term as a reserved analogy for the relation of Son and Father. But what we do know about it is that the Father gifts his own being to the Son, who now personally exemplifies that selfsame being in his own identity as Son and Word and agent of the Father. The Son does not possess a share in the Father's being. Nor does he happen simply to have an identically quantifiable nature (as two members of a family could each be said to be human) in a way that suggests there is a common nature to which both belong. On the contrary, the Son inhabits the Father's own nature: subsists in the Father's singleness of nature. In the way God qualifies and extends the divine outreach to the world we also learn that the Father has similarly gifted his own divine nature to the Holy Spirit. Not by begetting but by a manner scripture calls "procession." This means that both the Son and the Spirit now each subsist in the same singleness of the Father's unique being. They each have his being, or are his being; each individually (or hypostatically) instantiating that being of the Father. For Gregory, this is why Christians can say there is only one God, but that the One God is three personed. Gregory is the thinker who chiefly insists on the church clarifying its language to use in relation to the Trinity: three hypostases (or individuations) and one essence or nature (ousia).[32]

One can see, therefore, how the filioque radically disrupts what Gregory was teaching about the Trinitarian reality of God: how this giftedness of his being reaches out in a vast energy of communication. The divine outreach of the Trinitarian persons to the world is only an image, or shadow, of this more fundamental, transcendent communication by gift of the Father himself to the Son and Spirit. The filioque stops the Trinity from being a great outrush to the world; stops it also from being a model of how the world is saved. For Gregory also went on to suggest that as the Father moved out through the Son and the Spirit so the Church was brought, in the Spirit, to the Son and through the Son to the Father. The whole Christian energy of salvation was thus an intimate expression of the inner life of the Trinity becoming the inner dynamic of the Christian's life of grace. In the Western filioque version, the Trinity became static, a deadened image connoting nothing of much force. This is precisely why the Trinity lost the devotion and attachment of the Western Christian mind: it ceased to mean much to later Western believers, and so (to all real intent) fell into being a dead letter. For the Orthodox world the Trinity is a dynamic progression of grace experienced every day: to the Father through the Son in the Holy Spirit; and there is no Orthodox prayer, from the most exalted liturgy down to the humblest forms of individual devotion, that does not celebrate that mystery in numerous trinitarian doxologies each day.

One cannot stay too long with such an exalted mind as Saint Gregory's. But Gregory was not always stretching one's understanding this way. He was one of the most advanced intelligences of the ancient world, and also one of its great litterateurs. He composed many very beautiful and comparatively simple hymns to the Trinitarian Godhead, many of which are still sung in the Orthodox liturgies. It was he who, in his *Oration 21*, first called some of his predecessors "the Great." He named Bishops Athanasius of Alexandria and Basil of Caesarea "the Great," and these titles have remained with them to this day. There are many others to whom the church has affixed this honor. What Gregory was doing in this instance was to canonize some of his predecessors: name them as great saints. What he had in mind was not simply to commend them for their purity and holiness of life but more precisely to identity them as bearers of the Spirit of God. Such spirit bearers (*pneumatophoroi*) he saw as those men and women who through the ages carried the purity of the apostolic tradition most closely in their teaching. Many Christians can exemplify this by their fidelity, but these great souls were gifted with the teaching office. If a teacher goes wrong, he or she can lead many others astray. This is why Gregory felt that the only safe guides were those whom the church identified, retrospectively, as truly authentic and inspired teachers. Follow these, he argued, and do not listen to every voice, as the Apostle himself had first instructed (1 Jn. 4.2). This was, in effect, the formal identification of the principle of patristic theology. Patristic is a Latin word meaning "pertaining to the fathers." Gregory had put his finger on what the church had tended to do for a long time beforehand but was now going to do on a more systematic basis. Both the Latin and the Eastern Church followed the same path for a very long time afterward, though it tended to fade somewhat in the West. For Orthodoxy, however, this notion, that there are some theologians who are specially graced by the quality of their inspiration—the depth of their possession of the Spirit of God, the closeness of their hidden life in Christ, and thus the quality of their apprehension of the Father—that they have a privileged position in the ranks of Christian teachers, was one that took hold strongly.

The idea that there were noted fathers of the church whose teachings guided the church in each generation was a dramatic insistence that the apostolic tradition was not a dead thing but was renewed in every generation as the Spirit gave voice to inspired saints. Orthodoxy to this day prizes the ranks of those it calls the fathers, and it accumulates their wisdom in a careful collection and study of their work. It places less reliance on contemporary, living theologians and in each instance demands of its theological teachers that they conform their lives to the Gospel and to the preceding ranks of earlier teachers, so that the whole consensus of Orthodox theology will be organically linked in a tight communion of the Spirit. This is why Orthodox thought is dominated by the idea of precedent: Has this idea, whatever it is, been exemplified elsewhere in scripture? Or in the prayer and liturgical traditions of the church? Or in the teachings of its great theologians? Or in the lives of its holiest saints? If not, then how can it be seen as a positive aspect of the apostolic tradition? This is why patristic theology occupies a pride of place in Orthodox thinking, alongside the preeminent place of the scriptures. It does not preclude all other forms of thinking, especially about contemporary problems, but it is an approach that gives the Orthodox world great stability in its teaching ministry. What it teaches, it feels, has to be exemplified first: lived-out truths are more important than mere speculations. Gregory himself was soon adopted into the ranks of the greatest of the fathers of the church.

Saint Cyril of Alexandria and the Council of Ephesus (431)

Another major father of the Eastern Church is Saint Cyril, archbishop of Alexandria (378–444). I have chosen to list him in particular among our four great minds because if Saint Athanasius represents essential Orthodox thinking on the Incarnation and Saint Gregory represents its doctrine of the Trinity, then Cyril stands as someone who most acutely represents its theology of redemption by deifying grace. Anastasius of Sinai (died 700) expressed the sentiment of all the Orthodox churches when he called Cyril "the seal (*sphragis*) of the Fathers," in the sense that he set a royal seal on all that had gone before him. Cyril had closely read Saint Athanasius, Saint John Chrysostom, and Saint Gregory the Theologian, as well as the philosophers of the school of Damascius. His knowledge of the scripture is both subtle and deep: his theology being discursive and deeply engaged in a scriptural mesh long before he was drawn into more precise dogmatic arguments with his opponents. Chief among these were theologians who wanted to establish precision and order in Christian discourse, and who accused him of muddying the waters.

What had happened was that a new Syrian archbishop, named Nestorius, had been appointed in the capital city of

Constantinople in the year 428. The capital had been for many years past the Christian city that was claiming the ascendancy in church affairs. What it taught in its schools had a wide influence. When Nestorius began teaching that the church's language about Christ needed reform, Cyril sat up and paid attention with some anxiety because he recognized in the series of sermons issuing from Constantinople that he himself was a primary target of criticism. Nestorius had heard that the city he had inherited had a deep devotion to the Virgin Mary and acclaimed her in its prayers and litanies as the "Mother of God" (*Theotokos* in Greek).[33] This was something new to him, and he found it distasteful. Mary, he argued publicly, ought not to be called the Mother of God, since God, strictly speaking (*akribos*), had no mother but was eternal. So Mary should only be called the Mother of Christ, or the Mother of Jesus. What Nestorius meant to do by this was to institute a thoroughgoing reform of Christian discourse to eradicate what he saw as confusions. He felt that every time someone attributed to Jesus a divine characteristic this made for a terribly confused and mixed-up sense of how God was in Christ. He felt the language of piety that used such titles as Mother of God, or ideas like the sufferings of God on the Cross, was hopelessly wrong-headed. For Nestorius the main thing was to clarify and make exact (*akribeia*) Christological language. He argued that when one referred divine things to the Savior one ought to use the title "Word," or "Son of God." When one referred to things that applied to both the divine and the human reality of the Lord (miraculous powers, for example), one had to use the subject title "Christ," and when one referred to particularly human limitations (eating, ignorance, or suffering, for example), one had always to use the subject designation "Jesus." So, one should never say "God wept," only "Jesus wept," and so on for all the scriptural stories about Christ. In this way one could safely avoid two clashing rocks that would be disastrous for Christian thought: the Scylla of Arianism that was scandalized by any attribution of suffering or limitation if applied to a divine Christ, and the Charybdis of a pietistic view of a divine Jesus where his humanity was so mixed up in the divinity that it more or less disappeared into a picture of a divine Lord walking the earth like a god possessed of all superhuman powers.

Cyril was deeply puzzled by this attack on traditional piety and language. It seemed to him entirely an innovation, one that struck at the very heart of Orthodox theology. He put the idea simply at first, reversing the logic of Nestorius: "If Mary is not, strictly speaking (*akribos*), the Mother of God, then the One who was born from her is not, strictly speaking, God." When Nestorius protested that he was not attacking the concept of the divinity of Jesus, only the notion that some theological statements confused the divine and human in Jesus in such a way that they attributed suffering to the Godhead, and impassibility to the Manhood, in ways that were clearly illogical, Cyril deepened his argument. Nestorius, he said, seemed to be ashamed of attributing suffering to the divine Christ. He obviously felt it wholly inappropriate that Godhead should, in any way, be involved with humiliation and pain. And yet this was the decision of God himself who had freely elected to be born, in order to teach and suffer and die for the sake of men and women. If God, in Christ, had so elected the humiliation of the Cross, who was Nestorius to be offended by it? The Cross was a logical result of the Word's personal divine choice to be Incarnated.

For Cyril, Nestorius's God was more the Impassible Deity of the Greek philosophers than the God revealed to us in Christ's Incarnation, through the Gospels and the apostolic tradition. God, the Word, impassible and all-powerful in nature, had decided to enter into human history in this close and intimate relationship with the human race, and so had chosen the path of personal incarnation. This was the key to the uniqueness of Christian experience. For Cyril, the person subject of the Incarnate Lord was single and selfsame in all aspects of his being. In other words, the Logos of God was the single personal subject (hypostasis) of all of the following: the Second Person of the trinity, the Divine Word, the Son of God, the Christ, and Jesus of Nazareth. They were all one and the same subject. Obviously, the names of Divine Word, the Eternal Son, the Everlasting Wisdom of God, and other such titles of this single hypostasis were, properly speaking, eternal referents that referred to the life of the Word of God before the Incarnation. Equally, some names, such as Jesus of Nazareth, Rabbi, and Son of Man, were titles that specifically related to the life of the Lord in his incarnate state. Some titles were able to connote both the eternal life and the incarnate life, such as Son of God, Wisdom, Lord, Life and Light, and many others found in the New Testament.

Cyril pressed the point home that this singleness of subjectivity meant that it was the Divine and Eternal Word who had personally assumed the human life. There was not a man, called Jesus, whom God inhabited or inspired, in the way the older heretics, called Adoptionists, had once taught. There was only the Word who assumed flesh in the womb of the Virgin and was born from her as the Son of God, God from God, and Light from Light. In this way Mary, strictly and exactly speaking, was the Mother of God. The point Nestorius was making, that God has no Mother because of the definition of deity as Unoriginate, was perfectly true in itself, but was pedantically unnecessary in Christian discourse, because when the faithful confessed Mary was the Mother of God everybody understood that it was a way of speaking about the Eternal Son of God within his Incarnate state. This was so obvious it did not really need emphasis. If one denied this manner of speaking, however, then the implication was surely very heavy: to feel offended in saying Mary is Mother of God really meant that there was a certain reluctance in confessing Jesus really was divine.

As the bitterness of the dispute between Constantinople and Alexandria started to heat up, with each great see appealing outward to other sees, such as Rome and Antioch, each claiming that it represented the "proper" approach to the apostolic tradition, it became obvious that this was no longer a matter of individual concern. Sensing that he was truly defending the heartland of the Christian faith, Cyril pressed the theology more acutely, and this was where his own specific contributions shone out. Instead of agreeing on a compromise with Nestorius ("you have your low theology, and I'll have my high theology"), Cyril provocatively expressed his thought more succinctly by using a method of dramatic paradoxes. These were designed to shock his listeners at first, make them think about the statement, and then express their agreement that, in Christ, God had certainly come into human history, personally and directly, not in a mediated or distanced form. So, for example, Cyril used to speak about the Passion and the Cross as the "sufferings of God" and took delight in referring to the acts of Jesus as divine works. When Lazarus was raised, for example, he said: "God wept." He would deliberately cross over nature referents in the person and work of Christ, articulating boldly how Jesus of Nazareth was God in human form; how Jesus was the Eternal Son; how Mary was the Mother of God; how God wept at the tomb; and how God bled and died on the Cross. These things infuriated Nestorius. He started to think that Cyril had no theological sense whatsoever: not to know that Jesus's history did not preexist his birthday at Bethlehem, or that God could not be said to bleed or die. But Cyril was far from being naïve or ill-educated. What he meant by elevating these strong paradoxes was to make his Christology a set of *aporias:* philosophical puzzles that made the listeners supply the answer. It was a very old and established way of teaching in antiquity. The answer Cyril expected them to make, in fact led them to make, by this way of speaking, was that all these paradoxes that seemed illegitimately to refer acts and powers "to the wrong nature" became abundantly clear and perfectly correct when it was realized that they all referred to one and the same person.

If (but only if) Jesus of Nazareth's person was the selfsame as the Eternal Word of God, then what Jesus endured in the flesh was directly attributable to the Word of God; even though in his "own," or proper, nature as Second Person of the Trinity such things did not apply. In short, the Impassible Word could suffer and die because he had elected to be born in the flesh. Without leaving behind his divine glory he had willingly accepted the humility of the Incarnation. Just as he lifted up the Manhood into his own divine life, so too he lifted up along with it all the sufferings and limitations appropriate to that Manhood. Cyril went further. This, he argued, was exactly why the Incarnation happened in the first place. The

Word did not choose to come to earth, and live as a true human being, because he felt the need for a change of scenery. He came so as to embrace humanity into his own life as divine creator and refashioner, and, having embraced it so profoundly, thus to heal it. As he healed his own mortal nature, making what was evidently mortal and passible (as proved by Passion and death) into what was immortal and impassible, rendering the lowliness of death into the glorified body, so too did he elevate all human nature in that once and for all act. Cyril argued that the Incarnation was, therefore, nothing less than the second creation of humanity: a making of the Old Adam into the New Adam: making that death and corruption, which had so marked fallen Mankind, into a spring of life-giving grace that lifted the human race from death into life, through a new and intimate union with the Eternal Word-made-flesh. This complex idea is simply expressed as the "Communion of Idioms" (*antidosis idiomatum*) or "Exchange of Properties." It turns around the axial idea that there is but a single subject in the Incarnate Lord, and this means that all the acts of the Incarnate Savior are acts of the Logos-in-flesh. So if the Word is Eternal Lord of the angels and Jesus is a suffering and wounded figure, it is equally true to say Jesus is the Eternal Lord of the angels and the Word suffers and is wounded. In each case the paradox is resolved into sense by the understanding we are here always talking about the Word-made-flesh.

Nestorius was simply unable to embrace this concept in his thought. Cyril saw it as the very mainspring of the whole dynamic of salvation: why we were saved by the birth, life teachings, sufferings, death, and Resurrection of Christ, all of them acts that God the Word personally performed through the medium of the Incarnation. For Cyril it was not merely the death on the Cross that redeemed us but the ontological re-creation of our humanity that happened when the Divine Word did what was impossible and illogical (impossible to sophists and logicians, that is) and took up humanity into his own personal life, transfiguring it in the process. Christ himself, for Cyril, is the dynamic process of our salvation; and the life we are offered is life in communion with God through him. Cyril had learned most profoundly from Athanasius's old dictum, "The Word became Man so that Man might become god." But now he had expanded the idea to make all Christology into a clear and vivid doctrine of salvation. What is more, he had expressed this not only in high theology of a very intellectual order but even in the simplest of phrases suitable for the simpler believers. His thought now explained why one could say litanies of the form "Jesus my God; Jesus Pre-Eternal; Jesus Maker of the Angels": because the one who was born of Mary, late in time, and limited by his human nature, proved himself unlimited and timeless as well: his weakness also showing itself to be divine power; his humility and suffering manifesting itself as God's essential glory.

Where Nestorius seemed to find the Cross embarrassing, Cyril took Paul's point to heart and gloried in the Cross (Gal. 6.14). Nestorius's Christ was a servant of a distant God who kept his hands clean, as a respectable Greco-Roman divinity was expected to. Cyril's Christ was the God-Man who strode into the maelstrom of flesh and blood, in order to bring order and healing back to suffering men and women; in complete solidarity with them, yet lifting them out of their corruptibility into his own divine radiance if they would have his hand. This was why Cyril so doggedly fought against the alleged rational reforms that Nestorius wished to impose on his Constantinopolitan

Church. When an Ecumenical Council was called at Ephesus in 431 to resolve this conflict between the two archbishops, the great majority affirmed that it was Cyril's instinct and passion for the apostolic tradition that made it the one they recognized. To prove the point, Cyril brought to the council a whole dossier of patristic proof-texts to show how his thought was supported by many preceding great minds in Christian history.[34] From this time onward it has been customary in the Orthodox Church for anyone involved in a great theological question to collate such a body of evidence from precedence. To this extent Cyril added to the old ways of establishing apostolic authenticity (biblical proof-texts, liturgical supports, synodical agreements) this new pattern of collating patristic references. It would remain central to Orthodox and Catholic theological method ever after, and would always serve as a check to modern trends and opinions, to make sure that the church was always in touch with the times but never just conforming to the spirit of the age (Rom. 12.2). Cyril put the capstone on the church's traditions about Jesus's divine acts, or pressed the seal into the wax, as Anastasius had said. It is one of the reasons the Orthodox Church, which so greatly reveres Cyril, to this day has an approach to the Lord Jesus that is first and foremost a homely-mystical one: warmly sensing him as the Lord who transfigures all he touches into light and health and immortality.

Saint Maximus the Confessor and the Third Council of Constantinople (681)

If Saint Athanasius sums up the Council of Nicaea for Orthodoxy, and Saint Gregory represents the Council of Constantinople (381), and Cyril distills the Ecumenical Councils of Ephesus (431), Chalcedon (451), and Constantinople II (553) (which were a series of variations and clarifications on his master theme), then our fourth representative father of the church sums up the last of the great Christological councils, that of Constantinople III in 681. He did this even though he was not named in those acts or present for the council, having died a martyr for his defense of the faith. It is Saint Maximus the Confessor (c. 590–662). He is one of the most acute and brilliant minds of the late patristic/Byzantine era. His theology is deep and cosmic in scope, and it gives to most of what follows in the traditions of Orthodoxy the character of mystical ascent that Cyril had adumbrated and that now Maximus renders on a vast poetic canvas.

His skill was that of a brilliant philosophical theologian who was also a master synthesist. Maximus had the ability in the seventh century to review the whole gamut of the scriptures and also the complete range of the fathers who had written before him. But above all else he recognized that the theology of the Orthodox Church was meant for one thing only: not to present a face to the world but rather to clarify the way and method of the ascent to union with Christ for the believer. Theology was not just a theoretical discipline but also the path of salvation itself. It was no less than the spiritual life Christ had infused in the church. Maximus himself was a dedicated ascetic and monastic. He spent great amounts of his day in prayer and reflection. But he was also a deeply rooted scholar and an activist as well. He stood firmly for the truth that one becomes what one reads and prays. His overarching idea was that the Divine Word, or Logos, had not simply made the worlds of seen and unseen realities (in which humankind and the angels were the representative consciousnesses who served as priests of God) but had designed the structure of the cosmos to be the medium of revelation of God's love and communion. For Maximus, the Logos had set within the entire scheme of being a passionate drive, an Eros he calls it, of the deepest longing to go back to communion in God. Even though the mind and soul of an individual may not fully comprehend what is happening, all the driving forces in life that are good and clean and true serve to lift up the creature to a fuller sense of direction and a greater love for God. This love is ascentive in every sense: moral, intellectual, and metaphysical. In ascending through a pure life, one dedicated to prayer and compassion toward the neighbor, the soul of the individual realizes its innate priestly character. In beginning to understand the interior rationale of created things (their *logoi* in Greek), the priestly soul sees through the created structures to the Divine Logos who undergirds and empowers them all: then the mind offers praise, and in its wonderment at the profundity of God's mind, so barely glimpsed yet so transcendent, it lifts up the lesser-conscious creation around it in a priestly act of offering and refinement—as the ancient priest of old used to offer sacrifices of the first fruits. For Maximus this ascension of mind and soul demands study, for it is in clarifying our thought and our lifestyle that the presence of the Divine Logos in all things around us becomes clear, allowing the fire of divine love to grow in force, which leads us on even further still into an ever-deepening communion of love.

In his own time Maximus was faced with many who wished to stress that Jesus was so specially divine and separate from the created order that he did not have the same constitution as other human beings: he might be "Man" but he was not "a man" in the ordinary sense. This was an old temptation of pious Christians from early times: to mark Jesus off by not allowing that he had a mind, or a soul, or any other human defect. Maximus was pressured by the church authorities of his time, who were anxious to come up with an ecumenical compromise to bring together the Byzantine, Roman, Egyptian, and Syrian churches, to say that Jesus had only one will in his being: a divine one (monothelitism). Remembering his deep and close study of Gregory the Theologian, he replied that this would not only separate the Incarnate Lord from the nature he was redeeming by adopting it but also mean that he could hardly serve as a model of believers: since if his will was purely divine he could hardly be tempted as we are. Reminding his opponents of the Letter to Hebrews (Heb. 4.15) as well as of the sorrows of Jesus in Gethsemane when he wrestled for his ability to offer obedience to God (Lk. 22.42), Maximus insisted that Jesus had a divine will that flowed from his heavenly nature, as well as a human will that flowed from his human nature: for willing is a factor or aspect of a natural condition. Where his divine will was concerned with universal matters appropriate to his stature as Logos, his human will was exercised in all the concerns of his daily life and was the arena where he grew in stature and favor before God the Father (Lk. 2.52). What was unique about Jesus, however, was the manner in which his human will was so perfectly in tune with the divine will that he was truly, in every way, the model of how a human being would be perfected by communion with the Divine Word. What he was in himself and in his own being, we were called to be by his grace.

For his teachings, which he never ceased to proclaim against royal authority that tried to silence him, Maximus paid with his life. First he was arrested and sent into exile. Then, when he refused to be quiet and kept on writing, he was brought back to Constantinople and tried for treason and heresy. His tongue was cut out and his right hand was cut off as punishments, and he was sent back into exile at Lazica, on the Black Sea coast of modern Georgia. He died soon after from his wounds and so won the title "Confessor," which is given to a martyr who does not die immediately in the course of a persecution. Although he was never given credit for it until a very long time afterward, it was his theological preaching that underlined the sixth of the great Ecumenical Councils and that fixed the Orthodox theological tradition in a stability and comprehensiveness that it still possesses. Maximus's greatest influence on Orthodoxy was the stress that all striving in the church, all attempts to clarify and express the sense of God, were subordinate, in the end and in the beginning, to the task of living within God. What the mind often cannot grasp, the heart can always comprehend. To this day Orthodoxy is a faith that can embrace both intelligentsia and children with equal power.

SELECT ICONS OF ORTHODOX TRADITION

These four great theologians in a very real sense sum up all of Orthodox theology, and for that reason they have been offered here in an exemplarist fashion, so as to stand for a larger discourse on Orthodox thought, which would be out of place.[35] They collectively stride over the first six Ecumenical Councils, and their teachings still provide the key to understanding those foundational synods. Each one of these fathers of the church is steeped in knowledge and love of the scriptures and the church sacraments, which is why each demonstrates that profound linkage in Orthodoxy between scripture, synodical government,

Ecumenical Council, liturgy, and patristic theology: a synthesis of streams of spirituality that constitutes the Christian apostolic tradition and keeps the Orthodox Church ever ancient, yet makes it ever new; rooted with the firmest of anchors but always alive to respond to the spiritual needs and hopes of contemporary men and women. In the high Middle Ages another great saint of the Orthodox tradition, Symeon the New Theologian (949–1022), expressed this in a vivid image. Faith and Christian experience of the Spirit, he said, cannot be taught from a book, or even learned from deduction. It is like the flame of a candle. It can only be passed on, person to person, face to face, lit from one flame of a faithful soul to another in a personal encounter. This is the manner in which faith in the supreme hypostasis, that ultimate person of the Logos (from whom all other personal consciousnesses are fashioned) has made the process of spiritual "begetting." This is the faith of the Orthodox Church, which it received from the apostles, preserved through the long road of the ages, and still offers to all who are thirsty even to this present day.

CHAPTER FOUR

The Byzantine Imperial Church

BYZANTINE IDEAS OF CHURCH AND SOCIETY

The pre-Constantinian Church had suffered much from the hands of the state, especially in the fourth century when the emperors Diocletian and Galerius had specifically targeted the Christians in an attempt to bolster the traditional cults of the Roman gods. One might have expected Eastern Christianity to remain very skeptical about worldly powers. But when Constantine defied Galerius and rose to supreme power across both western and eastern provinces of the empire, it seemed that more than a dream had been fulfilled. The emperor had begun by granting great favor to the church and ended by being baptized himself. Even before his day the great theologian Origen had countered the claims of the Greco-Roman philosopher Kelsos that the church was a pathogen in the body politic, by musing how God himself had providentially laid down the infrastructures of Romanity in order to facilitate the spread of the Gospel to one people gathered together in a supranational identity: the religious spirit of Judaism refined by Christ and given to the world through the roads and institutions of civilization founded by Rome.[1] Other Christians had also seen a connection. Lactantius argued that Christ was the fulfillment of all the dreams of Rome for a golden age that had been diverted and misled by its brutal militarism.[2] Christ he depicted as the one whom the ancient prophecies of the Sibyls had been pointing toward. Many in the West saw the yearning and hopes of the *Aeneid* for a future Savior to come to Rome, as referring not to Augustus but rather to the one who was born in the reign of Augustus. Bishop Eusebius of Caesarea was not the first, then, to see Constantine's rise to power as a Christian emperor as the dawn of a new age. Many later Protestant theologians have tended to demonize this theology and ridicule it as "caesaro-papist."[3] Highly suspicious of the state's involvement in anything to do with religion, they find the close attachment of the church after the fourth century to state institutions as a corruption or at least a taking of a dangerously misleading road.

For the Orthodox world this is seen in a wholly different light. The rise of "Christ-loving emperors," as they are called, is seen as part of God's providential plan for the outreach of the mission of the church. It is the church's duty to be so involved in human society (not apart from it) that it acts as a leaven in the body mass, lifting and oxygenating it with the Good News of Christ's salvation. The Orthodox Church, once it had state support, immediately began to institute medical care for the poorest of the poor, which had hitherto been available only to the rich.[4] Gregory of Nazianzus and Basil of Caesarea solicited funds to found a great medical center (the Basiliad); and both of these figures, being monastics and among the highest theologians of the early church, offered an authoritative example for monks (who in the earlier ages had been withdrawn solitaries) and for nuns to offer their dedicated services in the education and care of children and orphans, and in medical services for the poor. Constantinople, in the early medieval period, had many charitable institutions operating as poor-relief houses, midwifery clinics, surgeries, orphanages, and schools. The very tight link between church institutions and the offering of public welfare programs was begun from the earliest times, and continued to build in medieval and early modern society. That linkage has only been broken in very recent times in societies with advanced welfare systems; but it remains in many places in the less developed world; and it stands as an abiding fact that it was the early Orthodox Church that taught the modern world the countercultural importance of care of the poor—something it needs to relearn in so many instances. This philosophy of care was called *philanthropia* in the Orthodox Church.

This took its lead from the Gospel injunction to love the neighbor and was seen as an imitation (a mimesis) of the philanthropia (literally, "loving-kindness for mankind") that the Divine Word expressed for the world in becoming incarnate. Love for the other, therefore, was always seen in the Orthodox tradition as more than simply human charity and rather an entrance into the sacrament of divine compassion and, as such, a profound act of worship. Saint Gregory the Theologian was the first writer, outside the scriptures, ever to go on record to theorize that the care of the poor, for their own sake and for the cause of the intrinsic dignity of the human person, was a godly act that demanded society's response.[5] Before him, in the long annals of Greek and Roman literature it had simply been presumed that the poor ought to go to the wall as part of the natural order.

As the fourth century advanced, the Orthodox bishops influenced Roman law under the Christian emperors to moderate its harshest aspects and to seek to bring it into an ever closer relationship with Christian values. By the early medieval period emperors themselves had published the law codes, together with relevant episcopal canon laws, so as to give Christian synodical legislation on morals and philanthropy a standing in law equal to civic regulations.[6] The Orthodox theologians sought after what was called *symphonia*, literally a harmony, between the church and the state in which each respected the remits of the other, and in which the emperor would stand as a protector and guardian of the church and a facilitator of its mission. Under these terms Orthodoxy became the state religion of the Roman Empire, now based in its capital at Constantinople, and thus often called "Byzantine"; though itself it always refused that nomenclature and designated itself "Roman." Symphonia meant that the emperor and the church would respect and facilitate each other but not intervene in the other's rightful affairs.

The emperor had charge of state security. The defense of the borders of the Christian Empire were seen as a sacred duty of defending the Kingdom of God as established on earth. The Eastern Orthodox bishops and priests were forbidden to bear arms at any time, but they had the duty to pray for the *basileus* and the armed forces. The emperor had the duty of calling an Ecumenical Council if he and the leading members of the state and the church saw a pressing need. It was his official decree, or *sacra*, that was necessary for such a council to meet and that gave the bishops the solemn duty of attending. It was also the emperor's decree, in the aftermath of the council, that gave the synod's decisions the status of imperial law. Both he and his courtiers, however, were forbidden to take part in the deliberations other than as observers. Deliberation was the priestly task of the bishops alone. Throughout the history of the Orthodox church from the fourth century to the fall of the Christian Empire in the mid-fifteenth century, the highest bishops of the church, especially the patriarch of Constantinople, served to guide and shape Byzantine imperial policy in marked ways. Politics, seen as the structuring of human society, is never understood in the Orthodox Church, to this day, as a secular matter. It is regarded, rather, as a fundamental part of the church's mission to bring Christ's presence and message into the ordering of human lives at the macro level. Western commentators often try to dismiss this approach as a dangerous Erastianism, or as desiring an enthralling theocracy; but their critiques generally demonstrate little if any understanding of the subtlety of the Orthodox viewpoint. Symphonia, meaning a harmonization of different musical notes, is quite precisely dependent on not one of those notes being drowned out by the other. This view of political balance caters to a variety of views and stances, not simply the supremacy of Orthodox Christianity. Constantine himself, for example, told the bishops present at Nicaea that he, as emperor and leader of the state, stood in the role of bishop for all those outside the church, then connoting pagans and Jews. His celebratory rites at the founding of Constantinople gave an example of wide religious diversity in their inclusive format. Even so, the Orthodox Church regards its mission of influencing the shaping of society and its laws as part of its basic role within the world of seeking to advance the great sacramental action of the Redemption—the ongoing deification (*theiopoiesis*) of the present world order by grace, embracing its sociology, its ecology, its governance, and its moral teleology.

The Western Church had a different path to this view of close symphonia of church and state. The West effectively lost its resident emperor in the fifth century and increasingly felt that the emperor at Constantinople had abandoned them. So they looked elsewhere. The pope at Rome became more than a merely symbolic leader and always exercised a profound influence. But as the old Western Roman Empire broke up into the rise of multiple nation-states, the kingly leaders of those new lands soon entered into a long-enduring struggle with the papacy for supremacy. For such reasons it is engrained in the Western consciousness that there ought to be a sharp separation of church and state. America and modern Europe are prime examples of that separatist philosophy. The early modern wars of religion only served to underline this belief, and this was why Protestantism emphasized it even more acutely. In the Eastern Empire, attitudes were quite different. The Orthodox world saw the emperor as a sacral figure but not as an absolute monarch. The church imposed upon the ancient world the view that even the king was subject to the laws of God, as established and taught by the church. The highest authority and the highest powers had to subordinate themselves to the Gospel injunctions and embody the mercy, justice, and compassion of Christ.

At Orthodox liturgies in the Byzantine Empire, the emperor himself would often play a symbolic role. At Easter, for example, he would process in the streets wearing pure white robes to iconize the Risen Christ. Every state occasion was accompanied by extensive prayers and liturgies in which he had an integral part. He alone, as a layman, was permitted to take Communion in the sanctuary of the cathedral, among the priests. His throne was always a double-seated one: but not to allow the empress to sit alongside him—rather to show there the jeweled Gospels and to demonstrate that he had his power as Christ's representative. Throughout the entirety of the Orthodox imperial period the boundaries of the empire were seen as the modern equivalent of the borders of the New Israel, and the emperor was the New King David.[7] This was taken in a more than merely symbolic way: political embodiedness was not separated from spirituality in the manner in which a kind of Platonizing consciousness so often permeated Western Christian thinking. The Orthodox Church really did see itself as the New Israel, with a new King David, setting the standard for a new Christ-loving society on earth, where the Gospel itself would be the supreme charter of civilization. If it did not succeed in fully establishing that dream, it nevertheless had it and tried to fulfill it. Orthodoxy even now, despite centuries of political oppression and occlusion, still aspires to it: a vision where this symphonia can be effected. This might explain why most of the Eastern European societies where Byzantine values underlie the social order are quite different in political and social theory from Western ones where secularism has made the notion of this priestly-kingly synthesis something to be held in suspicion. The ongoing difficulties of the Western democracies in understanding the mind-set of the Slavic states is one example of the continuing divide over political and religious values.

To the present day the Orthodox Church seeks, or at least expects to presume, a close relationship with the state authorities that it recognizes as God-given. At many times in its past, after the fall of the Byzantine Empire to the might of the conquering Ottoman Turks, it has had cause to regret the allegiance it has shown to the occupiers of the throne. The sultanate often proved deeply oppressive to it. The church in Russia also suffered much under the brutal reign of Tsar Ivan the Terrible. In more recent times, the Russian Orthodox Church venerated its tsars until the fall of Nicholas II in the Russian Revolution. But it also suffered considerably from state interference that often amounted to eras of stultifying suffocation. Today the governments of traditionally Orthodox countries such as Russia and Romania have a close relation to the church leaderships. In the whole of Europe and the Americas, only England's monarchy still represents that symbolic alliance.[8] Even there, the British government in power more actually exemplifies the strict separation of church and state that became the dominant model of religion and politics the West had evolved.

Orthodoxy's "God-beloved" and "Christ-loving" emperor has long gone. The Orthodox Church, however, still looks to that notion of the symphonia of the political and religious principles in society as an ideal. Symphonia in this understanding, the way in which two musical notes sound together in complementary ways to create a richer resonance than singly and separately, is a basic part of how Orthodoxy understands the mission of the church to be part of the very weave of all aspects of human life: the individual trying to live more truly and more nobly, as well as the societal whole, seeking to align its common legal and political values more fully with the evangelical spirit. It may seem a hopeless or whimsical thing for the Orthodox Church to still cling to this ideal in the present world order, but it is a mission to continue to plant the seed of Gospel in whatever ground it finds, friendly or not; and a task it has fulfilled in times past well enough to create a Christian ethos in many of its heartlands that it hopes can still outlast any spirit of atheism or secularist humanism that tries to extinguish and replace the lights of Christendom with less transcendent twinkling relativisms.

HARMONY AND DISSONANCE: COPTS, ARMENIANS, CHALDAEANS

When one speaks of Orthodoxy today, one thinks predominantly of the Byzantino-Slavic tradition. This can rightly be called the dominant tradition of Orthodoxy, and this book has been mainly concerned with it. Of course, in antiquity the Western Catholic Church was a core part of that Orthodox world. The pope was an integral authority, *primus inter pares* (first [in honor] among equals) in the consortium of the five ancient and greatest patriarchates of the ancient church: Rome, Constantinople, Alexandria, Antioch, and Jerusalem. After the great medieval rupture with the Western patriarchate, which thus became the sole patriarchate in the Western Hemisphere and was thereby set on the course of a monarchical inflation, Orthodoxy added more patriarchal churches to the roll call as more peoples and great nations were added to the flock. This was so especially after the conversion of the Slavs in the ninth century. In Russia the church became a patriarchal church, as in Serbia, Georgia, Bulgaria, and Romania. In Orthodox thought the pope is still regarded as the "missing" Western patriarch. Ecumenical relations between Orthodoxy and Roman Catholicism have immensely improved at official levels throughout the twentieth century, largely due to the courtesy and intelligence that have characterized recent dealings since the meeting of Pope Paul VI and Patriarch Athenagoras in Jerusalem in 1964. Even so, at a more popular level of the Orthodox faithful, a great suspicion remains in regard to Roman Catholicism, related to its past history of conversion campaigns aggressively mounted within the Orthodox world. Orthodoxy feels that when it was down in the dust after losing all orbits of independent power, with the exception of Russia, the papacy always undermined it rather than seeking to support it. It is this deep-rooted and ancient suspicion, on the Orthodox side, and basically a lack of knowledge and a dismissive disregard of the Eastern Christian world on the part of Western Catholicism, that today hinders real and substantive ecumenical rapprochement.

The Orthodox Church has warmer relations with British Anglicanism, which has habitually shown a very supportive face toward the Eastern churches that came to its knowledge both overseas and as immigrant communities in the West. Orthodoxy is a tradition that Western Catholicism recognizes as familial, of course. It differs in many significant respects from the churches representing the more radical Reformation. Protestantism's stripped-down sacramentality, and its several doctrinal departures from the ancient apostolic tradition, make it a more difficult communication for most Orthodox, and in recent years a few of the more easterly and more conservative Orthodox churches have resigned from membership of the World Council of Churches because of the spirit of liberal Protestantism felt to be prevalent there, triggering a lively debate among the Orthodox worldwide as to the nature and purpose of contemporary Christian ecumenism, and Orthodoxy's role within it.

But Orthodoxy's intimate relationship with religious dissidence did not begin in the twentieth century. From early times it made a very sharp and clear distinction between what it called "heresy," where a specific church community (or an individual person) was regarded as no longer meriting recognition as being authentically Orthodox Christian, and "schism," where a particular church (and those belonging to it) had become separated, perhaps in varying degrees of seriousness, from the mainstream of the Orthodox churches that were in communion with each other and maintaining the unity of Orthodoxy by their solidarity. This solidarity was represented by the way the bishops of all the Orthodox churches in communion (for world Orthodoxy still remains a system of churches in communion of doctrine and practice) shared with one another visits and eucharistic concelebrations. This sharp distinction meant that a church could be radically cut off from Orthodoxy if it damaged the apostolic tradition in any serious doctrinal matter. Such cutting off was regarded as applicable to the ancient separatist movements of the Gnostics, the Photinians, the Arians, and many others. These movements, of course, often regarded themselves as being perfectly Orthodox Christians. But if believers from such churches presented themselves in the mainstream Orthodox communities, the bishops would demand that they should be baptized before coming to the Eucharist. These rules date back to the early bishops Dionysius of Alexandria (died 264) and Basil of Caesarea (330–379), and they have been adjusted to meet the modern issue of a great variety of Christian denominations whose polity and doctrine vary considerably. The prior baptisms of those movements regarded as sects, not churches, were not regarded as having any force or validity; hence Orthodox practice was not so much a question of rebaptism as first baptism. Even today believers seeking to join the Orthodox Church from groups that differ from the apostolic tradition in substantive matters (such as nontrinitarian churches, for example) are required to be baptized with the full rites of the church, because their previous sacramental initiations are considered as having only a propaedeutic charismatic force (like forms of catechumenate of varying depth). This does not dismiss them as not being Christians at all; neither does it accept them as having been initiated fully. But Orthodoxy, worldwide, has not made its mind up in any full or determined sense about the status of the Reformed churches' ecclesial and sacramental polity. Most of the Orthodox bishops regard the Non-Chalcedonian Orthodox, Catholic, and Anglican churches' sacraments and traditions on a wholly different level.

The Non-Chalcedonian Orthodox churches are the closest, among all others, to the Orthodox Church's traditions and practices. They used to be called the "Oriental Orthodox," and some of them still prefer that designation though today it carries pejorative colonial associations in English-speaking lands. Oriental in this case, however, does not mean "Asian"; it refers to the *Provincia Orientalis* of the late antique Roman Empire. The group of churches covered by it were mainly centered in Egypt, Ethiopia, Syria, and Armenia. The separation occurred as a result of the slow-burning resentments that came in the aftermath of the great dispute between Cyril of Alexandria and Nestorius. The falling out was over the concept of the unity of Christ (how it was to be conceived and how expressed), and how that conflict was mediated by the imperial Byzantine government and the patriarch of

Constantinople. The antagonistic poles of Christian Syria and Alexandria were mediated by Constantinople, which was especially concerned to keep the Western traditions (represented by Rome) happy on all fronts. This mediating role, like many others that have been attempted in history, was destined to be unable to please everyone. Eventually the churches that favored a greater stress on the separateness of the natures of Christ (as Nestorius had argued for), which were especially located in the Syrian patriarchate, broke away from all the others and went their own way, rejecting all the common councils after the first two (at Nicaea in 325 and at Constantinople in 381). Those churches are now known as the Assyrian Church of the East. They used to be known, apologetically, as the Nestorian Church. Their missionaries went far afield: first to Ethiopia and then to China in the seventh century, and they were the first to evangelize that vast country.

The churches (mainly based in Egypt and some parts of Syria) that favored a view of the divine and human natures of Christ running together into a union that was no less than a single unity were increasingly disillusioned by the way Constantinople and Rome wanted to keep dialogue open and balance the polar views, and they eventually broke off relations with Rome and Constantinople, as well as with the aforementioned Syrian churches of the Nestorian tradition, whose theology they now claimed to see as corrupting even the Byzantine and Western churches. The members of these churches are now known (from their ancient language zone) as the Copts. Today they also include the Ethiopian Orthodox. They used to be called (again apologetically) the Monophysite churches. They include the Armenians. These communities regarded the Latins and Byzantines as having betrayed the proper Christological tradition after the Council of Ephesus in 431, and accordingly they refuse to accept any Ecumenical Council after that date. This is why they are also known, to the Byzantine and Roman traditions, as the Non-Chalcedonian churches.[9] The issue is at once disarmingly simple and yet maddeningly complex, which is why a resolution has been sought after for fifteen hundred years and is still elusive. The Roman and Byzantine Orthodox traditions put together (in the years after Cyril of Alexandria had set the tone and direction for Christology at Ephesus in 431) two simple principles for Orthodox thought. The first was this: if the Divine Word has brought two different natures, divine and human, into a Union through his Incarnation, this Union has to be accepted as indissoluble and total. Two things have become a one-ness. Christ is thus the God-Man. The second is this: it is also necessary to stress that in this totalist Union, the characteristics of each are not destroyed but rather given new and dynamic contexts: such that the impassible Godhead can enter into a wholly new way of working on earth (incarnate suffering redemption) and the human can assume powers and charisms beyond the range of mortality (the life-giving flesh of Christ, the immortal resurrection and so on). Nevertheless, the affirmation of totalist Union (*Henosis*) of the two natures into one must also confess that each nature is not confused with another, overridden, or submerged.

This was why, between them, the patriarchates of Constantinople and Rome affirmed a series of Ecumenical Councils (Chalcedon in 451, Constantinople II in 553, and Constantinople III in 681) designed to finesse and refine this question of balance in the form of acceptable axioms that would reconcile the differing parties. And so, this conciliar tradition basically taught that the Incarnate Lord had two natures made indissolubly one but "without confusion, without change, without separation and without division."¹⁰ The Coptic episcopal leadership was censured at Chalcedon for continuing to insist that any change to Saint Cyril's original formulae (when Cyril was apologetically bent on refuting Nestorius's radical separatism) was permissible for the church in future; and so the Egyptian contingent withdrew from participation in Chalcedon, and large parts of the Egyptian Church refused to accept the Chalcedonian settlement. Eventually this dissidence resulted in the establishment of parallel groups of bishops in the same areas: those who accepted the council of 451 and those who did not. Once a parallel hierarchy was established, the schism had come out into the open and was hardened over the centuries, made even worse as a matter of inter-Christian alienation when Egypt passed out of all Byzantine control in 639 and became a caliphate of Islam.¹¹ Much sniping fire has passed since then between the so-called Monophysites (one-naturers) of Egypt and the Diaphysites (two-naturers) who today represent the Christological traditions of Rome and the Western churches as well as those of the Eastern Orthodox.

Orthodoxy, however, fully endorses the basic principle of the Coptic confession: that the Incarnate Lord did indeed make a total and indissoluble union of the two natures in his incarnation, truly making them one in a new and dynamic resolution. It differs in this respect: that by confessing the Lord "has two natures" after the union, it does not deny the previous statement, only qualifies it by adding that these natures are not fused into a confusion but retain their properties in a newly enhanced and unique dynamic. The Orthodox tradition renounces Nestorian separatism, and this is why, whenever it does speak of two natures it always adds the four qualifying adverbs drawn up at Chalcedon. This is, to be sure, a clunky solution; but Orthodoxy maintains it as a symbol of the importance of keeping the communion of the churches intact under the system of ecumenical conciliar judgment having higher authority than any single person, be it an individual father of the church or a national episcopal leader. There has been much simplistic and offensive nonsense taught over the years about what the Orthodox are supposed to hold and what Monophysite or Miaphysite Christology is supposed to mean. There has been more serious study done over issues of rapprochement over the past generation than perhaps in the past fourteen hundred years.[12] But so little prior tradition has there been of meaningful and respectful dialogue that it will take more time to resolve deep-seated issues of this division that touches very closely on the heart of the Orthodox world.[13]

MONASTICS AND MYSTICS

Monasticism is a movement (originally) of lay men and women toward a radical lifestyle of solitude and social disconnection, meant to allow them to focus on God as the primary quest and orientation of their lives. It takes its name from the Greek term for solitary life. In Byzantine Orthodoxy it was also called the hesychastic life, from the word "hesychia" meaning "quietness." Saint Gregory the Theologian drew the comparison of monasticism's solitary goal with the Hellenistic philosophical ideal of seeking the illumination of the Demiurge or divinity presiding over the world. Their adage of *Monos pros Monon* (a single/solitary/celibate person seeking the One Who Is Alone, that is, God) was adapted by him for Christian use. The elegance is lost in translation, but the idea was part of Gregory's overall concern in adapting the highest aspects of Greek culture for Christianity.[14] Gregory it was who transitioned the more rough and ready Egyptian forms of Christian monasticism to a more sophisticated scholarly idea of a withdrawn life dedicated to theological studies and contemplation. These two types of monasticism, after the fourth century, remained standard aspects of the Orthodox Church. For simplicity's sake we shall call them the Syro-Egyptian monastic ideal and the Byzantine ideal, though conscious that they were both adapted all over the Christian world and entirely fused together in the end.

The beginnings of monastic life in the Orthodox Church appeared in third-century Syria and fourth-century Egypt. Later they moved westward and were adopted, to great effect, in the history of Latin Christianity too. In Egypt, which gave, perhaps, the classical expression of monastic institutions, the first exemplar was Antony the Great (251–356). His biography and exploits were celebrated in a very famous and popular text written by Athanasius the Great, who did much to spread the monastic practice through the Orthodox world.[15]

What we shall call the Egyptian model of monasticism was a radical battle with the simplicity of life in desert regions (Syria, Palestine, and Egypt excelling in this regard, for they each had extensive wilderness areas within relatively easy travel distance to the great centers of early Christianity: Alexandria, Antioch, and Jerusalem). Life in the desert meant that this solitary ideal, paradoxically, soon had to be tempered by the needs for survival that required small communities living out a subsistence economy. Woven baskets and other small craft wares for sale in the large city markets were the staple work of monks and allowed the desert dwellers to conduct their work manually while keeping their minds on matters of prayer and contemplation. Antony, one of the first renowned hermits, began by living in strict solitude and found that his intention to spend all day each day in prayer was a practical impossibility.[16] So he balanced his days out with revolving periods of prayer, manual work, psalm recitation, contemplative silent prayer, and the needs of his body, eating and sleeping in regulated small amounts. The nights were passed in prayer; sleep came after a small meal in the morning. Each day rotated in the same manner. Antony lived in a small cave for more than forty years. But quickly disciples had gathered around him and wanted to be associated with him. Antony's style of eremitical, solitary existence proved too hard for most to follow exactly. It soon became a lifestyle reserved for disciples who had spent many years in common life together in the desert and thus had proved their stability.

The life in common, that is, in small communities, was called the cenobitic monastic style.[17] It was based around a set of communal dwellings with a centrally located small church (*katholikon*) for purposes of worship. Cenobitic monks shared a common meal table and were under the supervision of a few leading superiors: the chief being the *higumen*, called in the West an abbot. In Latin monastic life the monks followed a set of rules written by a founder. Those of Saint Benedict are the most renowned, and his Rule (*Regula*) became a classic of the Western Church. In the Orthodox world the monks followed the instructions of the local founding teachers, and life was generally freer, though very strict and demanding from our modern viewpoint, and it was a life that followed in close obedience to the instructions of the higumen. After the ninth century many of the Orthodox monasteries started to follow a more commonalized tradition of life shaped around the charter and timetable of one of the greatest of Eastern monasteries: the great Stoudium at Constantinople. This charter (*typikon*) was founded by Saint Theodore the Stoudite. He and the earlier fourth-century teacher Saint Basil the Great are regarded as the leading monastic theorists of the Orthodox world, although there are many other figures whose writings and teachings about monastic life have been preserved and are venerated still to this day: among them Saint Pachomios, Saint John Klimakos, and Saints Barsanuphios and John.

Between the cenobitic lifestyle of the community organized in obedience to one leader, focused on many aspects of common works, and the eremitical lifestyle of the solitary living in seclusion and dedicated contemplation, there was also a mediating style of monastic life called the lavriotic. The term "lavra" originally meant back lane and was used by the Orthodox monks to connote the way that a valley with a great hermit in it at the closed end would often see a series of lesser hermitages springing up along the valley toward his cell. These were his loosely collected hermit disciples, seeking to be near the great man. In time this style became more popular. Instead of a common walled building with a central church and common rooms for sleeping and eating and working, the lavra remained a series of independent hermitages, peopled by senior monks, under allegiance to a presiding hermit, who exercised great moral and spiritual authority over the complex but did not need to concern himself with details of daily lifestyle or discipline, because of the advanced status of his disciples. Life was conducted on an individually secluded basis, and the pathway between the various houses was used for consultations, but the monks only gathered collectively once a week: on Saturday evening for prayers in common all through the night leading on into the celebration of the Eucharist together on the Sunday morning, with a meal and shared hospitality together until Sunday afternoon, when all returned once more to their separate dwellings.

In the golden age of desert monasticism, many lay people traveled out into the desert to seek the guidance of some of the more famed hermits. For those who could not travel, books were produced to give the flavor of some of these men and the tenor of their teachings. One such book that enjoyed great popularity in fifth-century Constantinople and then throughout the Eastern Empire was the *Lausiac History* written by one of the disciples of the great monastic theologian Evagrios of Pontos. Its author was the bishop of Helenopolis, Palladius of Galatia (c. 365–425). Books such as this and others from the same period, such as *The Sayings of the Desert Fathers*, became best sellers in the Christian capital cities and made the monastic life attractive (from a distance) to many of the laity.[18] Monasticism, formerly a phenomenon of deserted wilderness areas, spread to the cities themselves. At first they were seen in the suburbs where small farms supplied the needs for the townsfolk, but soon, as with institutions in all cities, the settlements were swallowed up within the city itself as suburbs became centralized because of urban spread. Constantinople and Rome were soon cities filled with urban monasteries, and in Constantinople the monks, being the most literarily educated class, were by the sixth century to be found extensively employed as a clerical elite, deeply inserted into imperial affairs.

While some monasteries retained a simple focus on manual labor and strict obedience, others developed academic and literary lifestyles. The great monastery of the Stoudium in the center of Constantinople had a world-renowned scriptorium where minuscule writing was invented: what we know today as lower-case handwriting. This speeded up the process of copying books immensely, and centers such as the Stoudium were responsible for the reproduction, transmission, and thus salvation, of the great classics of ancient Greek poetry and philosophy. When the monastic libraries of Constantinople were looted and exported to the West, after the Fourth Crusade in 1204 (and again after the fall of Constantinople in 1453), it was an influx of learning that would eventually jumpstart the Renaissance.

Monastic life, in all its rich variety, has remained a central aspect of Orthodox Christian experience to this very day. It never suffered from the wholesale repression it had to endure in the lands that followed the radical Protestant reform, or in England, where Henry Tudor's depredations served to fill the coffers of his restless and avaricious aristocracy. In many places of Eastern Europe, such as present-day Romania and Russia, the monasteries still serve as primary centers of spiritual and intellectual life in the Orthodox Church. Many parish communities will regularly make a pilgrimage there to seek out the spiritual elders and to ask their guidance. In Russian the elder is known as *starets* (plural *startsi*), and a vivid picture of one of these charismatic figures was given in Fyodor Dostoyevsky's Father Zosima in *The Brothers Karamazov*. Orthodox believers expect, still today, that the church's monastic ascetics will show the fruits of the spiritual ascent in an evidently dynamic and charismatic spirituality, meant to assist the laity in their own spiritual progress. In Orthodoxy, holiness is not regarded as an achievement for a few elite; it is considered the natural goal of all Christians, but it is something that needs guidance from those who are skilled in matters of the Spirit.

By the time of the sixth Ecumenical Council, held in 681, the major matters of theological doctrine had been well and truly settled in the Eastern Church. But the eighth century saw a monumental row brewing that would overshadow the entire generation ahead. It was the closest Eastern Orthodoxy ever came to having a reformation crisis; but it was resolved in a manner very different from the way in which the Western Reformation approached the issue of religious images— almost the polar opposite. The problem was concerned with the legitimacy of religious images (the Greek term is *ikons*) used in Christian worship. The questions that this controversy raised still serve to mark a significant difference in cultural and spiritual practice between the churches of the West and the Orthodox world.

Orthodoxy is a tradition that abounds in icons: the churches are full of them, and it would be rare for any private home of an Orthodox Christian not to have icons on the walls somewhere in the house. The Orthodox Church sees the images of the Trinity, or Christ, or the Virgin Mary, or saints and angels as highly important to a proper prayer life. In the church the icons assume an almost sacramental character. They are regarded as powerful channels of the grace of God, media that bring about the presence to the believer of the one who is depicted in the icon before which one is praying. They have often been described as doors, or windows, to the heavenly kingdom. At home most Orthodox will have an icon corner in a place where when one faces it one will be standing facing the East. Orthodox faithful will stand here (the traditional posture for prayer) when they say prayers; and they will often offer incense to God in front of the icons and very often have lamps burning before the icons as an act of reverence. In Russia the icon shelf is placed in what has become known as the "beautiful corner" (*krasny ugol*) of the house. In the Orthodox churches the major icons are placed on a screen that separates the altar area from the nave, known as the *iconostasis*.

The icon screen in Russian churches was greatly expanded in the late medieval period, and several other rows were added above these basic ones, so that in many Russian churches the screen goes almost all the way to the roof. The scheme of icons on these larger screens covers the great feasts of the church's year and various scenes from the Gospels. In the earlier years the icon screen was a more modest affair, and while it served to focus the worshippers' attention and devotion during the long unrolling of the eucharistic liturgies, it never cut off the people from the events happening at the altar. Several modern Orthodox churches have recently tried to combine the way the iconostasis sets apart the altar area as a specially sacred place, with the benefits of a more unrestricted view of the priestly actions at the altar in the course of the Eucharist. In the old Western churches the Rood Screen is an echo of this, though it was one of the architectural casualties of the Reformation.[19] Even so, many signs of its survival can be seen in numerous ancient English churches.

There is a central great opening to the altar, known as the royal doors. To the viewer's right is always placed a large icon of Christ, holding the Gospels and blessing the faithful. It is known as the Pantokrator Icon, confessing Christ, in his Incarnation, to be Lord and God: the Wisdom through whom the Father made the whole cosmos and keeps it in being; as well as the Lord who will come at the end of time to judge the world. To the viewer's left is always an icon of the Theotokos, Mary the Mother of God. She is often depicted in richly various forms, but the most common one shows her holding the child Jesus, with one of her hands gesturing toward him for the sake of the viewer. This icon is called the *Hodegitria*, meaning "She it is who shows the Way" (cf. Jn. 14.6). Adjacent to the Christ Icon on the altar screen is customarily an icon of John the Forerunner (*Prodromos*), known in the West as John the Baptist. Adjacent to the Virgin's icon is usually the icon of the patron saint of that particular church. This icon, in a smaller form, will also be placed just inside the main entrance to the church, and the faithful on entering church for worship will first stop in front of it, bow, and greet the saint— as if entering his or her private house and saluting the host— and then kiss the icon. Icons in Orthodoxy are not merely for looking at. They are designed for kissing: *aspasia* in Greek. This is at once an ancient form of greeting and a sign of veneration. It was what stirred up the great controversy of the Iconoclastic crisis.

The Byzantine Empire was ruled between 717 and 802 by the Isaurian dynasty. It was founded by Emperor Leo III. As the name suggests, Leo originated from the Syrian province of the empire (Commagene) and was a successful general of the armies before rising to power in a very troubled time.

Once he became emperor he seems to have been motivated by a strong desire to reform many aspects of church life. The more eastern, Syrian, parts of the Orthodox world had never been as devoted to icons in church life as were the Constantinopolitans. The precise reasons the emperor should have been so determinedly against the use of icons in worship is still not clear, but several factors point to possible solutions. He himself rose to power in the aftermath of a series of very weak emperors, who had seen the rising power of Islam come to the very gates of Constantinople in a twelve-month siege of the city. The evidence of the rapid ascent of Islam as a world power was taken (by them and by the Byzantines too) as a clear sign of favor from God. And yet the Orthodox Byzantines believed most firmly that they had been elected as the chosen nation under God on earth. So how could this loss of territories to Islam be happening? Leo probably concluded, on the basis of Old Testament antecedents of the "correction of Israel," that the military reversals were because of some great sin on the part of the empire. He may well have had an eye on the affairs of Islam, noticing how the Ummayad caliph Yazid II had issued an edict in 722 against his Christian subjects forbidding them the use of so-called idolatrous images in their churches. Idolatry, of course, was the most serious sin against the covenant establishing God's chosen people in all three religions: Judaism, Christianity, and Islam; so it is not unexpected that Leo might well see religious practice as a serious matter of state security. If icon veneration in the churches really was idolatry, it could certainly account for the apparent loss of God's assistance in the military reversals of the era. Recent scholarly work has also shown how complex the whole environment was, however, and the manner in which the pro- and anti-icon parties divided shows many aspects of class and regional differences. The military, the court, and the eastern provinces were more in favor of the imperial anti-icon policy. The monks, the women of the capital, the Byzantine theologians, and the western provinces were very much against it.

Leo's first set of reform legislation was designed to improve military and civic administration and the tax system. Then the emperor turned his attention to the spiritual life of his subjects. In 722 he called for an end to the religious pluralism that had been customary beforehand. He ordered mass compulsory baptisms of the empire's Jews and demanded that Christian heretics, such as the Montanists, who had been a minority presence since the second century, should be baptized in the Orthodox churches and conform under threat of severe penalties. Then, between 726 and 729, he issued a series of edicts against the use of icons in church. These he called idolatrous, using arguments that anticipated in many respects the arguments used by the radical reformers much later in the West. While the court officials and clergy around his circle supported him, the great majority of the monks (who formed a large part of the population of the city and the backbone of its civil service), the senior theologians, and the patriarch Germanos all opposed him strongly, as did the great majority of the Western Church under the leadership of Popes Gregory II and III. Gregory II called two councils at Rome (in 730 and 732), which censured the emperor's religious policies and excommunicated those who destroyed the icons. While the imperial party saw those who "worshipped" icons as idolaters (iconolaters), patriarch Germanos and his allies, notably Saint John of Damascus, called themselves instead iconodules (icon venerators). They named the imperial party icon smashers, or iconoclasts. The Iconoclasts accused the Orthodox of violating the biblical commands never to "worship graven images" (Exod. 20.4; Deut. 5.8). Much turned, evidently, on the precise meaning of the terms involved, and this dispute, perhaps more than others in the history of Byzantine theology, called for a very precise understanding of semantics. The emperor ousted Patriarch Germanos in 730, replacing him with a subservient iconoclastic patriarch, Anastasios.

When Leo died in 741, he was succeeded by his son Constantine V (741–775), who took the controversy one stage further by attempting to resolve it at a formal council held at Hieria in 754, where something in the region of three hundred and thirty bishops took part and issued edicts forbidding the use of images in churches. Constantine V pressed the whole iconoclast issue with more intellectual force than his father and so earned the great hostility of the Iconodule party. He has gone down in history as Constantine Copronymos: "He whose name is dung."

Constantine V suppressed many aspects of monastic life, knowing that this was the center of the opposition to his views. Even so, Constantine's son (Leo IV, 775–780) allowed the pressure to ebb from the controversy, and when he died and his son succeeded as a minor (Constantine VI, 780–797), his mother, the regent empress Irene, took the opportunity to call a major council to meet in Constantinople in 780, designed to restore the veneration of the icons in churches. The military garrison of Constantinople, hearing noise of its intentions, invaded the church of Hagia Sophia and put an end to the council. Biding her time, the empress acquiesced but slowly moved the Iconoclastic troops to other duties in various parts of the empire and, secure in her command of the garrisons, then reconvened the great council in the city of Nicaea in Bithynia. This met in 787, concerned with an official and comprehensive doctrine on how icons ought to be understood and used in Christian worship, and its decrees have been accepted by the Orthodox and Latin churches as the seventh Ecumenical Council, Nicaea II.

There was a second, and shorter, outbreak of imperial sponsored iconoclasm, once more led by the army and lasting between 815 until 843.[20] This time Leo V removed the famous icon of Christ on the Chalke Gate at Constantinople, replacing it with a simple cross symbol.[21] He reasserted the Iconoclast Council of Hieria as official imperial policy and set aside Nicaea II. Once again it was a regent empress, Theodora, who in 843 called an end to the imperial oppression during the reign of her son Emperor Michael III. Her celebration of a great festival to mark the restoration of icons in the churches of Constantinople in that year has been repeated ever afterward in the liturgical calendar of the Eastern Church. It is now called the Sunday of Orthodoxy and is observed on the first Sunday of Lent each year. In the course of the liturgy every heresy from ancient times is rehearsed, and the people symbolically reject each one. Iconoclasm thus assumes the status of one of the heresies appearing "late in time." In this second phase of Iconoclasm it was patriarch Nikephoros of Constantinople and Saint Theodore the Stoudite (759–826) who were the main intellectuals championing the importance of the icons. Together with the chief theologian of the first phase, Saint John Damascene, and the decrees of the seventh Ecumenical Council, these intellectuals gave to Orthodoxy its final and fullest theology of sacred art.

The doctrine of sacred art summarizes much of Orthodoxy's attitude to human culture, and it is not as negligible as it may seem to someone who has been brought up in Western Christianity's view of art as a peripheral (or even an objectionable) element of religious experience. The Orthodox Church has since 843 affirmed that the presence of icons in the churches is a vital sign of the health of the church's attitude to sacramentality. Comparable with the sacraments (what Orthodoxy calls the "Mysteries"), such as baptism or the Eucharist or the healing anointing, the icon stands as a symbol that is more than a mere symbol: rather it is a material sign that carries great spiritual effective power. While not adding icons to the major sacraments of the church, Orthodoxy regards them as sacramental in character. They are, in a real sense, sacramentals of the Incarnation. The Iconoclasts argued that no wooden painted board could ever stand in properly for the presence of the Lord. Only the Eucharist, they argued, could stand in as a proper symbol for Christ. All other Christian signs (such as the cross) were merely memorial signs, aids to memory. They were venerable but could not be "worshipped." The teaching of the Second Council of Nicaea argued against this that such a view rendered all sacraments merely symbolic. The Eucharist, in the conciliar argument, is far from being a valid symbol of Christ's presence in the church; rather it "is" Christ's presence in the church. This highly realist theology of the sacraments was a doctrine of "real presence" many centuries before such a thing was formulated in the Western Catholic world. The icon, however, is also a powerful symbol of Christ's presence. It carries a spiritual potency that is more than that of a simple memorial. When a believer stands before an icon of Christ and bows down before it, venerating it, the act of reverence done in that moment passes through and beyond the painted icon panel and ascends directly to the Lord himself. In this way a believer's veneration of the icon becomes a direct veneration of the person portrayed in that icon. This would also be true of an icon of the Virgin, an angel, or a saint. Whoever is portrayed in the icon actually receives the veneration given before that icon, veneration given not to the painted board itself but always in every instance given before the sacramental iconic form, passing directly to the person there represented.

This clearly involved the Iconodule theologians in a necessary clarification of the confused and woolly language of worship that had been in use beforehand. The Iconoclasts had evidently been confused by the manner in which the faithful of Constantinople were bowing down in front of icons and kissing them and carrying them around churches, believing they brought the spiritual presence of the saints and angels with them. They called such veneration worship and adoration and equated the two terms, thus making the practice they disliked into something idolatrous and superstitious. The Orthodox Iconodule theologians pointed out, however, that worship was quite different from adoration. Today our English concept of worship has once more equated these words and so has given rise to new generations of misunderstanding of the Orthodox position. The council of 787 determined that Christians use five distinct words for the collective experience of worship, which in itself precisely means "veneration." It only makes sense, from now on, to return to the Greek that was being used in this debate: for the Greek is a much more subtle and nuanced language than English.

The key terms are: *latreia, douleia, hyperdouleia, proskynesis,* and *aspasia,* which need to be exactly and consistently rendered as adoration, worship or reverence, special worship or reverence, bowing down, and kissing (the hand). English embraces all of these concepts with the single word "worship" but also uses it to connote the first (latreia), which is where all the confusion lies; because the Orthodox wish to make it clear that there are very clear degrees of worship and reverence (which we can take as synonyms here). One can reverence one's grandfather or the emperor, for example (give proskynesis*)*, or kiss the hand of one's elder mentors (aspasia), without committing idolatry.[22] But latreia, in all circumstances, is that special type of worship or reverence that is given to God and to God alone as an acknowledgment of his transcendent divinity. To give such "worship" to anyone or anything else would indeed be idolatry. Of course, the word "worship" here ought to be rendered more precisely as "adoration." So, according to the teachings of the seventh Ecumenical Council, Orthodoxy exalted the Iconodule position in the dispute and accepted that adoration can be given only to God. Reverence (douleia) can be given to the angels and the saints, especially exalted reverence (hyperdouleia) to the Virgin alone. This form of reverence in the context of Christian devotional practice is specific to saints and angels and the Virgin. It is not the same as that lower form of reverence that is offered (often using the same means, such as kissing or bowing down) to human personages we especially revere and honor.

In Orthodox churches the icons are frequently incensed during the course of the liturgy or common prayers. The priest will go before the icons and swing the censer in the form of a cross before each one (*thymiama*). Lay people will

come before icons in churches or at home and bow down before them (proskynesis) and often kiss the hand of the figure
depicted (aspasia). The people themselves are usually incensed at the same time, after the icons, to offer them honor
too as the living icons of God. The first time I was asked, as a
priest, to offer a short service of prayers for a mixed (mainly
Protestant) student community that was grieving over the recent dead after the Twin Towers disaster in New York, I remember the gasp of anxiety from some of the more radical
reform students present when this series of incensing took
place before the icons and the people. I knew their unease
related to this issue of whether a line had been crossed: was
this illegitimate worship? However, what is happening here in
the Orthodox practice is quite clearly understood by even the
youngest of the church faithful. The Ecumenical Council
taught the basic principle that the veneration offered before
an icon is passed directly through its medium to the person
who is depicted within that icon. So, when a believer bows
down and kisses an icon of Christ, what kind of veneration is
he or she offering? The church taught it was adoration, a
confession that the Christ here depicted receives the adoration (latreia) of his faithful as being the God Incarnate. Those
who bow down or reverence an icon of the Virgin are offering
hyperdouleia, or especially exalted reverence, to the Lady
Mother of God, not adoration. They venerate her as the
greatest creaturely vessel of the Spirit of God in history. The
icons of the saints and angels receive the reverence of douleia
because of their own possession of Christ's Holy Spirit. Both
they and the Blessed Virgin are vessels of Christ's divine grace
given through his Incarnation and his resurrectional power in
the world, which transfigures his church day by day.

The Orthodox Church sometimes iconizes God the Father, but rarely and in what is commonly regarded as a marginal and dubious tradition. Instead it images the divine Trinity in the scriptural symbolic form of the epiphany of three angels to Abraham at the Oak of Mamre (Gen. 18.1–33). Andrei Rublev's great icon of the "Hospitality of Abraham" is the most impressive form of this approach. The great work of art is a mystical and theological treatise in its own right. The church's preference, however, is for all icons of the divine to be mediated through that of Christ the High Priest, who mediates the Father to the world through the Incarnation: and this because Christ himself is the perfect "icon of the Unseen God" (Col. 1.15). For the Orthodox Church, therefore, the whole theory and practice of icon veneration relates to this idea of the grace that is mediated through the mystery of God the Word endowing materiality with spiritual power: first in his own divine incarnation as man, and then, by our participation (*methexis*), through the manner in which all earthly material can serve a divine function, if it is caught up into the ascent of grace. The Orthodox icon represents the manner in which all matter can be sacramentalized.

Using material forms (bread and wine, holy water, sanctified oil, blessed icons, fragrant incense) in all its modes of worship, Orthodoxy celebrates the startling fact that God incarnated and enfleshed himself among us in time and space. He is not the spiritually abstracted God of the Platonists but the God who gives himself to his faithful in the form of a meal. To this day Orthodox worship is an earthy experience that rises to a transcendental spiritual experience. The two things are never separated. In Orthodox services this is seen quite clearly and immediately. All the senses are engaged:

chanting, incense, lights, icons, relics of saints, full-bodied sacramental rituals—all being conducted with gusto. Whenever one enters an Orthodox church at service time, it always seems in full swing; and if the clergy are ever still for a moment, inevitably the people are on the move, bowing down, crossing themselves, kissing icons, lighting candles. There is a profound sense that God himself is in the midst, but that he is the Incarnate Lord of grace who has sanctified all material things when they are lifted up in prayer. In modern times several Orthodox thinkers have extended this ancient theory of worship from the seventh council and applied it to support a wider ecological theology. As the icon symbolizes the manner in which material things can serve as powerful doorways to the divine presence, so too all creation is graced with the marks of the Creator's energy. Thus, in Orthodoxy's spiritual sense there can never be a purely "secular thing": all created things, especially human beings, are created as iconic mysteries of grace with a hidden power and potential to shine in the transfiguration of Christ's holiness and light.

CHAPTER FIVE

The Church's Expansion

THE CHURCH OF THE RUS: KIEV AND MOSCOW

So far this story of the Orthodox Church has been focused on its ancient rootedness in the eastern provinces of the Roman Empire under the aegis of the Byzantine emperors. The Orthodox Church takes its name as Eastern Christianity from the fact that it originated in the eastern provinces of the empire (that is, the non-Latin-speaking areas, chiefly the Middle East and the Levant). Its first communities, the local Orthodox churches, were the Greek cities to which Saint Paul wrote in the New Testament: Philippi, Thessaloniki, Colossi, Corinth, Ephesus, and Galatia in the empire's Asian, Cappadocian, province. Only in writing to the Romans did Paul's attention embrace the western province. In the ancient system of organizing the Orthodox Church, of the five patriarchates of Rome, Constantinople, Alexandria, Antioch, and Jerusalem, only one, the first of them, was located in the West. For the whole of the first millennium, the "balance," as it were, of the Christian movement was Eastern. In this period, Constantinople was undoubtedly the axial point.[1] Its power and influence rose, while those of the other three eastern patriarchates dwindled under the shadow of the expanse of Islam.

Constantinople grew to take the pastoral care of a large set of Christian lands. But in one respect its missionary impetus was uniquely charged. The Council of Chalcedon in 451 had given the care of all new missionary territories (described as lands of the barbarians) to the patriarchate of Constantinople. The great scholar-patriarch Photios (c. 810–893) was one of the most important Orthodox theologians and canonists of the Eastern Church in the ninth century. He is regarded as a great saint in the East. The West regards him less sanguinely, for under his ecclesial leadership the Western pope was anathematized and the Western doctrine of filioque was censured.[2] His book *The Mystagogy of the Holy Spirit* stands alongside the works of Saint Gregory of Nazianzus as fundamental explanations of the Orthodox trinitarian theology.[3] Photios encouraged many Christian missions from Byzantium, including the first recorded mission to the Slavic tribes, in 867, when he sent them a resident bishop.

In 860 Photios had earlier sent two aristocratic Byzantine brothers, the deacon Constantine and his brother Michael, to oversee a mission to arrange the conversion of the khagan of the Khazars. The brothers are more universally known today by their ecclesiastical names: Michael as Monk Methodius, and Constantine as Cyril (after he was consecrated bishop in Rome). The khagan chose Judaism as his court religion, but many of the people followed the brothers, and one of the results of the mission was that Prince Ratislav of Moravia invited the brothers in late 862 to come and preach in his lands.[4]

This mission had a great success, and to facilitate it the brothers determined that the native peoples ought to be evangelized, and to worship, in their own native tongues. This became a standard aspect of all major Orthodox missions thereafter. Cyril and Methodius more or less invented the Cyrillic alphabet and laid the foundation for Slavic letters in the course of their mission. While their own work in Moravia was subsequently undermined by hostile Latin missionaries from Germany, it nevertheless set a tone and precedent for Orthodox missions emanating from Constantinople and (later) Russia, that the local civilization ought to be respected but always amplified and enriched by introducing a wider view of civilized letters and wider culture, with a sense of central communion and connection being established by the shared liturgical rites and prayers, though now in the native vernaculars. Because of this, Cyril and Methodius are called in the Orthodox tradition "equal to the apostles" (*isapostoloi*).

In its dealing with the Slavic tribes of Rus, Constantinople saw the opportunity for establishing a new mission, alongside the political treaties of trade alliance the imperial court wished to make.[5] There is an oft-told story from the Russian *Primary Chronicle* of how the Slavs converted after emissaries had been sent out to the world religions around them to see which one they should adopt: from all the choices they elected Byzantine Christianity. The group had been taken to experience the liturgy in Hagia Sophia, and they were so overwhelmed by the beauty that they reported back: "We did not know whether we were in heaven or on earth." The story is a romanticized synopsis of a nevertheless profound relationship with Constantinople (the Great City) that founded Russian Orthodoxy. The Russian *Primary Chronicle* also claims that Saint Andrew, brother of Peter, was the apostle who began Christianity in the eastern lands. There are no historical records to support this, but it is a tradition among the Eastern Orthodox Slavic and Balkan territories as deeply held as that of Saint Peter's foundation of the Church of Rome. Byzantine missionaries were first recorded as active among the Black Sea communities in the ninth century.[6] Patriarch Photius himself commented on the conversion of the people of Rus, but it is the conversion of the family of Prince Vladimir of Kiev that usually begins the story proper. In 955–956 Princess Olga, the grandmother of Vladimir, traveled on an official visit to Constantinople and was baptized there by Patriarch Polyeuctos in the presence of Emperor Constantine VII Porphyrogennetos, who thus became bonded to the family in kinship. It was therefore a political as well as a religious relationship that was entered into. Even so, while there may have been a minority of Christians in Kiev, the ruler, Olga's son Sviatoslav (reigned 963–972), remained a pagan, believing Christianity too pacifistic to command the interest of his troops. His son Yaropolk (reigned 972–980) tolerated Christianity as a pagan ruler. He fought for the sole right to the throne, killing his brother Oleg in the civil war that ensued, and causing his younger brother Vladimir to flee to Scandinavia. There Vladimir assembled an army and returned to overthrow Yaropolk at Novgorod, and he then moved on to base his command of the Rus at Kiev by 980. Prince Vladimir was himself baptized Orthodox Christian in the Greek Black Sea colony of Chersonesos in 988 and soon after returned to Kiev to supervise the baptism of the rest of his family and all the townspeople in the local Dnieper River.

Casting the wooden idols of the god Perun into the waters, in 989 the entire population followed their prince, though the old pagan rites remained strong for long after in the country regions. Byzantine missionaries were sent in larger numbers from the Greek capital and brought with them the exemplars of beautiful icons, liturgical texts, and ritual books. The missionaries evangelized the people in the vernacular Rus language, and by this means not only was the spread of Christianity accelerated but a distinctive tradition of the Kievan-Russian Church was born. The missionaries did not bring with them extensive exemplars of the sophisticated Greek literary culture that underpinned the Byzantine Orthodox tradition, focusing instead on monastic texts that mostly were liturgy, offices of prayer, and ascetical prayer. Writings of some of the great Greek fathers became commonly known throughout the Slavic Christian world, but not the works of the philosophers, and the Russian Orthodox tradition was, from the outset, highly monastically focused, with a very strong ascetical tradition of mysticism. The text was not the center of church life; rather the icon was. Russian adoption of the icon became a profoundly domestic religious force that has endured to this day. Many Russian Orthodox families still relate their personal history through the familial icons they have venerated in their homes.

This tendency to a highly liturgical, iconic, and mystical experience in Russia was encouraged by the manner in which monasticism became a powerful force in the organization of the Russian Church. The Cave Monastery at Kiev (Kyiv Pechersky Lavra) was established by the hermit Saint Antony (died 1073), who first inhabited cave cells dug out of the soft rock of the Dnieper banks, and developed further by Saint Theodosios (Feodosiy) (died 1091), who consolidated the complex into a large assembly of cenobitic monks alongside smaller numbers of hermits. By the mid-fifteenth century one hundred and fifty new monastic communities were known in Russia. The most famous of them included Valaam on Lake Ladoga, the community of Saint Cyril Belozersk, and Solovki, monasteries that endured as centers of Russian Christian civilization, sometimes despite their co-opting by the Soviets as forced-labor gulags.

Between 1237 and 1448 Russia was dominated by the Mongols, or Tartars, as the Russians called them. The church became a community of resistance to the often violent depredations, and the interest of the Russians in martyrdom, both real and symbolic, became a specific trend of their spirituality. The metropolitan archbishops of the Rus were based in Kiev, but the difficulties caused by the Golden Horde caused the seat of the church administration to be moved first to the city of Vladimir and then finally to Moscow, at a time when the princes of Moscow had assumed significant military power and a superior command over the other princes of the Rus. Up to 1448 Constantinople held a close rein on the affairs of the Russian Church in its higher clerical ranks. The metropolitans were frequently Greeks appointed by Constantinople, and in many of the major churches the liturgy was often celebrated in Greek. This would change after 1448. Moscow then took the ecclesial ascendancy and followed a line of independence, while Kiev remained under the aegis of Constantinople.

The reason for the shift in allegiances and dependencies was twofold. In the first instance, Constantinople in 1448 was a shadow of its former self. It had merely five more years of independent existence before it fell to the power of the Muslim Ottoman Turks and its patriarch became ethnarch of an enslaved Christian people. The Moscow princes knew this, of course, and having themselves just emerged from a long period of oppression by Islamic overlords, realized more than Byzantium did what inevitably lay before it. The second reason for the disaffection between Russia and Constantinople was the scandal caused to the Muscovites by the concessions the Byzantines made to the Catholic West. The emperor in Constantinople was trying desperately to find assistance from the Western armies. To facilitate that, he needed the support of the pope. And to gain that, he had to find a way to reconcile the churches of the Orthodox East and the Catholic West, each of which had, for some centuries past, regarded the other with more than simple suspicion and animosity. The Eastern Orthodox had begun to regard the Western Catholics as heretical because of their use of unleavened bread in the Eucharist, the quasi-monarchical power they had afforded to one supreme bishop in the form of the papacy, the changes in the Nicene Creed they had adopted at their worship, and lastly the altered trinitarian theology that the West had championed in the defense of the filioque interpolation.

The Western theology argued from the premise of the coequality of the trinitarian persons, that all acts of the deity were in common and that the Spirit of God proceeded from the Father and the Son equally. Greek classical patristic theology had argued, to the contrary, that the Son and the Spirit proceeded from the Father alone by the different subsistent modes of begetting and proceeding, in which the Father communicated to each of them his own single divine nature. This was why there was only one God: the personal nature of the Father was the common ontology of all three, making them one. The Latin theologians, by contrast, tended to argue that the divine nature was some form of common substrate to which all three persons had an equal claim. The Eastern Church felt that this wholly removed the dynamic, or taxis—that is, the inherent process of the divine life—and was not validated by any scriptural precedent. While the Greek theologians regarded the West as possibly heretical in many respects, the Latins in their turn regarded the Greeks as wholesale schismatics. For the Latins, the papacy had assumed such a major position in the understanding of their church structure that they were appalled by the way in which the Greeks regarded it as a strange *theologoumenon*, a type of opinion or piety that could be accepted or not but could never be mistaken for a cardinal aspect of the faith. On top of everything else, Constantinople had a long memory, and the Fourth Crusade was not something that was going to be forgotten soon. Responding to a call to arms from the pope in 1204, the crusading forces has diverted from the Holy Land for the easier task of the despoliation of Constantinople. Many of the emperor's subjects were afraid that papal assistance might only mean exchanging one form of oppressive domination for another. Many more were of the opinion that doing deals with the Western Church was a serious compromising of Orthodoxy.

In what proved to be a long-drawn-out series of conciliar meetings, beginning at Basel in 1431 and moving then from Ferrara to Florence between 1438 and 1439 on account of the plague, Pope Martin V negotiated with representatives of Emperor John VIII Palaiologos and his patriarch Joseph.[7] The emperor had petitioned for military assistance, and he, together with all his court, was very eager to come to terms that would allow the reconciliation of the churches so as to facilitate this. Patriarch Joseph of Constantinople died just before he was required to sign the decree of union. Letters were then (allegedly) found in his room assenting to the papal terms, and so an agreement with the Western Church was drawn up on July 6, 1439, without having to wait for his successor. There were thirty-one Greek delegates present and 117 Latins. All the Greeks, with the exception of Bishop Mark of Ephesus, signed the document in accord with the instructions of the emperor. The leading Orthodox theologians pressing the emperor's cause were Bessarion of Nicaea, George Scholarios, and Isidore the metropolitan of Kiev. When the delegates returned to Byzantine territory, they met with deep resistance from the wider body of Orthodox faithful, and in the empire generally the union was never accepted. Even the emperor lost interest in the idea when the promised military help barely materialized, though for some years there was great pressure placed on clergy to conform.

Isidore left Italy to foster the cause of unity in Russia, but on his arrival in Moscow in 1441 he found Grand Duke Vasily and the townspeople bitterly hostile to the proclamation of the union, regarding it as a betrayal of Orthodoxy.[8] Isidore nevertheless prayed for the pope by name in the Easter liturgy in the Kremlin cathedral (thus signaling the union as having effect in Russia), which caused so much popular anger that the prince arrested and imprisoned him in the Kremlin's Chudov monastery. After two years he escaped and fled to Rome, serving thereafter in the papal cardinals' college. Condemning Isidore, the Russian Church repudiated the Act of Union, and, as the Byzantine emperor continued to insist on it as a mark of the respect Russia should give to its founding mother church, the Russians suspended communion with

Constantinople and refused to consecrate any metropolitan to succeed Isidore, since Constantinople insisted on its customary right to propose the candidate. In 1448 the Russian bishops, encouraged by Prince Vasily, consecrated a metropolitan without seeking Constantinople's approval. After the fall of the city and the election of George Scholarios as the new patriarch, the idea of reunion with Rome was mutually abandoned, and Russia entered once more into communion with the church of Constantinople. But it never again sought permission from the old capital in relation to consecrating its own episcopal leader. In effect, it had declared its independence as a national church—known as autocephaly. In 1589 the princes of Moscow secured from the Greek patriarch Jeremias II (who had come begging for aid to them) the right for their church to be proclaimed a patriarchate like the ancient ones, but when Jeremias returned to Constantinople he called a synod there and declared that Russia would be ranked in honor only after Jerusalem as the fifth patriarchal see in precedence. Russia, at least, knew that, as the sole surviving independent princely power among the Christians of the East, effectively the patriarchate of Moscow was now the real leader and protector of global Orthodox affairs. This tension between notional or honorific leader of Orthodox affairs and real leadership has continued into the present, with much grating friction still observable between the two patriarchates of Constantinople and Moscow.

Moscow grew in status as the capital of the Russians, and soon the tsars were establishing stable dynasties.[9] Between 1613 and 1633 the intimately close relation between the tsar and his patriarch was abundantly demonstrated by Tsar Michael Romanov, who had his father, Philaret, as patriarch.

Their line would last until the abdication and execution of Nicholas II in 1917/1918.

If the ecclesiastical fortunes of Orthodoxy in Russia were in the ascent after the fifteenth century, though once more allied closely with the ruling dynasty on a Byzantine model of governance, the state of the great patriarchate of Constantinople was in a precipitous decline and circumscription, which at one and the same moment paradoxically redefined it for a long-lasting international role.

Mehmet II, the Ottoman prince, is known as Fatih Mehmet (the Conqueror) for his capture of Constantinople on May 29, 1453, after a long and ultimately bloody siege.[10] To the present the date is known among the Greek Orthodox as Black Tuesday, and the changing of the great cathedral of Hagia Sophia into the mosque of Mehmet and his successor sultans stands as the great symbol of the collapse of Christian Byzantine power.[11] With the city fell Eastern Orthodoxy's security in the former eastern provinces of the Roman Empire. The empire, often erroneously said by Western commentators to have ended in the fifth century, is regarded by the Eastern Orthodox as having ended on this day, with the death of the last Roman emperor, Constantine XI.[12]

In 1450 the patriarch of Constantinople, Gregory III (a collaborator of Patriarch Joseph at the Council of Florence), had been driven out of the city by popular demand, on account of his pro-papal policies. The city had realized by then that no substantive help was forthcoming from the West. The

Ottoman Empire had for long years past been strangling the city's supply routes, and the Roman Empire as a whole had been dwindling in size for centuries, losing territories to the expanse of Islamic power, until it could no longer sustain itself and had largely been reduced to a few colonies on the Black Sea and the Greek mainland, and the city environs. After Mehmet had built the castle of Rumeli Hisari on the Bosphorus Strait in 1452, he commanded the sea entrance to Constantinople, and the city's fate was more or less sealed. After several days of terrible looting, murder, rape, and enslavement of the local population, Mehmet intervened to call the city to order. He claimed the palaces and cathedral of Hagia Sophia for himself and, finding that the imperial palaces were run down to an irretrievable extent, he began the complex of a new set of residences, now known as the Topkapi Palace. The cathedral was taken as the main city mosque. Mehmet repopulated the city with Greeks from the region and set about stabilizing the chaos brought about by the collapse of the old structures of ecclesiastical and imperial administration.

To this end he looked around for a suitable replacement for the dead emperor and the patriarch who had fled to places unknown.[13] He selected George Scholarios (1400–1473) from the city's remaining Greek intellectuals. A former imperial judge and a renowned Aristotelian and theologian, George had been a leading voice against the policies of Emperor John VIII, and he had been retired to a monastic life in the Pantocrator monastery at the capital. In June 1453 he was selected by Mehmet to be the new patriarch of the Orthodox community. At his Christian consecration ceremony he was renamed Gennadios II and, by permission, used the Church of the

Holy Apostles to be his cathedral.[14] Mehmet instructed him now to serve as the ethnarch of all Christian subjects in the Ottoman dominion. Thus he became a fusion of the old civic authority and the religious, for all Christians. This was a new phenomenon, because it brought under the patriarchal authority Latin Christians in the Ottoman dominions, as well as all Orthodox believers in subjugated territories, and even the Oriental Orthodox communities, the Armenians, Syrians, Copts, and Ethiopians who refused allegiance to the Council of Chalcedon and had hitherto refused to recognize the ethnarch's authority.

As ethnarch the patriarch set the tax impost for Christian subjects under instruction from the Sublime Porte of the sultans.[15] Now endowed with great powers as the representative of the sultan, and serving a force that withstood no contradiction, the patriarchate of Constantinople became a massive organizing force for most aspects of Eastern Christianity, but because of this the patriarch was also a focus of much resentment, even among the core Orthodox faithful outside Constantinople. This was because his own administration (known as the Phanar from the district where it eventually settled) was so closely associated with a ruling power that while it ostensibly protected the Christian minority of the new empire, it was effectively bleeding it dry, removing substantive political rights and vetoing (under threat of death according to the terms of the Sharia code) its ability to function in any missionary sense at all. Phanariots, the administrative class of powerful Greek clerics and lay politicians, took charge of many Christian lands outside Russia, imposing Greek-style liturgy and a colonial-style Greek ruling class in many places, which would not be ousted for centuries to come. The losses of Orthodox Christian believers to Islam, enforced or heavily encouraged because of the oppressive environment, would be substantial over the centuries to come. Having lost its Christian aristocratic sponsors and protectors, its universities and schools for the intelligentsia (other than a few seminaries), and the majority of its churches, which had been sequestrated as mosques, the Eastern Orthodox came to call this period under Ottoman dominion the Great Captivity.[16] It would endure until the nineteenth-century independence movements that began to flare up as Ottoman power entered into its own terminal decline. After this, many Orthodox lands (especially those that had benefited from the patronage of the free Church of Russia) tried to shake off the hand of direct rule that came out of Constantinople, even that of the patriarchate, while still recognizing its central importance in Orthodox history.

What kept the flame of the Orthodox tradition alive in Eastern Europe and Asia Minor during this period was the heroism of local clergy and faithful believers, keeping the church and village schools functioning in circumstances of great poverty and political suffocation, and above all the Orthodox monasteries, which found it possible to continue in existence as corporations, being able to enter into treaties with the sultans when they were large enough, and especially paying taxes regularly and thus serving some useful and tolerable function in the eyes of the Ottoman powers. The monasteries served as training schools for clergy and were sources of celibate missionaries who could travel widely to serve the local needs for teachers and theologians of renown. In this period of the Great Captivity, the reputation of the Orthodox monastics rose to considerable heights. Quietly, local diocesan bishops started to assume clerical headgear that resembled the old imperial crown: a subtle statement that the emperor was now dead, but his role as central organizer of Christian civilized life had passed to the church. This spread to become the present-day bishop's mitre-crown, worn universally.

MONASTIC CENTERS OF CULTURE AND MEMORY

Mount Athos

Monasteries in Russia continued to flourish, to such an extent that they became the basic welfare system for the entire land and the greatest landowners apart from the highest aristocracy.[17] In Ottoman territory the great center of monastic life was clearly Mount Athos. This little mountain peninsula in northeastern Greece became known as the Holy Mountain.[18] It has endured to the present day as one of the great monastic centers of the Orthodox world, from the time the first monks settled there in the fourth century, but mainly from the issuing of the chrysobull of Emperor Basil I in 885 declaring all of Athos a reserved zone for male monastic habitation.[19] This status, meaning no women can settle or visit there, was reiterated over time and reaffirmed as recently as the treaty that marked Greece's entrance to the European Union. There are now twenty monasteries existing in a federated relationship on Mount Athos.

The Athonite monasteries represent the three classes of monastic lifestyle in the Orthodox Church. At the southern end of the peninsula there are still some cave hermits, and others dwelling in the most remote and ascetic form of tiny dwellings. There are then the major cenobitic monasteries built in Byzantine style, with a wall enclosing a central church (or katholikon) with monastic cells and common-usage refectories around the walls. And finally there are smaller, bungalow-type dwellings called sketes (sometimes these are quite large and can grow to be miniature versions of the larger houses). The skete was originally a smaller community of a few monks gathered around a particular *geron*, or spiritual father, seeking a more intense life of quiet and prayer than they felt could be found in the larger communities where physical labor and many church services were the rule. Some of the sketes would eventually grow to a considerable size, comparable to a small monastery.

A great number of the larger foundations have defensive towers and other fortifications, which served to protect them from the constant piratical raids they endured over the centuries. They could never have fought off Ottoman suzerainty; this they negotiated with, paying taxes from the incomes of the many properties their Christian patrons over the centuries (particularly the princes of Serbia, Romania, and Russia) had given them in various countries. By the middle of the tenth century the Athonite village of Karyes had already become the center of a global form of monastic organization, with the appointment of a protos, or senior monastic leader resolving common affairs for the hermits. The monasteries of Kolovos and Xeropotamou also appear in the imperial records at this time as having a significant size. A new era of building began with the arrival of Saint Athanasios the Athonite in 958. He was a friend and confidant of the emperor Nikephoros Phokas. He first built a richly endowed church at Protaton in Karyes, around which still revolves the overall administration of the monastic peninsula, now with the protos and a small council representative of the major monastic foundations. In 962 Saint Athanasios founded the central monastic complex of the Great Lavra. It is still the largest of the twenty monasteries of the mountain. From the outset it had imperial funds behind it and thereafter attracted the constant support of successive emperors.

From the eleventh century onward Athos attracted Serbian, Bulgarian, and Russian monastics, and each nation established a tradition of its own alongside the Byzantine Greeks. The Serbian royal house established a center there in 1198, when the prince-archbishop Saint Sava built a church and foundation called Hilandar. His father, the Serbian grand prince Stefan Nemanja, also retired there to live as a monk with his son. They began a long-enduring period of Serbian patronage of the colony. After the fall of Constantinople Romanian princes also offered extensive support. Today Saint Panteleimon's monastery is Russian; Hilandar is Serbian; Zographou is Bulgarian; and the Prodromos skete (a sizable stone foundation) together with the Lakkoskiti are Romanian, while the majority of houses are Greek.

Saint Catherine's in Sinai

Another venerable center of Orthodox monastic life also survived the fall of the Byzantine Empire. It was so far removed from the beaten path that it had existed as a contained unit for centuries beforehand and was able to negotiate with the Islamic powers, offering tax tribute in return for protection. This was the fortress monastery of Saint Catherine's in the Sinai Peninsula, at the very foot of Mount Sinai, where Moses had by tradition received the Ten Commandments and seen a glimpse of the "back" of God. This site had become a Christian pilgrimage focus from early times, and by the era of Constantine the Great a fortified tower had been built (on the site of the present Reception House of the monastery) to commemorate the Theophany of the Burning Bush and to serve as a defensive fallback for the numerous Christian hermits who lived in caves in the vicinity.[20] Those caves continued to be used for centuries to come, for other important hermits and theologians, while the fortress started to be a nucleus of buildings that began to house a cenobitic community of monks.[21] The Byzantine emperor Justinian endowed the site lavishly in the sixth century, giving it massive defensive walls around a veritable small-town square. It is one of the wonders of the ancient world still surviving intact.

At this period in the sixth century, a new basilica-shaped church was built, and both it and the monastery were dedicated to the Transfiguration of Christ. Justinian presented the church with two remarkable icons. One was the Pantokrator Christ of Sinai. For centuries it was the chief icon of the church but was retired from use and is now found in the dedicated art gallery in the monastery walls. It ranks alongside the Mona Lisa, Fra Angelico's frescoes, and Michelangelo's Sistine Chapel ceiling as one of the greatest of all artworks. An adjoining chapel was consecrated as the site, and shrine, of the burning bush. All who entered this were required to remove their shoes in memory of the Sinai theophany. In the Middle Ages, when Latin pilgrims were more numerous in the Holy Land, the story of Saint Catherine of Alexandria (whose body was said in the *Golden Legend* to have been miraculously found on Mount Sinai) caught their imagination and started a new life of the monastery as a major pilgrimage destination.[22] It led eventually to the monastery being renamed Saint Catherine's.

To this day pilgrims who visit the monastery church and venerate the saint's relics are given a small silver-colored ring as a token of their pilgrimage.

The Sinai monastery grew throughout its long history in terms of moral reputation, not least in the number of its martyrs, saints, and theologians, and became more independent as regular communications under Islamic power were made more difficult with Jerusalem's hierarchs. It had begun as a part of the diocese of Pharan under the patriarchate of Jerusalem. After the council of 681, when the bishop of Pharan was deposed for adherence to the Monothelite heresy, the episcopal see was moved to the monastery, and then it also subsumed the diocese of Raithu, which had seen its monastic headquarters devastated by Saracen raids. In 1575 (and again in 1782) the patriarch of Constantinople gave the monastery autonomous status as an Orthodox church. Today the archbishop is elected solely by the monks of the monastery (which suggests it is an Autocephalous church among the Orthodox) but is also consecrated as archbishop by the patriarch of Jerusalem, which suggests that Sinai is an Autonomous church. It is certainly a unique case of a tiny independent communion within the greater body of the Orthodox churches.

Its radical desert environment made the monastery a center for hesychastic prayer. This is the mystically interior style called the prayer of the heart, favored in many parts of the Orthodox world, of which Sinai and Mount Athos have long been the champions.[23] Saint Catherine's, however, also was renowned for more mainstream forms of ascetical theology, advocating a lifestyle of regular prayer services, physical forms of penance, and fasting, as advocated in the book of instruction for young monks written by one of its early higumens,

Saint John Klimakos (died 649). He takes his name now from the book he wrote, *The Ladder of Divine Ascent*.[24] Imagining the ascetical life following Christ as a ladder of thirty steps, the book gives a picture of how to acquire virtues, with many wisdom sayings and pithy forms of advice for neophyte monks. John himself had entered monastic life at Sinai aged sixteen, and as a mature monk spent twenty years in a hermit's cave nearby. The cave is still shown to visitors willing to make the trek. When he was seventy-five the monks asked him to return and lead the Sinai community at Saint Catherine's. It was around this time that he composed his guide to monastic life. It is a text that is even to this day given to monastic novices in the Orthodox world and is read out in all monastic refectories during Great Lent.

As Islamic control spread over the Middle East and the Levant, all the treasured Christian literature of the Middle Eastern churches started to make its way slowly but inexorably toward the library of the Sinai monastery, like fine sand running down to the lowest point of multiple surfaces. Today it is one of the greatest treasure houses of ancient religious manuscripts in the world. Sinai was so remote that the bindings on the books in many cases are the originals. The collection once housed the famous Codex Sinaiticus, one of the complete editions of the Bible (Pandects) commissioned by Constantine the Great from the scriptorium of Bishop Eusebius of Caesarea for the new churches he founded in the Middle East. Constantine Tischendorf, the manuscript scholar, claimed that he rescued the codex from ignorant desert monks who were going to burn it as fuel for the stove. The fact that he is named in the monastery as "Tischendorf the thief" may suggest there is an alternative story to that commonly received (one of his own generating). The manuscript is now in the British Library. It is one of the most beautiful exemplars of ancient Christian writing. It is an extraordinary experience to sit in the evening outside the Church of the Transfiguration and listen to the purity of Sinai's all-pervading silence; or to attend the radiant Greek liturgy in the early candlelit hours of the morning in an environment that has barely changed since the time of Justinian the Great.

Mar Saba

There are several surviving ancient monasteries from that time in the Holy Land (its golden age was the seventh century) when Christian Byzantine emperors protected the territory and saw it as an essential heartland of the Christian world. Many more keep turning up as great ancient monuments (often lying buried under the sands until recent excavations show how large they once were). Many of the monasteries near Jerusalem were built and developed because of the great pilgrim traffic that once made the Christian churches of Jerusalem and Bethlehem world centers of interest. The crypt at the Saxon monastery church at Ripon in England was constructed as a mimicry of the holy tomb by returning pilgrims who had been so impressed by all they found on their journey to the Middle East. These tiny subterranean rooms were meant to offer English pilgrims at Eastertime a similar liturgical experience, at the tomb, to what the traveling monks had witnessed firsthand in Jerusalem. Jerusalem's liturgical life, revolving around processional liturgies in and around the holy sites, had from earliest times impressed worldwide Christianity and set a standard for international churches to emulate. Most Christian churches celebrating

Holy Week are, perhaps, unaware today of how many of their customs derive from the Byzantine-era Jerusalem rites.

But by the tenth century the Christian emperors at Constantinople were losing their military grip. The Western kings sent the mercenary armies we now know as the Crusades in several waves (generally to the annoyance of the emperors), and in the long term the Christian hold over the Holy Land progressively slipped away. Pilgrimage became dangerous, and the shrines themselves passed from having extensive wealth flowing through them to extreme poverty, relying on international support, and much political negotiation, to keep them in existence. It was in this context that one of the important Palestinian monasteries rose up to a second life of significance for Orthodoxy: this time as a great memory keeper for liturgical ritual. The place was Mar Saba monastery.

It was founded by Saint Sabas in the year 484. *Mar* is the Aramaic word for lord or saint, and *saba* was originally a title for elder. Saint Sabas himself was such a major monastic leader that it was felt sufficient to call him *the* elder. Even today his monks are called the Sabbaites. In Byzantine times the house (which is rather a collection of houses grown up over centuries to form a walled complex) was known as the Holy or Great Lavra. It is located in the Kidron Valley, not far from Bethlehem, and from its beginnings attracted some of the most skilled and intellectual ascetics of the early Christian world. Sabas came from a Christian family, but even as a youth he had won the admiration of the monks of Palestine. He served as a disciple of one of the greatest of them, Euthymios, and after spending many years in a regular monastery of the common life, he moved to become a strict hermit. When his

reputation as a man of prayer started to spread internationally, many monastic disciples from near and far came to ask his
guidance, and so he arranged to build cells around a difficult
but easily defended gorge. The monastery today is an amaz-
ing sight, dropping down the cliff to which it clings.[25] In his
lifetime Sabas had several conflicts with the monastics who
did not always appreciate his guidance. Many of the more intellectual monks resisted his deep simplicity and spirit of renunciation, and against his wishes they insisted that an ascetic
ought to be learned and skilled to be a teacher in Christian
traditions. Sabas moved away from the Great Lavra and
founded another, which would be called the New Lavra. His
body (the relics became an important site of pilgrimage in
their own right) was eventually laid to rest in the original
lavra, where they remained until the twelfth century, when
Latin Crusaders took them home with them. It was a great
occasion in Eastern Orthodoxy in 1965 when Pope Paul VI
returned them to the Great Lavra as a gesture of reconciliation between the Roman Catholics and the Orthodox East, an
act that began the thaw of many centuries of cold estrange-
ment between the churches.

In the time when the Christian Holy Land started to become even more remote than it had been in the fifth century,
in those times when it was only a short journey to the great
ritual centers of Jerusalem and Bethlehem, Mar Saba monastery began its second life as a kind of stored memory of an
earlier golden age. Its library began to store foundational
texts with much greater security than was possible in Jerusalem. Its great obscurity in the desert also served to protect
the monastery from marauders and even from the easy reach
of Christian emperors who wanted to interfere. The great

theologian Saint John of Damascus (676–749) lived and was buried here, and here he wrote in defense of the icons against emperors who wished to eradicate them. John and several other Sabbaite monks also composed numerous hymns for liturgical use that are still today at the core of many Orthodox church services. The members of the monastic community of Mar Saba, seeing the decline of the city churches, were all the more determined that the full glory of the Orthodox liturgical rituals should be celebrated within their walls. So it was that they soon became known for the purity and extent of their liturgical tradition. How they did things there (known as the typikon) became a gold standard. By the ninth century their reputation stood unchallenged in international Orthodox monasticism.

By this time the great founding center of the Palestinian and Egyptian deserts had been overcome and largely silenced by Islamic power, but the monasteries of Constantinople were still flourishing, and they looked very closely at what the Sabbaite monks were doing. This is how the later Orthodox liturgy came to its contemporary, classical, form. The rituals of Constantinople were often highly colored by the ceremonies involving the emperor and court aristocrats: gorgeous vestments, much ceremonial procession, repetitive litanies the crowds could join in with simple refrains, and highly elaborate singing of poetry commissioned from great rhetoricians and performers. This shaped the character of the Constantinopolitan rite, and its effects are still visible in the elaborate ceremonies of the Orthodox Church. The monks of Mar Saba, however, kept the rituals of the Jerusalem church to the fore. They also celebrated worship with a much more simplified and ascetical diet of psalms and prayers of petition, as was appropriate for monastics living in such a simple environment. The monks loved to spend entire nights at prayer, and so the Sabbaite ritual developed with long prayer services involving many psalms, celebrated in a very sober style. Someone who has only witnessed the Orthodox paschal services (reminiscent of Constantinopolitan style) would be surprised if they attended weekday Vespers or Matins of prayers, which would be very biblical and very long indeed—often too long for a congregation not made up of monks. It was in the great monastery of the Stoudium, at Constantinople, sometime in the tenth century that a fusion started to take place between the two liturgical approaches, and it is this Sabbaite-Constantinopolitan compromise that spread out from the imperial city to become the dominant worship style of the entire Orthodox world in those important last four hundred years before Constantinople itself fell before Islamic power and the pace of future church developments fell into somnolence.

CHAPTER SIX

Orthodox Life under and after Islamic Dominion

THE SLAVIC ORTHODOX EXPERIENCE: MEDIEVAL TIMES TO THE NINETEENTH CENTURY

The Russian Church was entering its greatest period of consolidation and development at the same time that the Greek East was entering its long twilight under the Ottoman domination of the fifteenth century. The Muscovite princes, having moved the central see of the Russian Church from Kiev to their own capital, and having conquered the armies of the Tartars, whose incessant raids had so troubled the earlier peace of the church, were now widely seen as the God-favored inheritors of all the old Constantinopolitan rights and duties. The Russian ecclesiastical historian Filofei of Pskov wrote to Tsar Basil III at this time, "Now Moscow alone shines over all the earth more radiantly than the sun," and he attributed its rise in stature to the manner in which it had kept the strictness of the Orthodox faith in contrast to the laxity of the Greeks willing to indulge in ecumenical compromises.[1]

In the late fifteenth and early sixteenth centuries the Russian Church was divided by significant tensions between two highly influential camps of monastic leaders. They were known as the Possessors and the Non-Possessors. As the names suggest, the issue was whether monastic poverty meant the renunciation of all possessions for both individual and associations of monks, or whether it meant that property should not be held individually but used communally for the advancement of the monastic and ecclesial cause. The leader of the Possessors was the abbot Joseph of Volotsk (1439–1515), who argued that the manner in which the Russian monasteries accumulated land and holdings was a sign of the health of the church and augured well for the way the church could strongly influence the governance of the state through its influence on the princes as an equal voice of authority in the land. The Non-Possessors were led by Nil of Sora (1433–1508). He was opposed to extensive monastic landholdings and said that all monastic life had to be always characterized by extreme simplicity and abnegation, with possessions only held for purposes of active charity among the faithful. He was also very wary of the monastics being involved with the governance of state affairs. Typically, both men are venerated in the Russian Church calendar as saints, a symbol in a real sense of how the Russian Church simply conflated and embraced political principles and spiritual attitudes that to outsiders seemed incompatible.[2]

The Slavic character of Russian Orthodoxy was underscored by a highly significant moment in 1499 when Gennadii, the archbishop of Novgorod, issued in manuscript the first complete Church Slavonic Bible. This became a literary treasure for the entire Slavic world and had an untold influence on later publishing history. Almost a century later Prince Konstantin Konstantinovich of Ostrog would issue the first printed Slavonic Bible based upon it. In 1551, Tsar Ivan IV and his patriarch Makarii of Moscow convened a council known as the Stoglav, or Council of One Hundred Chapters. It was a moment in the life of the Russian Church that brought under stricter control the fluid and often local practices in terms of icon painting, devotions in church, variations in ecclesiastical service books, and a wide variety of operative forms of the calendar of feast days. Rules were issued, and a more centralized form of church governance was applied so that a conformity could be established for the future. The distinctive practices of Russian ritual were held up as laudatory, not deviational. Makarii issued a massive edition of the (Greek) *Menologion*, or definitive texts for the feast days to be celebrated throughout the year. Entitled the *Velikii Minei-Chetii* (the Great Book of Monthly Readings), it brought a definite and thoroughgoing Slavic spirit to the Russian Church and symbolically marked its emergence from its origins as a Byzantine daughter church. Ever afterward this style of saints' lives and devotion shaped the character of Russian Orthodoxy with a distinct symbiosis of biblical archetype, saintly ascetical and humble endeavor, and sacramental liturgical ethos.

The deepening Russian Orthodox character of uncompromising conservatism, and increasingly centralized control, came soon enough to cause a severe problem for church life. The Kievan Orthodox Church had oversight over Ukrainian and Belo-Russian territories but was drawn ever more deeply by the sixteenth century into the ambit of Polish and Lithuanian state princes who belonged to the Latin Catholic world. The Orthodox bishops reacted to the higher social standing of their Latin counterparts in many cases by looking to Rome for support, and to the West generally with an eye to its clearly higher educational standards.[3] A significant number of Orthodox bishops met in council at the city of Brest in 1596 and declared a reunion with the patriarchate of Rome. The terms of the *Unia* meant that the Orthodox bishops would continue with their distinctive Eastern Christian customs (married clergy, liturgy of Saint John Chrysostom) but accept the Orthodoxy of the Roman Church and submit to the ultimate authority of the pope. What this would mean in the longer historical term was a progressive alignment with (some would say submerging under) Latin practices and doctrines. In the immediate term, however, it caused a major split, or schism, between those who now accepted papal authority and the Orthodox who refused it, thus renouncing the authority of the Uniate bishops as schismatics.[4] Strong feelings were roused among the Orthodox communities, who suspected that Rome had undermined the Eastern Church's essential unity by offering prizes of political stability and the benefits of the more advanced West. These tensions remain to this day in the churches on Russia's western border regions, and they implanted in the heartland of the Russian Orthodox Church as deep a distrust of the Western proselytizing churches (both Catholic and Protestant) as of the armed intrusions of Islam.

One of the leading archimandrites of the Kiev Caves (Pechersky) Lavra, which had remained a center of Ukrainian Orthodox life, assumed the Orthodox metropolitanate of Kiev. He was Peter Mohyla (1596–1647) and was destined to have a large impact on Orthodoxy up to and through the nineteenth century. He had been raised in Poland and grew up aware of the educational standards of the West. Contrasting them with the general educational standard of the Ukrainian and Russian people, but especially that of the clergy, he was determined to do something radical to raise Orthodox standards of culture. To this end he established an academy in Kiev with a curriculum that included Greek, Slavonic, and Latin learning.[5] It soon produced generations of leading intellectuals who spread over the Orthodox world as chief administrators and higher clergy, taking the ideals of raising standards of culture with them. Mohyla was deeply impressed by the power of the West's printing presses and by the systematic nature of Western Catholic theology. Like the Western Church, he was moved by the perceived need to offset the articulate Protestant preaching missions, and so he galvanized Orthodox efforts to upgrade the tertiary level of education in the clergy and to begin issuing books and printed materials for use in evangelization. Many in his own time and many subsequent Orthodox historians have accused him of excessively Westernizing the way the Orthodox Church articulates its mission. Though overstated, this accusation recognizes that Mohyla did in fact introduce a scholastic element into Orthodox texts of this era that was not native to it and was a style of thought that in many ways tended to paralyze one's ability to read the original sources more clearly in their own ethos. It would take the church until well into the early decades of the twentieth century before this scholastically oppressive style of thinking could be diminished (just as it was eventually dismantled in the Western churches too).

On the positive front, however, Mohyla had sounded the bell that the Russian Church needed to take a lead in the educational reform of its clergy, for purposes of preserving the purity of its mission, and his call was never forgotten by generations of great Russian hierarchs after him. There was never a dearth of bishops who, from a monastic upbringing, had scant regard for academics or traditions of learning, preferring a simple faith and trying to hold the line of unthinking monastic obedience imposed on all levels of their churches, even the laity. But equally there was formed a tradition of hierarchs who were ordained because of the spiritual quality of their lives allied with the strength of their intelligence; this combination produced some of the very best examples of the flourishing of the Russian Church in the early modern period. As with the conflict between Possessors and Non-Possessors, this once more produced conflicting attitudes in the Russian Church between its Byzantine past and the cultural attractions of an ascendant West, resulting not so much in an either-or as rather a both-and. The schism of the Old Believers shows the same aspect occurring once again.

Patriarch Nikon (1605–1681) and his tsar, Alexei Mihailovich (1629–1676), became very conscious of the extent of the local differences in practice and church service books between the Russians, the Ukrainians, and the Greeks. This issue was precipitated by a visit to Moscow from the Greek patriarch of Jerusalem, who was critical of the liturgical differences he noticed prevalent in Russia. Since the Ukrainians also tended to follow the Greek (Byzantine) ritual forms, the Moscow patriarchate's practices stood out as anomalous, and the Greeks claimed that since they provided the original source, their books had to be regarded as the authentic exemplars and the Russian traditions had to be regarded as deviations. In fact the Russian conservatism in force since the church's foundation in the tenth century made it, in many cases, hold to original historical forms of service and custom that the Greeks had more or less unconsciously altered over the years in a gradual series of reforms and developments. Nikon was anxious to make the Russian Church impervious to these accusations of deviation, since Russia had redefined Orthodoxy (originally the Greek term for "right-thinking") in Slavonic as *Pravoslavie*, that is, "right-worshipping."

The patriarch, with the young tsar's blessing, began to collate Russian service books against Greek exemplars. The Greek texts he took to base his work on, however, were not the Byzantine manuscripts, now inaccessible to the Russians, but rather printed Greek books emanating from seventeenth-century Venice, and others coming from the Polish-Lithuanian commonwealth that had been influenced by a certain Latinization. Throughout Russia, but especially among its most conservative church circles, the reforms were regarded as a heresy. The spiritual leader of the opposition was Archpriest Avvakum (Habbakuk), who publicly accused Nikon of "defiling the faith" and "pouring wrathful fury upon the Russian land."[6] One of Nikon's proposed changes concerned restoring the sign of the cross with three fingers (symbolizing the Trinity) as opposed to the traditional Russian way of two fingers (symbolizing the two natures united of the Incarnate Lord).[7] This apparently small change ignited into a major revolution against Nikon's authority.[8] The base issue, of course, was one of authenticity of spirit and who had the right (and to what remit this extended) to speak for the wholesale Russian Orthodox tradition.

While the young tsar supported him Nikon was safe enough, and he showed an unyielding and sometimes cruel attitude to those who stood against him. But the tsar himself grew tired of Nikon and his imperious manner and lost confidence in him. Nikon reacted by dramatically stripping off his patriarchal vestments and retiring to the New Jerusalem monastery outside Moscow. Perhaps he hoped he would be recalled as indispensable, but the see remained vacant for years. The tsar finally decided to rid himself of a former ally who had now come to be an embarrassment and abandoned Nikon to his enemies. There were enough of them to demand a synod of bishops to assemble between 1666 and 1667 to adjudicate the disputes.

Tsar Alexei called the patriarchs of Antioch and Alexandria to preside over it. The synod deposed Nikon for his autocratic behavior and imprisoned him; but it also upheld the liturgical reforms he had set in motion as commendable; this despite the fact that most Orthodox laity and most members of the lower clergy radically detested them. In the end a sizable group of faithful and clergy refused to accept the new ritual instructions and broke off relations with the Moscow church authorities. These were the so-called Old Believers, also known as Old Ritualists.⁹ They developed soon enough into two distinct streams, the Priestly Ones (*Popovtsy*) and the Priestless Ones (*Bezpopovtsy*), depending on how closely each group reflected the sacramental and liturgical life of the Orthodox Church. Neither had much interest in ecumenism, increasingly regarding the main Orthodox Church (the Nikon Church, as they called it) as hopelessly immured in faithlessness. The members of the Priestless sect regarded the church as having died out on earth, and general society as having apostasized. Accordingly, their duty was to cut themselves off from the evil around them and endure without sacraments or priests through the era of the Antichrist. Though represented at first by many merchants and Boyars, the Old Believers eventually became a highly exclusionist, inward-looking, and eschatological movement of the only-surviving pure ones. Growing preference for life in obscure rural retreats (often to which they had fled for protection from persecution) made them an ascetically severe movement living out a simple and prayerful lifestyle. The state regarded them as a constant nuisance. Regarded askance by the mainline Orthodox Church, the Old Believers were often afforded much greater respect from the larger body of Orthodox faithful, who recognized in them the ancient simplicity of the old Russian traditions. Before the 1917 Revolution in Russia there were an estimated twenty million Old Ritualists. After great sufferings during the twentieth-century Soviet regime, there are now only an estimated two million surviving. In 1971 the Moscow patriarchate officially removed the historical anathemas that had been pronounced against them. A small movement for reconciliation with the mainline Orthodox Church resulted in the 1800s in the formation of the *Edinovertsy* community of churches (meaning "people of the same faith") which was a compromise offered by the patriarchate for converts from the Old Believer Popovtsy, who could reconcile within the mainstream Orthodox family but still retain their pre-Nikon ritual differences. There are still several churches of the latter movement within the Russian Orthodox communion today.

Though a religiously observant ruler, Tsar Peter the Great (1672–1725) had little time for the deep conservatism of the clergy and faithful of the Russian Orthodox Church. He had his mind set on energetic reforms that would bring his country into greater alignment with the rapid cultural and technological developments he saw taking place in the West. He moved his capital from Moscow to his new city of Saint

Petersburg to facilitate his moves at every level to modernize Russia.[10] Knowing that he had to take a firm stance with the church if he was to succeed in this, he abolished the patriarchate by simply refusing to appoint a successor when Patriarch Adrian died in 1700, and making his adjutant bishop, Stefan, stand in for the duties for twenty-one years until Peter then officially named him metropolitan archbishop of Moscow. Peter radically redesigned the system of church administration, creating government by episcopal synod, but a synod that now had significant executive involvement of court-appointed officials. Every Russian bishop henceforth had to be appointed with the tsar's approval. Peter also moved against the monasteries by making it illegal for anyone to become a monk under the age of fifty. The clerical ranks increasingly came to be seen as a backwater career. To advance his cause Peter imported into positions of seniority many hierarchs from Ukraine whom he felt were more open to new ideas. Under Peter and Catherine the Great (empress 1762–1796) the church was drastically sidelined from the close partnership it had once enjoyed with previous rulers. The standards of its education and culture also fell.

Under the later Romanovs, the church, though it was always protected and patronized by the tsars, would never again see a patriarch who was a real political power in the land. Peter's decisive pushing of the church off the visible tracks to secular success reinforced Russian Orthodoxy's character as an ascetical mystical force, one that often seemed to turn away from a secular environment seen as hostile and corrupt. This context partly led to a significant tendency among lay intellectuals and some monastics in the latter part of the nineteenth century in Russia that has come to be known as the

Slavophile Movement. The group of intellectuals who first began it was a mixed group of religious, literary, and philosophical thinkers. The theologian Aleksei Khomyakov (1804–1860) was the main originating figure, along with the critic and philosopher Ivan Kireyevsky (1806–1856). Their call for a revival of the traditional values of Slavic culture had a broad appeal and drew in a range of other thinkers such as the writers Nikolai Gogol (1809–1852) and Fyodor Dostoyevsky (1821–1881), the poet Fyodor Tyutchev, and even the Russian composers known as "the Five" (Mily Balakirev, César Cui, Modest Mussorgsky, Nikolai Rimsky-Korsakov, and Alexander Borodin). All the Slavophiles tended to regard the Orthodox Church as a force and systemic organization that encapsulated the elusive "Russian soul" that had to be liberated from oppressive Westernizing elements. The movement was, then, in its origins a clear attempt to throw off the bureaucratic heritage of Peter the Great, but it also tended to give rise to an ever-deepening sense of suspicion of the traditions of Western Europe, and certainly to a fear of engaging with non-Orthodox Christianity, which was often felt to be interested only in proselytizing a simpler and less aggressively missionizing church. Several of the Slavophiles worked up the trope that Orthodoxy represented the ideal principle of spiritual freedom in Christianity, as distinct from the excessive control manifested by the Roman Catholic ecclesial spirit and the individualistic anarchy seen in Protestantism. This tendency to think in such antinomies became a marked characteristic of much Russian Orthodox thought running on from the late nineteenth century and throughout the twentieth.

The perceived state-sponsored suppression of freedom of spirit in church life also certainly encouraged the monastic element in the church to rise to great spiritual and moral prominence, something that can be seen when, shortly, we turn to look at the so-called hesychastic revival. Unlike Nikon and Philaret, patriarchs who had challenged the tsar's supremacy, a tradition flourished in Russian spirituality that looked back to the sons of Grand Prince Vladimir, Boris and Gleb, from the earliest days of Russian Christianity.[11] As the monastic chronicler tells the tale, knowing that their pagan brother Sviatapolk had contested their right to rule after the death of their father, they went meekly to their own murders rather than advance the civil war (1015–1019). They were designated passion bearers (*strastoterptsy*) in the church traditions and were regarded as pure icons of the meekness and self-sacrificing attitude of Jesus himself. This tradition of seeking to exemplify the interior humility and abnegation of the passion bearer ran deep in many aspects of Russian spirituality, and it continues to this day among both monastics and many Orthodox lay people.

RUSSIA'S NEIGHBORS: BULGARIAN, SERBIAN, AND ROMANIAN ORTHODOXY

Throughout all the period of the ascendancy of Ottoman Islam in the Balkans and the Levant, Russia stood out as the great Orthodox power and real defender of Christian rights. Within the shade of the great Russian Orthodox tree, however, several other local Orthodox churches were able to grow; though, as with all such sheltering plants, their growth was not just simply encouraged by the overshadowing form but oftentimes restricted by it too. For our purposes here, the indigenous Orthodox traditions of Bulgaria, Serbia, and Romania can stand as brief examples.

Bulgaria

Orthodoxy came to Bulgaria much earlier than it did to Russia. Geographically, Bulgaria was centered in the ancient Roman regions of Thrace and Illyria, the first of which was adjacent in a northerly direction to Constantinople's closest province, north of the Danube, and the second of which was located on the Adriatic Coast. The area was thus intimately known at an early stage to the Byzantine Empire. By the late seventh century Bulgar (Turkic) tribes had crossed the Danube southward and formed the basis of a kingdom under the khans. It is Khan Asparuch who is traditionally credited with establishing the Bulgarian state at the beginning of his reign (681–700), crossing the Danube into undefended Roman imperial territory and settling there, mingling with many Slavic tribes. In 811 Khan Krum (803–814) fought with and killed the Byzantine emperor Nikephoros I, who had come to exert dominion and dismantle the state. In 813 he fought off Emperor Michael I in addition to putting the Byzantine city of Adrianople to the sword and advancing even up to the walls of Constantinople. This was the point at which Khan Krum died, and his successors decided to negotiate with the Byzantines, turning their territorial ambitions away from the south, the heartland of the empire, and toward the West, to Macedonia. There had been some long-standing Christian elements among the Slavic tribes already in Bulgaria, but when the son of Khan Omurtag (814–831), Prince Enravotas, embraced Byzantine Orthodoxy, he was immediately executed by his father. And yet, more and more of the people and the ruling classes turned to Christianity. The conversion of Bulgaria to Orthodoxy is traditionally dated from 865, when

Khan Boris accepted baptism and entered into a closer allegiance with the empire. A shared Christianity helped the consolidation of the Bulgarian nation, still notably split into its Turkic and Slavic constituencies.

Though Khan Boris was willing to accept the advantages of the Christian faith, he was not so eager to be overwhelmed by the influence of Byzantines, and so in 862 he renewed the relationship his ancestor Omurtag had first established with the Frankish kingdom, meeting with the Western leader King Louis in that year and asking the king to send Latin missionaries to evangelize his people.[12] The Byzantine state reacted strongly, demanding that Boris break off all relations with the Franks and receive only the Orthodox faith. Though he was compelled to accept this, and so was personally allied to the emperor in his Orthodox baptism of 865, he was nevertheless also happy to allow the argument between the patriarchs of Rome and Constantinople to simmer on (as it would for generations to come), as to which rite was the real founder of Bulgarian Christendom, and which one should exercise ecclesiastical jurisdiction. Trying to negotiate the independence of his own state's church, he was frustrated by both the Eastern and the Western patriarchs independently. Pope Nicholas I and Patriarch Photios of Constantinople clashed bitterly over the Bulgarian issue, but eventually Boris was satisfied when an imperial council of 869–870 definitively assigned Bulgaria to the Byzantine Orthodox Church and also granted it a fairly autonomous archbishop of its own. After 885, the missionary disciples of Saints Cyril and Methodios who had been expelled from Moravia, led by their disciple Kliment, moved to assist in the evangelization of Bulgaria and the Macedonian Slavs, introducing the Slavonic language to the country. In

894 Boris abdicated and retired to life in a monastery. His son Tsar Simeon then promoted Kliment to be the metropolitan archbishop of Ohrid, which became the leading see of the nation and a long-enduring seat (until 1767) of Byzantino-Slavonic learning and Christian culture.

By the tenth century, Bulgarian Orthodoxy had been extensively Byzantinized, but in a Slavonic form, and was rooted in the affairs of the ruling classes. At this point the tsar, Peter I, gained decisive victories over the Byzantines and in 919 encouraged his national synod to declare the autocephaly of the church, in the form of an independent patriarchate, a fait accompli as far as Constantinople was concerned. The wider Bulgarian Church experienced a growing sense of alienation among the poorer classes, who started to regard the ecclesiastical world as belonging more to their rich rulers than themselves. A deep-seated movement arose among the poorer classes led by the priest Bogomil, who encouraged all his followers to live radically ascetic lives because the world, as he saw it, was irredeemably corrupt. His movement caught on and increasingly came to represent dualistic ideas (probably present in the earlier folk religion of the area): that there was an evil god and a good god warring for souls. This world's sufferings were the creations of the evil god; radical renunciation of sex and rich foods would save the souls of the elect; the visible sacraments were worth little.

Many of the Bogomils reacted to their oppression by state and church leaders by simply hiding in plain sight, attending the Orthodox churches but renouncing their customs and doctrines in their own private prayer sessions. Even into the thirteenth century the leaders of the church were meeting to discuss how to eradicate Bogomilism from its midst. By 972 the Byzantine armies again started to erode Bulgarian independence. By 1018 Byzantium had gained the upper hand politically once more, with the victorious Emperor Basil I (the Bulgar Slayer) acknowledging its autocephaly as a church but deliberately depriving it of the title of a patriarchate and reducing it to an archiepiscopal see based at Ohrid, most of whose subsequent incumbents the Byzantines ensured would be Greeks. In 1235 the patriarch of Constantinople convened a council in Lampsakos to restore the patriarchal title to the Bulgarians, which served to acknowledge Bulgaria's decision yet again to renounce allegiance to the Roman popes, which it had used as a bargaining counter.

By the late fourteenth century, Ottoman military advances had started to enclose the Bulgarian kingdom. The Bulgarian patriarch Evtimi was then seated in the city of Tarnovo, but this fell to the Ottomans in 1393. His expulsion marked the end of the Bulgarian patriarchate as well as the end of the independent kingdom. In 1394 the patriarch of Constantinople, Antony IV, appointed the Moldavian metropolitan Jeremias as exarch to superintend Bulgarian Church affairs. For the next five hundred years Bulgarian Orthodoxy survived under the Ottomans. Though it was supposedly a tolerated religion in terms of the Koran, across the nation the Orthodox were offered many inducements, not excluding terror, to convert to Islam. After the fall of Constantinople itself, less than a generation later, the Bulgarian Orthodox were, like all other Christians in the Ottoman dominions, placed under the governance of the ethnarch appointed by the sultan, namely, the patriarch of Constantinople. His administration, as was the pattern in many other Slavic areas administered by the Phanariot ruling classes of Constantinople, led to an increasing reservation of the highest state and ecclesiastical offices for these superintendent Greeks themselves. The introduction of the Greek language into the services was but the spearhead of a thoroughgoing Hellenization of the Bulgarian Church for the next five hundred years, and the profound overshadowing of its indigenous Slavonic traditions. This would not be reversed until the nineteenth century, which saw a widespread monastic revival of the church that went hand in hand with renewed efforts of the Bulgarians to throw off Ottoman domination and reassert their political independence.

The Zographou monastery on Mount Athos had served throughout this long period as a repository of the Orthodox Bulgarian memory and aspirations. The Bulgarian monk Paisy of Hilandar (1722–1798), who had also lived at Zographou for thirty years, was the first to signal this symbolic revival, with his work *Slavo-Bulgarian History*, an account of the long endurance of the church in which he pointed an admonitory finger at both Islamic rule and Phanariot domination. His work circulated extensively in manuscript form, disseminated by Bulgarian monastics and intellectuals, and was certainly a lively spark for the encouragement of the Bulgarian national liberation movement of the nineteenth century. This would eventually result in both independence and the restoration of the Bulgarian patriarchate, but the latter not until 1953, and never again with its former rank and prestige. Today the Bulgarian Orthodox Church has an estimated six million believers in the homelands and a further two million in the diaspora.

Serbia

Serbia is today the sixth-ranking patriarchate of the Orthodox Church. In medieval times its ecclesial territory covered a larger area of the Balkan Peninsula than present-day Serbia.

The Balkan Peninsula became a focus of Slavic tribal migration from the seventh century onward, and the tribes there were caught up into Orthodoxy by the mission of Saints Methodius and Cyril, receiving from them too the Slavonic literary culture that would eventually form the tribes into a nation. Nationhood and the Orthodox Church have ever since been closely associated by the Serbs. The twelfth-century prince Stefan Nemanja (1109–1199) fashioned the tribes into a powerful state, centered in the mountainous region bordering modern-day Kosovo and Metohij; the latter name derives its meaning from "the land of monasteries." Up to the fourteenth century the Serbian state expanded, largely at the expense of Byzantine territory. Stefan's son Prince Ratsko (1175–1235) left the court to become a monastic founder on Mount Athos. Under his name of Saint Sava the Enlightener, he remains the most revered of all Serbian Orthodox saints. When his father joined him there and assumed the name of Simeon, they together founded the great Serbian monastery of Hilandar, which was from that time on a center of Serbian religious, intellectual, and spiritual culture.

In 1219 Sava and Simeon, working once more in the homeland, convinced the patriarch of Constantinople (then in exile in Nicaea because of the Latin occupation of Constantinople) to give the Serbian Church its independence (autocephaly). Sava was consecrated as the chief archbishop of the church, and he extensively reorganized and expanded his dioceses. Many of the monasteries founded during this period (such as Studenica, Gracanika, Visoki, Pec, and Sopocani) are today considered among the world heritage sites representing the Serbian people. Sava insisted on the church using the Slavonic language, not Greek, and underscored its Slavic heritage. In the mid-fourteenth century the Serbian Church and the Serbian state had expanded to the point that they had aspirations to take over from Byzantium (then reviving its fortunes). The ruler Stefan Dusic Nemanjic, without asking or waiting for Constantinople's agreement, instructed the bishops to appoint the senior hierarch Joanikije to be the patriarch of a truly independent national church; and in 1346 Joanikije consecrated and crowned Stefan "emperor and autocrat of the Serbs and Greeks," causing a major row with Byzantium, whose patriarch excommunicated the entire church in 1353.[13]

There was a patched-up reconciliation of some form in the years that followed. But politically Serbian state fortunes declined consistently and rapidly. The Ottomans advanced into the southeastern territories. Two catastrophic battles (Maritsa in 1371 and Kosovo in 1389) saw the fatal damaging of the small empire, and the capital, Smederevo, fell to the invaders in 1459. The patriarchate itself was abolished by the Ottoman powers after the death of Arsenije II in 1463, and the church administration was relocated to the archbishopric of Ohrid. Through the fourteenth-century decline Serbian Orthodox had more and more become aligned with the Greek Byzantine tradition. Under Ottoman rule, and as part of the *Millet* system, where local Christians were administered separately as a subject people, the Serbian Church was, paradoxically, to receive more independence than before. In 1557 the sultan's grand vizier, Mehmet Sokollu Pasha, showed his early origins as a conscripted Christian boy in Serbia by arranging the restoration of the Serbian patriarchate in Pec and appointing to the post his relative Makarije Sokolovic.[14] The patriarchate then had a jurisdictional role stretching to the north from southern Hungary, to the south in Macedonia, and from the Dalmatian Coast in the west, to parts of Bulgaria to the east. Ottoman rule, however, also caused many Christian Orthodox Serbs to flee from the country, and the Serbian presence at this period also moved outward through significant immigration to the Austro-Hungarian Empire, especially after the defeat of the great revolt in 1690. Even today there is a very large Serb Orthodox diaspora in the New World.

The seventeenth and eighteenth centuries were a marked low point for Serbian Orthodox fortunes; the church was profoundly weakened. In 1766 the Ottomans once more abolished the patriarchate and placed it under the direct jurisdiction of Constantinople. Thereafter the Phanariot Greek nobles in charge once more tried to Hellenize the church as much as possible but were largely unsuccessful, and on the borders of the Hapsburg Empire the emperors there started to offer their own resident Serbs political and religious advantages if they served as a border defensive force. The Orthodox Serbs within the Hapsburg Empire were organized around the metropolitanate of Karlovac, to which, in one of its last independent acts in 1710, the Serbian patriarchate at Pec had given autonomous status. In the mid-nineteenth century the weakened state of the Ottoman Empire would finally allow the Serbian Orthodox to reassert their independence, but the two parts would not be reunited until after the First World War, when the Austro-Hungarian Empire itself collapsed. In 1920 the modern Serbian Orthodox patriarchate was reinstated with the agreement and recognition of the patriarch of Constantinople.

Romania

Today, Romania is the second largest of the Orthodox lands, after Russia, numbering just fewer than sixteen and a half million self-styling believers in the 2011 census of mainland Romania, as well as almost three-quarters of a million faithful living in the adjacent Republic of Moldova.[15] There are also dioceses of the Romanian Church supervising what is an extensive diaspora population of twelve million Romanian Orthodox in Serbia, Hungary, Central and Western Europe, the Americas, and Oceania. It is by far the largest of all Orthodox churches within the European Union and the only Orthodox church that uses a Romance language in its liturgies and services.

Its existence as Christian church stretches back to apostolic times, when the faith was preached in the region south of the Danube, occupied then by Illyrians, Thracians, Dacians, and Greeks (the present-day regions of Serbia, Bulgaria, and Greece). The resulting Romanian culture is a rich blend of Latin, Greek, and Slavic influences. On the eastern borders of the Danube there exist remains of episcopal sees already established in the fourth century, and a metropolitan see at Tomis (modern Constanta) in what was then Roman Scythia Minor. Two of the early Scythian theologians had international reputations in the ancient church: Saint John Cassian, the great monastic theologian who eventually settled in Marseilles, and Saint Dionysius Exiguus, the theologian and historian who gave to the world the time schema that pivoted on the Incarnation of the Lord: A.D. and A.C. (the latter more commonly seen in English abbreviation as B.C.).[16]

The original Illyrian territories were extensively Latin speaking, and related to the Roman patriarchate, but the second and fourth Ecumenical Councils placed the northern Danubian lands under the aegis of the patriarchate of Constantinople. This diocesan structure more or less eroded between the seventh and tenth centuries under the wave of Avaro-Slavic tribal migrations. The Slav settlement permeated the

Dacian-Romanian language. Slavonic became increasingly used in church services, as Russian Orthodoxy extended its influence, and eventually became dominant until about the end of the seventeenth century, even though the common people did not understand it. Romanian began to be used after the sixteenth century and in 1863 was declared to be the only official language of the Romanian Orthodox Church.

In the middle of the fourteenth century, two Romanian principalities emerged, Wallachia (1330) and Moldavia (1359).[17] Constantinople recognized the metropolitan status of the first in 1359 and that of the second in 1401. Subordinate dioceses grew from this, and some, especially those in Transylvania, were in the territory of the Catholic kings of Hungary and were frequently hampered and sometimes suppressed by the Hapsburg rulers. The princes of Wallachia and Moldavia, however, were great patrons of the Romanian Orthodox Church, and many of its hierarchs were men of distinguished learning. Voivode (Prince) Stephen the Great (1457–1504) is remembered by all Romanians as a great national hero, opposing the sultans and developing the Romanian state (sometimes with the military support of Voivode Vlad III Dracula of Wallachia). Stephen built numerous churches in a distinctive Gothic-Orthodox style, which are today among the most beautiful examples of Orthodox ecclesial culture.[18] The church became a repository of Romanian language and culture as well as the national religious focus. Its ecclesiastical authors, chiefly monastics, issued Slavonic printed liturgical texts in Wallachia after 1507. The monasteries were centers of hesychastic spiritual life and became important to the development of the nation. From the sixteenth century, the Orthodox Church was seen as the bearer of the whole national tradition, and when Romania finally became a kingdom, it was without question the state church. This very intimate relationship between church and statehood served Romanian Orthodoxy well under later times of Russian Communist oppression, for the pro-Soviet regimes tended to turn their antireligious oppressions onto individuals who spoke out, rather than onto church institutions as such, which were being used by the state as a form of cultural and nationalist buffer between itself and its Muscovite masters. Accordingly, the Romanian church infrastructure would survive extensively after communism, unlike several other Soviet-zone churches.

In the late seventeenth and early eighteenth centuries the Roman Catholic Church, with state aid from imperial Vienna, launched extensive missionary campaigns in Transylvania. The principalities of Wallachia and Moldavia remained strongly Orthodox, but the Jesuits effected a union of some of the Transylvanian churches with Rome, and the Greek-Catholic Romanian Church was created, placed under the Roman Catholic archbishop of Esztergom. The center was later moved to Fagaras, near Sibiu, and then to Blaj, where the pope raised it to metropolitan status in 1853. The Orthodox episcopate in Transylvania was suppressed until 1761, when a revolt forced the Viennese authorities to appoint a Serbian Orthodox bishop to take care of the people. A Romanian bishop was not able to be elected until 1810. The important scholar-theologian Andrei Saguna eventually succeeded to the see, and in 1864 he proved capable of raising it to metropolitan status at Sibiu, thereby reasserting the development of the largest ecclesial body in Transylvania. The Communist governments after 1948 would severely suppress the Greek Catholic Church organization there, forcing its merging with the Romanian Orthodox establishment until the liberation following the revolution of 1989.

In 1859 the Romanian principalities of Wallachia and Moldavia politically merged and declared themselves the Romanian state and nation. In 1864, Prince Alexandru Ioan Cuza declared the nationalization of all Romanian monasteries and lands, effectively removing them from the control of the patriarchate of Constantinople, which still exercised rights over the church that the sultan had given to the Phanariot administration. The prince also declared the Romanian Church's independence from Constantinople, affirming its autocephaly on his own authority. The following year the archbishop of Bucharest was declared to be the metropolitan primate of Romania. In 1872 the Holy Synod of the Romanian Church was organized, led by the metropolitan of Bucharest. The patriarch of Constantinople, Joachim IV, acknowledged the Romanian autocephaly in 1885 (following the 1877–1878 Russo-Turkish War when Romania and Bulgaria shared the Russian victory over Turkey and deconstructed Ottoman influence in the Balkans). In 1925 the senior Romanian metropolitan, Miron Cristea, was duly acknowledged as a patriarch, and since then there have been five others in succession. The Romanian patriarchate is the second largest in terms of Orthodox numbers, and ranks seventh in order of precedence.[19]

THE GREEKS AND THE OTTOMAN EXPERIENCE

The fall of Constantinople was a shattering experience for the Greek Christian world. Constantinopolitan Christianity in its golden age was outward looking, culture making, world dominating. After the fall of the capital to the Latin forces in the Fourth Crusade of 1204, the political and cultural fortunes of the Byzantine Orthodox world went into an unstoppable decline, while those of the Western Church rose in the scales. The greatest losses of all were not always the most obvious ones, such as loss of political freedom, territory, wealth, and power. What was more damaging in the longer term to Eastern Orthodox Christianity was the new Islamic ascendancy that forbade the Christians to preach their faith. Christian religion could be followed liturgically within the churches that were not sequestrated, but it could not be proclaimed or advanced in any way outside them. This, and the removal of almost every Greek aristocrat who could serve as a protective patron, meant that schools and libraries, considered tertiary-level centers of Greek scholarship, all but collapsed in the aftermath of 1453. Monasteries remained important centers of Greek Christian culture and today, the libraries at Sinai or the Athonite houses testify to the often heroic efforts the Greek Christians made to keep the flame of learning and spiritual culture alive under Islamic domination in the East.

The very real fear that Greek learning, for so long a lighthouse that had illuminated the entire Christian world, East and West, might be dead and soon forgotten (for the Roman Church had no desire to record its achievements in its own version of church history) led the Greek Orthodox Christians clustered around the patriarchate of Constantinople to be overzealous in propagating their Christian Byzantine culture in the various diaspora colonies over which the sultans gave them supervision. As we have already seen, these Phanariots, the noble or merchant families surviving around the patriarch in the Phanar district of Constantinople, not only administered the sultan's Christian subjects in the conquered dominions of the Ottoman Empire but also aggressively Hellenized the churches there too, almost always trying to suppress local traditions in the cause of creating a series of little Constantinoples outside Byzantium. Under the Ottomans, between Moscow on the one side and the Phanar on the other, colonization seemed to be the order of the day, and the smaller Orthodox churches in the Balkans were the ones who largely paid the price.

To this day many local churches raise a somewhat skeptical eyebrow when the Greek or Russian Orthodox happen to speak about the leadership roles and rights of either church. Many remember the historical manner in which both churches, in the times when they held actual power, did little to preserve the indigenous rights of any of the other local Orthodox communities or paid little more than lip service to the global Orthodox idea that the local church is present in all its fullness and perfection in the person of the local bishop assembled in his local eucharistic communion. This latter idea of local groundedness, something encapsulated in the later principle of subsidiarity, and fully endorsed by Orthodoxy's commitment to collegial synodical governance from ancient times, has often been the victim of waves of ecclesial imperialism that have washed over it. When the various national revolutions against Ottoman rule began, chiefly in the nineteenth century, and brought with them the progressive dismemberment of Phanariot ecclesiastical control, the patriarch of Constantinople issued a statement in 1872 condemning phyletism as a corrupting element in Orthodox life.[20] The term (from Greek) is a disparagement of the new nationalist movements (most seeking ecclesial independence) as a fragmenting tribalism that corrodes the essentially catholic, that is, universal, nature of the church. Constantinople, however, could not see that its own policy of ecclesial Hellenization looked very much like the same kind of thing from outside its own small viewing balcony.

Through the long Ottoman twilight, the Greek clergy maintained Hellenic letters with great fidelity and devotion. Their memories of a Greek glory that stretched back even before Byzantium (one that included the New Testament saints, the fathers of the church, and also the pre-Christian philosophers) sustained their self-identity in most difficult times. The local schoolmasters were often the heroes of the day, keeping histories and memories alive in the local Greek schools, against the background of an impoverished educational world stripped of resources and in a context where denunciation for alleged evangelization was a rapid death sentence. The clergy sustained Orthodox life by a much more concentrated liturgical cycle. Since the Orthodox faith could be celebrated only inside church buildings by any Greek in the Ottoman domains, the focusing of all Orthodox life within the liturgical cycle was an inevitable outcome. This made the Greek Church inward looking, detached from politics and wider culture, in a way that the Russian Church did not know. It encouraged a certain form of withdrawn, devotional spirituality that reserved its secrets for the interior life.

This would partially change when the Greek mainland rose in rebellion against the sultan in the war of independence between 1821 and 1830. The powers of Russia, Great Britain, and France eventually intervened to prevent an Ottoman rout and ensured the Greek victory. The London Conference and the Treaty of Constantinople soon after allowed for the recognition of the Greek kingdom in 1832 when Otto of Bavaria became the first king based in Athens. But this was not before the patriarch of Constantinople had been hanged by order of the sultan from his own gate at his church in the Phanar, for failing to secure the loyalty of his people.[21] From then until the collapse of Ottoman power, the sultans treated the patriarch and the Phanariots with the deepest suspicion and distaste. The law court in Athens declared the autocephaly of the Greek mainland church in 1833, and the church was recognized by the patriarchate of Constantinople in 1850, even though there were then only four bishops making up the Greek Church and serving in the royal (mainly Protestant) establishment. The outlying Greek islands, the largest of which was Crete, remained under the supervision of the patriarch of Constantinople, as did all the very extensive Greek diaspora in America and Oceania. Greek government laws of 1833 closed all monasteries with fewer than five inhabitants, and though there were several spiritual and intellectual revivals attempted through the nineteenth century, designed to offset the more secularist attitude of the German ruling establishment, the state of the church remained predominantly rural and moribund with clergy that were, in the main, not educated beyond elementary level. Priests were an integral part of peasant rural society and, as in Ottoman days, kept themselves in the main to serving the liturgy on Sundays and performing numerous blessings and exorcisms for their farming and seagoing communities. Less frequently the bishops would send around a more educated priest-monk on a tour of the more remote villages, who would preach to the people and counsel the local clergy. The monasteries and the elders of Mount Athos always remained a focal point for the admiration of the Greek people.

SAINT PAISY VELICHOVSKY AND THE HESYCHASTIC RENEWAL

The Greek Church revivals of the 1840s and the 1880s (the Anaplasis movement) were in some senses reminiscent of a more profound spiritual movement that had taken its origin on Mount Athos in the eighteenth century, but they would grow throughout the nineteenth and twentieth centuries to become a formative spirit of contemporary world Orthodoxy. This Athonite spiritual tradition departed in significant ways from the mainland Athenian revivalist movements. The latter were always hostile to the concept of Western educational principles and attitudes but ended up, paradoxically, deeply immersed in the most scholastic forms of theology (heavily influenced by Germanic school models). The Athonite-inspired hesychastic revival looked back to a classical patristic golden age of spiritual writing and from the start was interested in manuscripts, in oral traditions, and in finding a quality of life from the past that was not merely antiquarian but rather a pathway to a more fulfilling spiritual dimension. From its inception it represented a synthesis of Greek, Ukrainian, Russian, and Romanian Orthodox monastic streams, monks who circulated on Athos to begin with but disseminated from that central point to all the Eastern Orthodox world.

It has also been called the Philokalic Revival, from the title of the most famous book (or rather collection of books) that it produced: the *Philokalia* in Greek, and the *Dobrotolubiye* in Slavonic. The term "Philokalic" (literally) means "a Lover of Wisdom" but is more properly understood as a Byzantine-era term for a florilegium. The *Philokalia* was a collation of the most important writings from the patristic era to the late Byzantine period.[22] It covered much of the great patristic-era writings on prayer and how these were commented on and expanded in the medieval-era Eastern monasteries. Because of the heavy Byzantine-era editing of these collected spiritual writings, great stress is placed on the spirituality of the heart; that is, the hesychastic tradition of interior stillness and contemplation. All these texts stand in a close familial relation with one another and represent a massive body of a spiritual tradition that is, in many ways, the heart and soul of Eastern Orthodoxy. When other church institutions fell before hostile powers in the East, the inner life of the church, upheld by its monastics, carried on the secret fire. In free Orthodox lands such as Russia, the spiritual tradition of the *Philokalia* reached far and wide, influencing Orthodox culture throughout the past three centuries, being as it were a *ressourciement* movement of renewal that spread out in the latter part of the twentieth century and became a spiritual pattern of prayer for the laity too.

The main protagonists in this first Philokalic effort were bishop Macarius (surnamed Notaras) of Corinth (1731–1805), Hieromonk Nikodemos (Kallivroutsis) the Hagiorite (1749–1809), and Paisy (Velichkovsky) of Neamt (1722–1794). Macarius was a cleric from a wealthy Greek family who was consecrated bishop but was unable to take up his see because of political turmoil. He retired to an ascetic and scholarly life and commissioned the monk Nikodemos to prepare for him an edition of the best spiritual texts from Orthodox antiquity. Nikodemos was a whirlwind of a writer, an indefatigable collector, editor, and publisher of numerous manuscripts. Supported by Macarius, his work extended to a greater size than had ever been first envisaged. It is now represented by the

Philokalia in five volumes in Greek, containing the most important mystical texts of Byzantine Greek monasticism, written from the fourth through the fifteenth centuries.[23] Paisy Velichkovsky performed the same kind of task, more or less independently, for the Slavonic-reading Orthodox world. Like Nikodemos, Paisy was a fire of energy and fervor. All three Philokalic collators have since been canonized by the Orthodox Church as great saints.

Paisy began to develop his approach to the spiritual literature and its heritage when he arrived on Mount Athos as a monk from Ukraine.[24] He had been a monastic disciple of the great spiritual teacher Basil of Poiana Marului in Moldavia but had been deeply disappointed when he came to Mount Athos thinking to find another spiritual guide who could take him into the advanced stages of prayer. He found the state of monastic life there stultified and the monastics obsessed with the saying of prayers, especially in the form of the recited hours. He began on Mount Athos in 1746 as a strict and poor hermit but after a visit from his former elder Basil, four years later, he was advised to open his life to a small community of disciples. His zeal for contemplation soon attracted followers from the Greek and Slavic worlds. Paisy arranged for his small monastic family to have two separate worship-language experiences. The closeness of the group led him to understand the importance of the ancient tradition of the spiritual father, the starets: someone who could guide a disciple along the highway of prayer and the deeper Christian observance, precisely because he had trodden it before them and knew the easy tracks and the pitfalls in advance. Paisy lamented the fact that he had hoped to discover good guides everywhere on the mountain but could not find even one who practiced the prayer of the heart in the advanced way.²⁵ So he set himself the task of going around to the great monastery libraries on Athos to see what texts they had that spoke of the inner life. Soon he had his team of disciples making translations of the Greek manuscripts into Slavonic, for their own use and study. These two projects were the hallmarks of his apostolate: the gathering of a close body of zealous followers around himself as spiritual father and leader of a monastic family; and the gathering of the best sources on prayer from the ancient tradition. The two things have been closely associated ever afterward in the modern hesychastic revival in Orthodoxy.

After Paisy had spent eighteen years on Athos, Moldavia's Prince Grigore III Ghica invited him to come to his dominion and renew the monastic life there. So he came to Dragomirna monastery in Bucovina with sixty-four of his followers. It was here that the monk Raphael began to translate some of the Philokalic texts into Romanian. When the Austro-Hungarian Empire annexed Bucovina, the future of Orthodox monasticism looked bleak, so Paisy relocated his base to what became the great Romanian spiritual center of Neamt. He had presided over three hundred and fifty monks at Dragomirna, and now the Neamt community grew quickly to number seven hundred followers. It was at Neamt that Paisy completed the translation project of the Slavonic Philokalia. The manuscript, a truly massive one, is today preserved in the library of the Romanian Academy. The work was printed in Russia in 1793 and had an immediate and profound effect on Russian monasticism. Paisy's senior disciples spread out to take leadership positions across Romania, Ukraine, and Russia, bringing with them the deeply interior hesychastic tradition of monastic life: a life turning around inner prayer of the heart as the core purpose underlying all the manual labors and the church offices.

The Russian monastery of Optina was heavily influenced by Paisy, through his disciple Feodor Ushakov, who brought the Philokalic tradition to the monastery. Another of his disciples, Dosifei of Kiev, was the starets who gave the great Saint Seraphim of Sarov the blessing to begin his own renowned monastic path. Optina grew to become one of the greatest of the Russian spiritual centers. In 1821 it built a special center adjacent to the main communal monastery, to house the hermit elders, or startsi, and spiritual eldership became a great emphasis here that renewed Paisy's vision of spiritual fatherhood throughout the Slavic-speaking Orthodox world. Following the tradition of Paisy, the startsi repaired the bureaucratic spirit that had entered Russian monastic life after the so-called reforms of Peter the Great and Catherine the Great, pulling it back into the mystical tradition of prayer that stood as the root of its actions. This renewal movement was also popularized in the late nineteenth century by Russian monks in Ukraine and on Mount Athos who popularized the concept of constant prayer in the novelette form of the *Way of the Pilgrim*, a book that had an equally great impact on modern Western readers in its many twentieth-century translations, and captured a younger readership after its appearance in J. D. Salinger's novel *Franny and Zooey*.[26] At Optina between the nineteenth and twentieth centuries a steady stream of all the notables of Russia, alongside the peasants, came for spiritual guidance and direction. They included the writers Dostoyevsky, Gogol, Zhukovsky, Tolstoy, Turgenev, and Rozanov. Optina's history boasts many great saints and clairvoyants. Saint Ambrose (Amvrosiy

Grenkov) (1812–1891) was one of the great Optina elders thought to have been the model for the saintly Father Zosima in Dostoyevsky's *Brothers Karamazov*. Optina was one of the first of the confiscated monasteries returned to the Russian Orthodox Church in 1987 after the relaxation of Soviet totalitarianism. It had been used by the Soviet Communists as a gulag for prisoners, and its own last higumen, or abbot, had been executed in 1938. Today it is once more a thriving monastic center and looks to its many saintly startsi as an inspiration for a new generation of monks and nuns.

CHAPTER SEVEN

Orthodoxy under the Communists

THE RUSSIAN CHURCH
UNDER THE COMMUNISTS

The repurposing of historic monasteries in Russia after 1917 was a common factor under the Soviets. Often the more the place was renowned for holiness in its past tradition, the more it seemed the state powers used it for purposes of evil oppression of the human spirit. If the Greek Church knew its modern martyrdom under the early modern Ottoman domination, the Russian Orthodox certainly found it under the Communists of the early part of the twentieth century. In 1917 after the abdication of the tsar, a church council was held to consider reform and progress for the future. All knew that it was a tense and troubled time, but few had envisaged how quickly the Bolsheviks, under Lenin, Leon Trotsky, and Joseph Stalin, would push the country first into civil war and then into a second, far-reaching social revolution that established a Communist totalitarian state. The 1917–1918 Moscow Church Council was interrupted by the sound of gunfire that signaled the arrival of the Bolsheviks; but before it broke up it had reestablished the ancient Russian patriarchate and set terms for what it hoped would be a renovation of the Russian Church—one that surely lamented the loss of its tsar but was also able to have great hope that it could establish a greater autonomy after the dissolution of the strict control the tsars had enforced over the bishops hitherto. The council was composed of an innovative number of lay representatives alongside the bishops and priests. There were 299 laity present alongside the 264 clergy. The saintly Tikhon Belavin was elected as the restored (eleventh) patriarch of Moscow and All Russia. When the Bolsheviks attacked, the council dissolved, planning to reconvene in 1921—which would never happen.

As soon as the Bolsheviks were secure in their power, in 1922, they declared the new Union of Soviet Socialist Republics to be officially an atheistic state. Holy Mother Russia was to be no more. Seeing how closely the Russian Orthodox Church had been allied with the tsarist regimes, and how it elevated the figure of the tsar-emperor in an ideologically important role, comparable to the position of the Byzantine emperor-priest in the medieval Eastern Church (one God, one church, under one monarchical ruler), the Soviets knew they had to do a radical deconstruction of the power of Orthodoxy if they were to secure the Russian people's enduring allegiance. Lenin wrote a policy essay entitled "On the Attitude of the Working Party to Religion," in which he spelled out the position clearly for all to understand: "Religion is the opium of the people. This saying of Marx is the cornerstone of the entire ideology of Marxism about religion. All modern religions and churches, and every kind of religious organization, are always to be considered by Marxism as the organs of bourgeois reaction, used for the protection of the exploitation and the stupefaction of the working class." In a letter of 1913 he had already compared religious belief to syphilis: "Religion is a most dangerous foulness, the most shameful of all diseases," and in a speech on October 20, 1920, he openly professed: "We (Bolsheviks) do not believe in God . . . all worship of a divinity is an act of necrophilia."[1] Lenin's disciple Stalin systematized the hostility even further: "The party cannot be neutral to religion. It conducts an anti-religious struggle against all and any religious prejudices."[2]

So, active moves were not slow in coming once the Bolsheviks assumed power. In November 1917 the lands and properties of the church were declared to belong to the nation. The next step was to institute a classical Bolshevik policy and attempt a serious disruption of the internal structures of the opposition. To this end the Bolsheviks seized on fracture lines of unity within the church and exploited them. They appealed to a smaller group of bishops and priests who wanted to push social reform quickly and offered them state support to constitute a so-called Living Church, separate from the (implied) dead wood of the established church. Once they had set this up it caused, of course, an immediate schism within the fabric of Russian Orthodoxy, since the acquiescence in such a level of state direction had rarely been seen even under the tsars, and the process of instituting this new system of governance was contrary to all the classical canons of the church.

Following on from this, sterner measures were taken against the clergy, the monks and nuns especially, who were the most bitter opponents of all attempts to suppress Christianity's Russian traditions. It is certainly the case (though contrary to the global imagination of Christianity) that the persecution of the Russian Church between 1917 and 1939 exceeded by far the total of all the Roman persecutions of the early church era. In the three years between 1918 and 1921, 673 monasteries were forcibly closed, many left to rot, and several turned into prison gulags, state farms, factory warehouses, and psychiatric institutions where numbers of clergy were harshly imprisoned on the basis that their faith constituted an ineradicable neurosis.

The Bolshevik government began a systematic process of encouraging "scientific atheism." Religion was forbidden to be taught by the church. State schools inculcated atheism as the normal intelligent view. Children were encouraged to inform on the retrograde beliefs of their parents. Faith in God was not officially proscribed, but it was openly ridiculed as a neurotic throwback of bourgeois existence. It became commonly known that anyone hoping for a career ought not to profess Orthodox belief and should never be seen attending church services. The church liturgies tended to be populated by old grandmothers (*babushkas*) who had no career prospects they needed to protect, and were served by clergy who were increasingly winnowed out, removing the zealous and leaving in place, more and more, those who could be counted on to conform (and inform on their people). A deep distrust began to grow up between the observant faithful and the clergy who continued to be seen occupying church positions in public.

In 1925 the government, with Trotsky and Lenin's direct encouragement, founded the League of Militant Atheists as a propaganda force to counter aggressively the claims of the churches and unravel the preaching of the clergy in towns and villages. Priests were only allowed to conduct their profession within the church buildings, never with any outside events, such as the procession that used to mark the feasts of the Russian Church, or a youth club, or any educational extra-worship meeting of any kind. Religious intelligentsia were forbidden access to mass media, and the famed "ships of philosophers" actually exiled a whole generation of Russian theologians and writers in 1922, paradoxically making Paris, in the latter part of the twentieth century, the focal point where Russian theology and spirituality survived and first reached a truly international audience.

The Bolsheviks hoped that what they saw as lingering religious superstition would soon evaporate when the glories of the socialist golden age replaced dreams of the Kingdom of God. When this did not prove to be the case, a more savage era of suppression opened up, beginning with a killing spree of previously unknown proportions. Between 1918 and 1919, twenty-eight Orthodox bishops were assassinated. Between 1923 and 1926, fifty more bishops were killed. By 1926, two thousand seven hundred Russian priests, two thousand monks, and three thousand four hundred nuns had been executed by the Bolsheviks.[3] These executed clergy, of course, were not randomly chosen. Rather, they represented the brightest church leaders among those who had not been forced into exile. Most of the seminaries were forcibly closed, and religious publications were generally suppressed. Institutions (such as the Kremlin cathedrals) or church publications that survived were merely empty showcases, heavily controlled for propaganda purposes.

By the beginning of the Second World War more than eighty thousand Russian clergy, comprising bishops, priests, deacons, monks, and nuns, had been eliminated, either by execution (the favored NKVD and Cheka process was by a bullet in the back of the skull) or by forced labor, starvation, and disease in one of the horrendous Soviet gulags.[4] The number of Orthodox laymen and -women who were imprisoned and died for their faith cannot be estimated, as all religious people were simply classed as subversive dissidents by the Soviets. A 1995 Russian Presidential Commission announced the results of its retrospective survey of official Communist files and concluded that the Communist religious persecution had killed two hundred thousand clergy in all. It reported methods ranging from live mutilation, to crucifixion of priests in their churches, to making priests into pillars of ice in the Siberian wilderness. It estimated that a further half million clergy and laity had also suffered nonfatal persecution in gulags and other forms of oppression.[5] By 1937 one-third of all the regions of the USSR were left completely without churches, and in another third only five survived. Hardly any of the monasteries were any longer active as religious houses. The most visible and historic churches were turned into museums, some of them being themed as museums of atheism. Of the fifty-four thousand Russian Orthodox churches functioning before the First World War, there were only five hundred that remained open for worship by 1941. By June of that year, when Hitler's Operation Barbarossa began the attack on Russia, only four Russian bishops remained active in their diocesan sees.

In some ways the legitimate fear Stalin had that his regime might collapse because of the Nazi advances brought an end to a level of persecution that could have been even worse. In 1925 he had seen with his own eyes in Moscow that the roots of the Orthodox Christian faith might not be so easily eradicated by his terror methods when three hundred thousand people turned up to pay silent respects on the death of the patriarch Tikhon. He had died suddenly of heart failure after several years of trying to reason with Stalin. Many, probably rightly, suspected that the sudden and fatal symptoms were a covert assassination ordered from the Kremlin.

In 1927 Sergey Stragorodsky, then the metropolitan of Moscow, since Stalin had refused to allow the continuation of the patriarchate, issued a rebuke to Russian bishops outside the country who had dared to suggest, to other Christian bodies, that religious oppression was burdening the homeland. Metropolitan Sergey self-righteously insisted that the church was entirely free and had a marvelous relationship with the state, thus publicly demonstrating to what extent he was a stooge of the Communist powers. Before the White Russian resistance collapsed, many of the Russian hierarchs had been killed, but many others had fled into exile. From France and Germany and America they organized the "Russian Orthodox Church Outside Russia" (ROCOR) with a synod of their own exiled bishops at Sremski Karlovci in 1922, in what was then free Yugoslavia. They were highly suspicious of the continuing Russian hierarchs, whom they regarded (largely rightly) of being, under duress, often entirely under the thumb of Communist atheist supervisors.

After metropolitan Sergey's ridiculous censure, the Russian bishops outside Russia met in a further synod and decided that under present circumstances the Russian Church could no longer be presumed to operate freely, and so, invoking an emergency measure that Patriarch Tikhon himself had drawn up in 1920, concerning what should be the procedure if civil unrest made a diocese unable to communicate with the central ecclesial administration, the free Russian hierarchs

- formally set themselves up as the surviving voice of Russian Orthodoxy. The resulting clash between them and Moscow resulted in a refusal of mutual recognition (a great schism, in effect, the first to strike Russia since the time of Patriarch Nikon, and one that was not healed until the 21st century).[6]

In 1941, facing the bleak prospect of Nazi invasion, Stalin offered the church concessions if it would mobilize the faithful, and wider society, around the idea that defense of the motherland was a patriotic and moral duty. He allowed the patriarchate to be reestablished, ensuring that his own candidate, Sergius, was elected. He also stripped the church of the remaining treasures not looted in the 1920s: silver chalices and church artifacts that could be sold internationally to gain currency. It was in this period that thousands of Russian icons were sold by the state and collectors in the West became more conversant with Russian Orthodox art. Paradoxically, this impoverishment of Russia was yet another means by which the icon reached out to become, by the end of the twentieth century, a well-known and much loved aspect of most Western Christian experience. Before that it was more or less unknown and frowned on as a medium of religious tradition in the West. But the thaw Stalin initiated lasted. By the time Nikita Khrushchev came to power after him, twenty-two thousand Russian churches had been reopened and were functioning once more. Some religious publications had also been allowed to be resurrected. Eight seminaries and two theological academies had been allowed to reopen (none was in existence in 1941). Public church membership was once more growing.

All of this frightened Khrushchev, who in 1959 decided to clamp down once more on Russian Orthodoxy. This time the campaign against the Orthodox Church centered on a renewed wave of antireligious propaganda conducted by state organs. Measures were adopted that were designed to choke off church finances and starve the remaining structures, placing great stress on the relationships between clergy and hierarchs. In the early 1960s, children were, by law, forbidden to attend church services. More churches were closed in this period, and it was underlined that any signs of religious affiliation would count badly against anyone hoping to make a career in the USSR. Of the eight seminaries still functioning across the country, Khrushchev ordered the closing of five. Students who applied to the remainder were strictly monitored by the authorities, and those with a university-level education were usually forbidden by the state to enter training for the priesthood. By 1962 only two monasteries remained active in the territory of the entire Russian Federation. By 1966 seven thousand five hundred churches remained active for divine service in the USSR, but of those only two thousand were in the Russian territories proper. The majority of the active ones were in Ukraine or the satellite Baltic states. The Khrushchev era, however, saw the beginnings of a new movement of intelligentsia taking an interest in the affairs and condition of the Orthodox Church, something that had not been seen since the Slavophile movement of the end of the nineteenth century and turn of the twentieth. A whole raft of dissident thinkers, critical of the failing Communist state in the late 1960s, began to make their voices heard on how Russia needed a moral conscience and a spiritual tradition to withstand the banality of state-sponsored atheism in Communist form.[7] More and more they voiced the argument that the Orthodox Church's purgation by martyrdom, along with its foundational role in Russian history, had won for it that right.

The antireligious policy was continued less stringently by Khrushchev's successor, Brezhnev. By 1975 only seven thousand churches were allowed to function, and a wave of imprisonments had been adopted to try to cow the clergy into submission. Docile bishops who would support the regime were given the honorary rank of colonels in the KGB, the state security service. Even so, a lively underground church flourished despite all the state efforts. From the very beginning the priests who had been deprived of their parishes and all visible forms of structured religious service and the monks and nuns who had been thrown out of their monasteries merged in civil society, and they often continued a hidden ministry in the form of pamphlets circulated among a closed set of circles, secret services held in homes, and so on. Believers would often meet for pilgrimages disguised as picnics that just happened to be on the site of holy places now demolished. At the surviving ruined walls of dynamited city churches old grandmothers would habitually stop to say a prayer. All of this quiet dissidence was, in fact, a radical new form of the old system of spiritual fatherhood, now with the starets or starissa being acknowledged for bravery and apostolic zeal among a loyal community of believers who followed them and absorbed their teaching in a very personal and zealous manner. It was sometimes known as the Inner Church movement, where, devoid of external supports and Christian structures, believers really had to take a personal stance. The inner spiritual life and the orientations of the heart were given precedence, and the aim was to keep the fire of the Gospel alive until the age of the persecutors passed. The teachings and admonitions of the startsi, the new "confessors," were generally held in higher honor than the guidance statements made by the surviving hierarchs, who were seen (and necessarily so, of course) as complicit with the regime.[8] Russia's ancient traditions of mystical interiority and the stress it had always laid on passion bearers (strastoterptsy) as the highest exemplars of Christian fidelity came now to the fore and gave the Inner Church a fiery disposition. This was rooted in the belief that the suffering Christ mirrored himself with especial loving-kindness in the sufferings of his faithful followers, and that in the midst of great sorrows remarkable spiritual graces abounded.

The real thaw began for Orthodoxy during the glasnost era initiated by Mikhail Gorbachev. His administration overlapped with the anniversary of the millennium of Russian Orthodox faith in 1988. The state encouraged the church to celebrate this as part of a moral reclamation of Russian identity. Many churches and monasteries were returned to the church, and new arrangements were made for financial reparation and support. When the Communist system collapsed in 1991, the church remained as one of the most solid institutions around which politicians hoped to rebuild a civic culture from the ruins. The early post-Communist years in Russia were chaotic, and church leaders, after so many decades of having been starved in terms of education and isolated in their culture, were not particularly well equipped to deal with the many challenges of an economy and society that felt as if it had been blown out to sea without an anchor. But eventually the church responded by ordaining many younger and energetic clergy to the higher offices and by instituting a pastorally creative movement to rebuild parishes and Christian social institutions. Patriarch Alexei II (Ridiger) began the renovation, and it was continued after his death in 2008 by Patriarch Kirill (Gundiaev).

The Russian Federation today is now officially a secular state (no longer a militantly atheistic one) and aspires to be multinational and multireligious. But there is no question that Russian Orthodoxy has risen to a position of great eminence as the most extensive center of Christianity in Russia. Its long history and its tradition of noble and suffering resistance outweigh the examples of conformism and betrayal it manifested under unbelievably harsh oppression. Today, many polls bear witness to the fact that the Orthodox Church is seen by the Russian people as one of the most trusted institutions of society. Western observers often do not realize the extent of their own Protestant mental formation when they express great distrust about a church that sees no wrong in close alliance with the state powers. Outrage is regularly voiced in the Western secular media when President Vladimir Putin is seen in church alongside Patriarch Kirill. But the strict separation of church and state seen by the Puritans as a consummation devoutly to be wished never formed part of the Eastern Orthodox mind-set. From Byzantium onward, ruling power was always seen as something to be blessed, encouraged in the good, softened in the bad, and whenever possible co-opted for the advancement of the Gospel. It is a Byzantine model of church-state relations that underpins so much of Orthodox attitudes, but that still strikes a dissonant note with many Western observers who do not share that ancestral tradition.

THE COMMUNIST EMPIRE

The victory of the Allies after World War II left Soviet Russia a dominating force in Eastern Europe. What the Bolsheviks had done to the church within Russia became an example held up to all the satellite governments Moscow increasingly came to install and supervise in the growing extended empire it created, out of a dozen different states with their own historical traditions. All of these were ploughed under by Stalin's zeal to spread the gospel of an atheistic Communist way of life.[9] On March 5, 1946, giving a speech at Westminster College in Missouri, Winston Churchill famously said: "From Stettin in the Baltic to Trieste in the Adriatic an iron curtain has descended across the continent. Behind that line lie all the capitals of the ancient states of Central and Eastern Europe. Warsaw, Berlin, Prague, Vienna, Budapest, Belgrade, Bucharest and Sofia; all these famous cities and the populations around them lie in what I must call the Soviet sphere, and all are subject, in one form or another, not only to Soviet influence but to a very high, and in some cases increasing, measure of control from Moscow."[10] The Iron Curtain was largely meant as Moscow's way of sealing off its satellites from seduction by, or comparison with, Western European nations. The majority of these now trapped and oppressed nations had Orthodox Christianity as their ancestral form of Christian faith, though there was a good admixture too of Muslim populations and Roman Catholics. Romania, Serbia, Bulgaria, and Ukraine were the largest of the Orthodox nations that now fell under Soviet control. In each of them the contact with Russian Orthodoxy in times past had been creative and fruitful. Now Stalin's grip over the Russian Church became a tool to use church connections as a measure of control. The independent church organizations were more or less subjected to Moscow's ecclesiastical as well as political control. Patriarchal traditions and processes were sometimes simply abolished in an imperialist manner. In some ways, this Stalinist policy was a continuation of old habits.

When tsarist Russia annexed Georgia in 1811, for example, it simply abolished the eight-hundred-year-old Georgian patriarchate on the spot. When the Bolsheviks overthrew the tsar, the Georgian bishops quickly reconvened in synod and declared their patriarchate restored. Moscow only acknowledged this (by church and state decree) in 1943, when Stalin needed church assistance in the war. The patriarchate of Constantinople only concurred with the de facto decision in 1990. Life was always difficult in satellite countries for any church leaders who nurtured hopes of freedom. The Communist authorities in Georgia decided to execute the Georgian patriarch Amvrosi for daring to send an independent letter to the International Genoa Peace Conference in 1922. Only a threatened riot after widespread street demonstrations in his support averted the decision. The Georgian Church, however, like the churches in many of the other oppressed states, was able to list a considerable number of candidates for canonization as "new martyrs" in the years after the collapse of Soviet power. Overall the Georgian Church suffered just as severe a treatment from the Communist authorities as did the Russian. The country had just over two thousand functioning churches in 1917. By the late 1980s, when the Soviet grip was slackened, only two hundred were still open.

Very heavy oppression fell upon the Ukrainian and Belo-Russian churches, especially those that had declared autocephaly and had strong nationalistic leanings. They were heavily oppressed both in the 1920s and once more after 1944 (after they had renewed their structures under the Nazi occupation with its policy of church tolerance). The higher clergy were decimated, with many village and town parish priests shot or sent to camps.

In 1918, Serbia was strongly influenced by the Pan-Slav ideals of the Slavophile Russian movement. It was a concept that imagined a greater Slav common consciousness based in Orthodox religious philosophy and nationalism, and the movement led to the creation, in that year, of the state of Southern Slavs, or Yugoslavia, bringing into unity the differing Serbs, Croats, and Slovenes. This was pressed further, ecclesiastically, in 1920 when the patriarchate of Karlovci was merged with the metropolitan see of Belgrade and relaunched as the refoundation of the patriarchate of Serbia. During the Second World War the Orthodox Serbs suffered considerably under the Nazis, who regarded them as ideologically suspicious and racially inferior. Pressure was put on the laity to assimilate to Roman Catholicism. In Croatia, Bosnia-Herzegovina, and Macedonia, four Serbian Orthodox bishops and more than two hundred priests were killed. In Montenegro the Communists killed the metropolitan archbishop Joanikije and more than 120 of the lower clergy. When the lands fell under Communist domination Josip Tito at first continued a strong policy of religious suppression but then relaxed his brutality somewhat.

In 1952 Tito's Communist government expelled the entire Faculty of Theology from the University of Belgrade. It had to continue its work after that point solely as a church school. In 1967 the Communist authorities encouraged the Macedonian clergy to declare their secession from the Serbian patriarchate. To add to their difficulties, in 1964 the Serbian Orthodox diaspora in Western Europe and America publicly accused the homeland church of collusion with the

Communists and declared their own independence. The Serbian patriarch between 1957 and 1990, German Doric, is largely credited with steering his church wisely and cautiously during this period, ensuring its ultimate survival and eventual regeneration. In the 1990s, when other Orthodox nations were reestablishing themselves after the fall of communism, the bloody civil war that engulfed Croatia, Bosnia, and Kosovo pulled the Serbian Church down into ethnic and interreligious chaos for many years.

In Bulgarian affairs the tension between the Bulgarian Orthodox exarchate and Constantinople, which claimed rights of being a superintendent mother church, dominated matters. In 1913 the Bulgarian Church leader Joseph moved his residence and administration from Constantinople to Sofia, and relations broke down between the two bodies. After the end of the Balkan Wars and the First World War, the treaties established at the cessation of hostilities saw the Bulgarian Church being trimmed down by being deprived of its (extraterritorial) dioceses of Macedonia and Aegean Thrace. When the Bulgarian patriarch Joseph died in 1913, a new Bulgarian leader could not be elected again for more than three decades. It was not until the end of the Second World War that matters changed. The patriarchate of Constantinople finally agreed to recognize the independence of Bulgarian Orthodoxy, and in 1950 its local synod composed a new charter that led, in 1953, to the restoration of the ancient Bulgarian patriarchate and the election of Archbishop Cyril of Plovdiv as patriarch. All of this happened because the post-1945 Communist authorities wished to elevate the nation and saw the church as one of the tools to make progress. In Bulgaria, for the period of Communist domination, it was probably the case that the church was more co-opted than persecuted. There was an exception in the period between 1947 and 1949, when attempts were made to damage the church structure, and several prominent clergy were assassinated. Though the usual Communist system of atheistic propaganda and massive ecclesial restriction was in place, the Bulgarian Orthodox Church was regarded by the local Communist authorities as more or less an organ of state. The resulting suffocation that fell over the church often proved more damaging than persecutions that elsewhere had roused up fiery martyrial opposition.

Romania was the largest of all the satellite countries taken over by Russia after the Second World War. It was radically set on a new course, from a rightist-orientated monarchical system to a socialist republic. Romanian Orthodoxy suffered a paradoxical fate. It was suppressed, certainly, and subjected to close scrutiny and limitation by special delegates of the Communist state. But the church was also looked upon with some pride as an ancient system that had lifted the Romanians into unity and a greater identity. Oppression and savagery were often directed at individuals professing their religion, therefore, rather than at the systems and structures. In the towns and countryside Orthodoxy had deep and extensive support among the people. And yet the Communist state security system, the Securitate, was by far more savage than the Russian security services. The Romanian Communist secret police liked to play with the minds of its perceived dissidents. Many of those arrested in Romania for their Orthodox faith (and for several other religious affiliations) suffered intensely and savagely.

Romanian Orthodoxy had emerged as a patriarchal church in 1925, marking the collaborative merging of most of the various provinces inhabited by Romanians after the First World War. The Second World War saw Romania subject to the Nazi occupation and soon afterward to the Communists. In 1947 the Romanian Workers' Party assumed power under Russian patronage and immediately set about subordinating the Church, by initiating the usual repressive anti-ecclesiastical measures and treating harshly any who showed a spirit of resistance. The higher clergy were extensively purged and deposed, and three bishops who had publicly denounced the Communists died suddenly in mysterious circumstances. Thirteen other bishops who were regarded as potentially subversive were sent to prison. Communist laws of 1947 ensured that the state controlled a mandatory retirement age for bishops and the processes of electing new ones. In this way the Communists ensured that all future appointments met their standards. The theological schools of Sibiu and Bucharest, both of which had long and high traditions, were systematically starved of resources. At the same time, the churches and resources of the Romanian Greek Catholic Church, now suppressed, were forcibly seized and transferred to the Orthodox. The state took over control of all the church schools, higher and lower, but also made itself responsible for paying clergy salaries. Infiltrating all the structures of church governance, it systematically weeded out all overt expressions of dissidence among the clergy. In May 1948 when Patriarch Nicodim died, the state ensured the election of a more enthusiastically socialist patriarch Justinian Marina (patr. 1948–1977). By 1953 there were something approaching five hundred Romanian priests and monastics held in gulags. Monasticism was more difficult to control. Accordingly, between 1958 and 1962 a new antichurch policy was put into practice. Half of the country's many monasteries were closed and their properties and lands expropriated by the state. Two thousand monks and nuns were forced out and made to take up secular jobs. Roughly a quarter (fifteen hundred) of the country's active priests and lay activists were harassed or imprisoned during this period. The patriarch dutifully assured the faithful inside (and observers outside) the country that these were (allegedly) not persecutions on account of the faith.[11]

After 1962, the Communist authorities in Romania started to adopt a much more nationalistic policy, striking a line as independent of Russia as they dared. Accordingly, they coopted the Orthodox Church to assist them, giving it more freedom in return for its prestige as a historic and widely popular aspect of Romanian cultural identity and using its moral pressure in teaching conformity. The schools of theology were allowed more latitude, and theological journals were permitted to be published. Nicolae Ceaucescu, the state leader, arranged for his daughter's church wedding to be broadcast on national television. Even so, in order to build his vast presidential palace in the heart of Bucharest, he ordered the demolition of more than twenty urban churches, some of them of great historical significance. None of the hierarchy dared to raise an objection lest something worse might be imposed. By 1975 the Romanian clergy numbered close to twelve thousand in all. After a bitter struggle in the late 1980s, when hardliners in the army and the security forces vainly tried to fight off the revolution to freedom, the church began to breathe more freely and felt the terrifying hold of the Securitate fall away. It began to assert its right to restitution of properties and received significant government subvention for its ongoing life. Several of the leading clergy made public apology for "not having the courage of martyrs" during the Communist period. The church, after communism, remained very popular with the great majority of Romanians and quickly emerged, after the Russian, as the largest, and one of the most lively, of all the modern Orthodox churches.

CHAPTER EIGHT

The Twentieth-Century Orthodox Diaspora

THE MOVEMENT OF PEOPLES

The late nineteenth and early twentieth centuries witnessed a large wave of emigrations from Central and Eastern Europe, largely of peasant classes attempting to find a better life by moving to America and Oceania. This was accelerated after the massive population disruptions following the Second World War, when many more who were able fled Eastern Europe as the Communist takeover was set in motion. The Greek Civil War also sent many Greeks on a second wave of emigration. In addition, the twentieth-century British occupation of Cyprus encouraged a large Cypriot population to establish itself in many of the larger cities of the United Kingdom. Because of this the ancient Roman imperial distinctions between Eastern and Western churches began to have less and less relevance. Today there are more Orthodox Christians in England than there are Baptists, and Orthodox parishes with supportive diocesan structures are found all over America, Oceania, and Europe. By relentless processes of emigration, then, the Eastern Orthodox Church has come West too. Whereas by the turn of the twentieth century Orthodoxy might have been as remotely exotic as Tibetan Buddhism for most Western Christians, it is the case today that anyone who cares to can actually meet Orthodox believers and attend their church services, to see for themselves that these are not exotics but rather ordinary Christians following an extraordinarily ancient form of Christian profession.

One significant aspect of this movement westward and establishment of parish life in a new world, however, is that it was not planned in any way. It just happened that as Orthodox people moved, so too they wanted a church where they could worship, led by an Orthodox priest, preferably of their own national origin. This effectively meant that they had to build their parish church while they were about the business of building up all the other aspects of their new life. It also often was the case that this movement of church planting was laity led. After the fall of Communism and the reinstatement of the abilities of Orthodox mother church synods to exercise supervision over the affairs of their faithful in different countries, this occasioned no small amount of conflict over who had the rights of ownership and jurisdiction. During the Communist era the Orthodox parishes in the West were often so anti-Communist that they refused to have much to do with the home synods, which they regarded as having been overrun by Communist infiltrators. After the fall of communism it would take at least another twenty-five years before relations between the different factions of the same traditions (for example, the Russian Orthodox Church Outside Russia and the Moscow patriarchate, the Romanian churches in America in communion with the Romanian Patriarchal Synod, and the

Romanian diocese within the ambit of the Orthodox Church of America) came to the point of discussing unity. In the latter example union never properly occurred, and the Romanian Synod refounded its own archdiocese of the Americas.

THE ORTHODOX IN AMERICA

The Orthodox came to the United States almost as soon as the country had advertised itself universally by its Declaration of Independence.[1] Little attempt to make any permanent church organization was manifested in these early days of the late eighteenth century. The Greeks had a trading settlement called New Smyrna, near Saint Augustine in Florida, but it never seems to have had its own priest. The first notable mission came from the other end of the country, when Alaska still belonged to Russia. The tsar (Catherine the Great) appointed a mission of eight monks from the renowned New Valaam monastery. The group was led by Archimandrite Joasaph and his deputy, Monk Herman. They were sent out with the blessing of Metropolitan Gabriel of Saint Petersburg. Their first task was to supply clergy and sacraments to the colony of Russian fur traders who had settled there. Grigoriy Ivanovich Shelikov was the director of the Russian American Company of Traders. In Saint Petersburg he painted a picture of the spiritual need of the traders and gave the church authorities the impression that all was in readiness for the arrival of clergy, who needed to be educated so as to take over the school and church building prepared for them. When they came the church would be properly furnished, all at company expense. When the missionaries arrived, however, they found that Shelikov had retired permanently to Russia, and nothing whatsoever was waiting in readiness for them. The missionaries were also shocked by the lax standards of the Russian traders, who lived with native families while married to Russian wives at home and when returning to Russia took the children with them as dependent servants but left the concubines behind. They also found that the company used native hunters in an abusive way, barely rewarding them for dangerous and unprotected work they would not undertake themselves. Archimandrite Joasaph soon returned to Irkutsk in Siberia to report on the company's behavior, leaving Herman in charge. While he was in Siberia the church consecrated him as bishop of Alaskan Kodiak, meaning he now had civil authority over the local director of the fur company. With two other monks of the original eight, he set off for Alaska on the steamship *Phoenix*. It came close to Kodiak but sank offshore, with no survivors. Meanwhile, another of the original eight, Priest-Monk Juvenaly, had gone to make first contact to evangelize a native tribe but died under a volley of arrows from its warriors, who feared a strange shaman coming to them. His last act was to bless them with the sign of the cross.[2] The mission, though reduced now to four monks, had by 1800 converted seven thousand of the natives, who freely came to services and found a strong affinity with the warmth of the Russian Orthodox liturgical ceremonies.

Director Baranov of the trading company continued to outrage the missionaries by his abuse of the native population, and so an appeal to the Holy Synod of Russia by the community resulted in the sending of Priest-Monk Gideon to supervise. Things improved at Kodiak while he was there but reverted to the old situation as soon as he left in 1807. One of the monks, named Herman, decided to make a protest by leaving the service of the main church and retiring to a more solitary and independent existence on Spruce Island. At first he dug out and lived in a cave, then built a wooden chapel and ministered attentively and graciously to the natives who started to come to him. Subsequently, he built another wooden building to serve as a schoolhouse for the many orphaned native children whom he gathered and cared for. He died in 1837, and in 1970 was the first saint canonized by the Orthodox Church in America and given the title Saint Herman of Alaska. Another later missionary, a married priest, Father John Veniaminov, arrived with his family on the island of Unalaska in 1824. He was the first to translate the Gospel of Matthew into Aleut, with the help of the local chief, Ivan Pan'kov. After his wife's death he became a priest-monk, and in 1840 Moscow appointed him bishop of the newly created diocese of Kamchatka and the Aleutian Islands. As was the custom, he took the new name Innokent. In 1850, after a replacement bishop was sent, Innokent returned to Russia, leaving his closest assistant, the priest Netsvetov, who was of mixed Russian and Aleut descent, to continue the work of translating church texts into the native dialects. Netsvetov made a lasting impact on Orthodox Aleut culture, creating a church ethos that was sensitive to native traditions, but that also led the tribes decisively away from the old traditions of solving disputes by internecine battles. Innokent returned to Siberia in order to study more languages to advance his missionary work. In 1868 his fame was such that he was elected metropolitan bishop of Moscow. In this role he still maintained his missionary interests and in 1870 founded the Orthodox Missionary Society. He died in 1879, and in 1977 he too was canonized by the Russian Orthodox Church.

In 1867 the sale of all of Alaska to the United States brought the Orthodox mission into the American experience. At first the new government authorities worked hand in glove with newly arrived Presbyterian missionaries, in order to effect a radical deculturing of the Aleuts, attempting to bring them forcibly away from Russianism (including Orthodoxy) to become good Protestant Americans. The protests of the Orthodox missionaries and those of the local native chiefs fell on deaf ears. It would be several more decades before the collusion of the Alaskan government and Protestant missionaries would fade.

The Russian Church meanwhile had received an appeal for a sponsored mission to the American mainland from the many Russians who had left Alaska after the sale of the territory. These included Bishop John Mitropolsky, who petitioned to have the Russian diocesan headquarters moved to San Francisco, where there was a sizable Russian contingent. The Moscow synod approved the proposal in 1872, and two years later the church of Saint Alexander Nevsky became the new cathedral there. This was now one of only four Orthodox churches fully functioning as parishes in the whole of the mainland United States: Father Nicholas Bjerring's parish in New York City; a Greek parish with Orthodox of many ethnic backgrounds in Galveston, Texas (founded in 1862); and a similar parish in New Orleans (founded in 1864).[3] The Orthodox numbers did not significantly grow until the late 1890s, when immigration started to change the American demographic.

Important figures of this time were Archimandrite Sebastian Dabovich, born in America in 1863 to a Serbian immigrant family. He was one of the first who imagined a Native

American Orthodox Church in the new country and also ministered to the extensive Serbian immigrants. Bishop Tikhon (Belavin) meanwhile served the diocese of Alaska and the Aleutian Islands from 1898 to 1907. His pastoral travels took him the length of America from Alaska to San Francisco and across to New York, where he visited the Russian parish now established by Father Alexander Hotovitsky. The Moscow synod gave Tikhon an assistant bishop for Alaska, and soon after they both ordained Bishop Raphael Hawaweeny to take charge in Brooklyn as bishop with special charge of all Arabic Orthodox in America. Tikhon also wished Father Dabovich to be given a similar role in relation to the Serbs. He moved his diocesan headquarters to New York, laying the cornerstone of a new cathedral, Saint Nicholas, on Ninety-seventh Street off Fifth Avenue, in 1901. He then drew up for the Moscow synod a plan to make an Archdiocese of America, where all the various ethnic Orthodox groups had their own presiding bishop who took care of the various ethnic communities, but where all the different bishops would participate in one synod under the archbishop appointed by the Russian mission. This was a new notion, put forward formally in 1904, since in all previous church canon law dioceses had been created in terms of civic areas and not, ostensibly, on ethnic lines.

Several things conspired to prevent this vision of unity under the jurisdictional control of the Russian mission from ever being realized. Tikhon himself was recalled to Moscow as the new metropolitan of Yaroslavl in 1907, and he would eventually be elected patriarch of Moscow and All Russia, merely a few days after the Bolsheviks seized power in 1917. The Russian Church itself was undergoing great social upheavals consequent on the disastrous First World War. The main obstacle to Tikhon's vision of a multiethnic single collaborative of the Orthodox in America, however, was simply that the Greeks, who were the majority lay Orthodox population in America at that time, were primarily focused on establishing parishes for their own people. The Greeks, as was true of most other ethnic Orthodox groups, and ultimately true of Tikhon himself, of course—though he did have a deeper appreciation of the unique American situation than any other hierarch of the time—looked first, and instinctively, to their homelands to supply ecclesiastical support and governance.

The patriarch of Constantinople, Joakim III, citing a canon of the Council of Chalcedon in 451 that placed future discovered "barbarian lands" under his own special patronage, claimed a jurisdictional right over all New World territories Orthodoxy entered into. He independently transferred the rights of supervision over American Greek parishes to the synod of the mainland Greek Church in 1908, and their hierarchs certainly did not recognize any prior jurisdictional claims from the Russian side. The first ever African American Orthodox priest, Robert Josias Morgan, traveled from the Greek parish in Philadelphia to be ordained in the patriarchate at Constantinople in 1907, returning as Father Raphael. He traveled once more to Athens, in 1911, to be tonsured as a priest-monk serving in America, and had a long and faithful pastoral career.

The ongoing waves of immigration in the early days of the twentieth century brought more and more Orthodox who were neither Greek nor Russian: Romanians, Macedonians, Serbs, and Ukrainians. All of these home synods established direct and separate episcopal governance over the parishes that they saw as an external mission of their own national churches. The two world wars brought further crisis and division among all the Orthodox families. The Greeks were split into two factions in America, the monarchists, who favored King Constantine's leaning toward Germany, and the Venizelists, who opposed the king. This split affected everyone down to parish level and across families. The Eastern European nations, beginning with Russia and Ukraine, were progressively stifled under the hand of the Communists. Slavic American Orthodox churches became battered in the winds emanating from Russia.

The Communist authorities early on had invented a movement called the Living Church meant to inculcate socialist values in Orthodoxy while disrupting it from within at the same time. They appointed married socialist priests as bishops to lead it—which the rest of the Orthodox world considered a scandalous departure from canon law. The Communist government sent out Father John Kedrovsky as the new archbishop of the Orthodox Living Church of North America. He made numerous claims for possession of all the Russian Church properties across the United States. He generally failed to secure them given the opposition of the local Orthodox congregants, but he was successful in gaining possession of Saint Nicholas Cathedral in New York, on the grounds that the late Tsar Nicholas had provided a very large subsidy to pay for it, and the local judge felt that his successor was now Lenin. The local congregation had to find another building downtown and relocated to Second Street by Second Avenue. Russian Orthodox bishops fleeing Russia were assisted by the Serbian hierarchs to set up their own synod in exile and constituted themselves as the Russian Orthodox Church Outside Russia (ROCOR), with headquarters in New York. The majority Russian Orthodox parishes regrouped under allegiance to their own American-based hierarchy, and in 1924 when this synod declared that it was now "temporarily" disconnecting from its Moscow allegiance because of the Communist infiltration of the church, it became known as the Metropolia.

Three disconnected groups, therefore, had emerged in America in place of the old united Russian mission. The divisions would not be resolved until the Communists abandoned their support of the Living Church by allowing the Moscow archbishop to take control of the New York cathedral in 1933, and until the Russian synod gave its blessing to an independent American Russian Metropolia in 1970.[4] This then became known as the Orthodox Church in America (OCA) and looked back to Tikhon's original vision as its inspiration and charter to put itself forward as the Orthodox Church "of" America—in the sense that it would be the claimant to being the first truly indigenized American-language Orthodox Church. The division between the ROCOR and the Moscow synod would not be repaired until the twenty-first century. The ROCOR hierarchs, however, immediately denounced the legitimacy of the Metropolia receiving autocephaly, or full ecclesiastical independence, from the Moscow synod still under the sway of the communists.[5] The patriarch of Constantinople, all the other Greek churches, and most of the remaining world Orthodox communities also refused to recognize the independent ecclesial status of the OCA. Though they accepted its full reality as an Orthodox communion (it soon became a shelter for several ethnic-based Orthodox episcopates in exile, such as the Bulgarians and part of the Romanians and the Syrians), most of the worldwide Ortho-

dox did not regard it as a fully canonical autocephalous entity
as such. Some wondered if this intra-American chaos that had
been caused by the move to grant the Metropolia independence was not a ploy of the Soviet Communists in 1970 to
cause confused dissension in the churches wherever they
could. Hierarchs of the two Russian Orthodox jurisdictions in
America would not concelebrate the Eucharist together until
2011, and even that symbolic gesture did not serve to bring
them into any fuller unity in practice to the present day. The
same unease in relations between American parishes and their
homeland churches under Communist control affected every
other ethnic group too, and often resulted in parallel organizations and counterclaims for being in schism that have still
not entirely been resolved even thirty years after the fall of
Eastern European Communist governance.

This rather formalist account of origins and divisions of
the Orthodox in America, however, should not mask the underlying fact that Orthodox parish life grew and flourished
throughout the twentieth century to the point that there are
now roughly one million self-identified Orthodox faithful living in America, less than 0.5 percent of the world Orthodox
population (260 million). This total Orthodox number, however, makes up merely 0.4 percent of American Christianity.
The demands imposed on parishes to meet the pastoral and
educational needs of successive generations of youth who
have never lived in the originating homelands and to welcome
new waves of Eastern European immigration from the 1980s
onward—the first group wishing to abandon the use of
Eastern European languages in worship and the second
group feeling the need to cling to them—have led to a lively
awareness among the new generation of Orthodox clergy

that Orthodoxy must adapt to its new Western home in more ways than style of worship.

If life in the West has opened up layers of new opportunities for Orthodox faithful who are proud of their ancestral faith and worship traditions, equally it has served to bring the presence of Orthodoxy into the light in countries where before it had only been a rumor. The Orthodox in America, with a considerable number of clergy educated to a high degree in a modern country that has its very origins in immigration, are perhaps among the most advanced in the Orthodox world in terms of thinking out the issues of what constitutes Orthodox identity beyond nationalistic traditions and how Pan-Orthodox mutual openness might revive the awareness of the fundamental catholicity of the Orthodox Church. The Metropolia and its descendant, the OCA, in particular were blessed with a generation of founding fathers who were of exceptional intellectual acumen. They collectively emerged as the most powerful voices articulating Orthodoxy in the Western environment in the latter part of the twentieth century. Fathers Georges Florovsky, Alexander Schmemann, John Meyendorff, and their modern successor Father John Behr put the OCA seminary of Saint Vladimir in New York on the intellectual map of the Orthodox world in a relatively short span of time, making it one of the centers of theological reflection and founding the SVS press on the campus. This press, beginning with liturgical and devotional texts, very quickly became the repository for the finest Orthodox pastoral, scriptural, and theological publications worldwide. The Greek seminary of the Holy Cross in Brookline in Boston also founded a high-quality theological journal and has issued largely devotional and liturgical works from its press.

The period after World War II saw an unprecedented influx of immigrants to Oceania. From 1950 to the present, the population of Australia, for example, grew from seven million to twenty-two million. Six million immigrants arrived after 1945, and today one-quarter of all Australians were born elsewhere, representing a total of more than one hundred different countries of origination. The Greeks were the first to establish an Orthodox presence in Australia. Modest trickles of immigrants in the early decades of the twentieth century did as the Greeks did everywhere else: built Orthodox churches where they settled.[6] Their numbers in 1901 were little more than a thousand. By 1947 they numbered seventeen times that, and are still the largest single group of Orthodox in the land. After the refugee crisis of World War II, many Eastern Orthodox came into the country. This increased after the government offered free passage to Greeks and Yugoslavs caught up in the fighting of their civil wars. Many other Orthodox, particularly Russian, Ukrainian, and Romanian, fled there for refuge too. By 1971 the Orthodox in Australia numbered three hundred and forty thousand, which was 2.6 percent of the national population. Later, Lebanese immigrants fleeing the Arab-Israeli War of 1967, and then the civil war of the mid-1970s, added more Orthodox numbers. The 2006 census indicated that there were then more than half a million Orthodox in the country, representing the Greek, Macedonian, Serbian, Russian, Ukrainian, and Romanian traditions (listed in terms of the groups' respective sizes).

ORTHODOXY IN WESTERN EUROPE

The modern visitor to London's bohemian Soho district will notice a main thoroughfare there called Greek Street. The name is the last relic of the fact that in 1677 the Greek community of London chose what was then a very fashionable part of town to open their first Greek Orthodox Church, dedicated to the *Panagia*, the All Holy Virgin Mary. The Anglican bishop of London, Lord Henry Compton, at first had given them permission. Many Anglicans of the time regarded Constantinople and the Greek Church as a potential ally in the ongoing struggle against "Romanism." When Bishop Compton found out what Orthodoxy actually looked like, he was appalled. The Greeks had icons in their churches; they believed in the tangible presence of the embodied and Risen Christ in their eucharistic devotion; they valued monasticism; they venerated and prayed to the Blessed Virgin Mary; they called upon the assistance of saints and even prayed for the dead. No: none of this would do. Bishop Compton acted, and at first insisted that the Greek parish remove all its icons, stop praying to the saints, denounce what he called the Romish doctrine of Transubstantiation, and for good measure denounce the Orthodox bishops' conclusions at their recent synod of Jerusalem (1672), which had roundly rebuked a list of Calvinist-themed doctrines as heretical and strongly reaffirmed the doctrine of the real eucharistic presence, along with the efficacy of the eucharistic sacrifice for the departed faithful.[7] This council, which was a belated and negative response to cardinal aspects of the Reformation, basically made a clear signal that Protestant theologians could certainly not count on Orthodox support to claim that theirs was a true reading that either renovated or reformed the ancient Christian tradition.[8]

All of this outraged the very evangelical Bishop Compton. How the Greek community reacted is not entirely clear. What he demanded of them was not just ceremonial adaptations but basically a refutation of the faith and order established by the seven Ecumenical Councils. The community informed the patriarch of Constantinople of the matter, and the patriarch approached the British ambassador in the city, Sir Robert Finch, who dryly gave him to understand he would receive no support whatsoever from the British government. He gave the patriarch the answer that "it was illegal for any public church in England to express Romish beliefs, and that it was just as bad to have them professed in Greek as in Latin."[9] The London Greek parish was forcibly closed in 1684, and its buildings were handed over for the use of the exiled Protestant Huguenot refugees from France. By the time another Orthodox Church was opened in London in 1838, after years of the Greek Orthodox community using the chapel of the Russian Embassy in London for worship, no external interference was recorded at all. The Greeks began to build larger, more permanent churches in London at the turn of the century, which presaged the real beginning of a permanent and expanding Greek Orthodox presence in Great Britain as the decades progressed.[10] In 1922 the patriarchate of Constantinople recognized and incorporated the parishes as the Greek archdiocese of Thyateira and Great Britain with its episcopal headquarters in London.[11] It would struggle, however, to find a national footing, instead relying on Greek seminaries to train successive generations of its priests. Without the focal point of a theological academy it has never been able to mount a significant publishing program of accessible English works on, or about, Orthodoxy in the United Kingdom.[12]

Throughout the twentieth century many more Orthodox groups other than the Greeks arrived and settled in England, and the parishes they instituted also attracted a growing number of English converts from both Catholicism and Protestantism. The postrevolution Russian émigrés, having lost the use of the Orthodox chapel of the Russian Embassy in Finchley, took a lease on a redundant church in Kensington and eventually purchased the church in Ennismore Gardens as their cathedral. It became a renowned center of Russian Orthodoxy under the saintly and inspired leadership of Metropolitan Anthony Bloom (1914–2003), who gained a high reputation for spiritual wisdom among the wider English intelligentsia. His administration favored the regular use of English for the converts in his community, and the Russians were the first to establish a regular tradition of English-language celebration of the liturgy, a practice that is growing in the wider representation of all parishes in the United Kingdom today. His cathedral attracted the composer Sir John Taverner, who converted to the Orthodox faith and composed numerous works imbued with Orthodox sensibility, sometimes working with Mother Thekla, the last surviving founder of the Normanby *hesychasterion* (monastery) near Whitby. The monastery of Archimandrite Sophrony, a renowned starets from Athos who founded twin communities of men and women at Tolleshunt Knights in Essex, has grown to be a vital center of monastic life in Great Britain. It also has its own small press. Today, Orthodoxy is a small but vibrant and developing church on the British scene. There are currently almost 150 worshipping Orthodox communities in the United

Kingdom. Not all of them have churches of their own; the single largest focal accumulation of churches is in London, where the immigrant communities first congregated. The national U.K. Orthodox population is now thought to be in the region of 11 percent of all British active (regularly worshipping) Christians.[13]

France and Spain, more traditionally Roman Catholic countries, have, like England, become heavily secularized in culture since the Second World War. Orthodoxy has arrived in them by extensive immigration, especially after the fall of Communist control over Eastern Europe and under the aegis of the European Union, which encouraged an open movement of labor forces. Many Eastern European countries, once their populations could move, lost numbers of Orthodox to France and Spain, who, once settled, began to organize their respective parishes. Romanian Orthodoxy particularly spread westward after the fall of Ceausescu's brutal regime in the 1990s.

Paris was the first gateway for Orthodoxy reaching the West with a notable profile in the twentieth century. Lenin was so incensed by the prevalence of idealist philosophy among Slavophile intellectuals in Russia at the time of the October Revolution that, since shooting them would be bad publicity for the new movement, he thought the best course would be to round them up and ship them into exile. The exile has come to be known as the "ships of philosophers," as the first notable group came out by ship, though later in 1922 other groups were sent by train to Latvia and others by sea to Istanbul.[14] One hundred and sixty members of the intelligentsia with their families were set on the German ships *Oberbürgermeister Haken* and *Preussen* in November 1922, including some of the leading lights in Russian sociology, the arts, psychology, and philosophy. Among those exiled were a tight group of Orthodox religious philosopher-theologians whose combined writings would make Orthodox theological style suddenly appear like an unexpected starburst among Western religious thinkers at a period when reductionist materialism was the fashion elsewhere and the churches of Western Europe were deep into the process of the so-called demythologizing of the Christian narrative.

The main thinkers in this group were Nikolai Berdyaev, Sergius Bulgakov, Semyon Frank, and Nikolai Lossky. To these could be added Georges Florovsky when he too arrived in France as an exile. Bulgakov and Florovsky soon after became ordained as priests and were, together with the Romanian intellectual priest Dumitru Staniloae (1903–1993), among the most highly influential Orthodox theologians of the twentieth century, both through their writings and by their zealous actions on behalf of the church. Staniloae had to endure life-long oppression by the Communist regime that included periods of imprisonment. Yet he sustained a professorial and pastoral career that included a monumental output of religious works, including a new *Philokalia* and a powerful church dogmatics that has only recently appeared in English. Most of the other intellectuals came from the Russian tradition. Arriving first in Germany, they soon gravitated to the new headquarters of the White Russian émigrés, Paris. The Saint Alexander Nevsky Cathedral (founded in 1861) at 12 rue Daru became the central focal meeting point. It refused allegiance to the Moscow patriarchate in the time of the Soviets and came under the protection of the patriarchate of Constantinople.[15] Florovsky became a leading light in the early years of the World Council of Churches. With a close eye on the Jesuits of France who were working assiduously in this area, he also set a new standard for scientific patristic theology among the Orthodox. Bulgakov inspired the foundation of the Fellowship of Saint Alban and Saint Sergius in England and set the tone for future generations of close rapport between the Orthodox and Anglican churches. His theology, detested and censured in his lifetime by the Russian Church in Exile as being too innovative, has since come to be reassessed and appreciated as having engaged with profound issues in a unique way that was both traditionalist and forward looking. Bulgakov's stature as one of the great Christian thinkers of the twentieth century, of any church, is unmistakable.

Berdyaev and Lossky's considerable philosophical standing showed how Orthodoxy was, as the ancient Greek fathers had long contested, itself a philosophical view of the world that was simultaneously phenomenologically personalist, idealist, and ontologically realist: challenging all the various factions of the philosophical schools of the day. Nikolai Lossky's son, Vladimir, in 1944 brought out a deeply influential monograph that was soon translated into English as *The Mystical Theology of the Eastern Church*, showing how the spiritual traditions of Orthodoxy are not separate from its philosophical or doctrinal traditions but form a coherent whole woven around the mystery of the deification (*theiopoiesis*) of humanity through the Incarnation of the Divine Word of God in time and space. The work stimulated generations of later scholars to go back to the ancient Orthodox writers, no longer in the spirit of early twentieth century theological books (assembling apologetic propositions to justify already held positions), but rather to see how the inner spirit and ethos of

Christianity worked to change the heart and soul of the individual. Through the work of these scholars now being accessible in modern European languages, no longer only in Greek, Russian, or Slavonic, the inner spirit and heart of Orthodox mysticism has been shown to be highly relevant to a modern society starved of spiritual leadership. Their influence also led to a great boost to American Orthodoxy, and the intellectuals founding the Orthodox Church in America, Schmemann and Meyendorff in particular, were deeply inspired by their example and continued their tradition.

Through the Paris exiles, clustered around the rue Daru Nevsky Cathedral, Orthodoxy not only came West but it left its poor-immigrant clothing behind and entered the lists along with some of the highest intellectuals of Europe, now using a widely comprehensible set of languages. This not only showcased a more illuminated Orthodoxy to the Western world, long accustomed to dismiss it as a backward peasant religion (from the British imperial oversight of it in the post-Ottoman Middle East context), but also served to inspire and stimulate world Orthodoxy internally and started to bring together, for the first time in centuries, all the varied forms of Orthodox tradition, including the Non-Chalcedonian churches, which began to realize that they had far more in common with each other than they had differences. It is no exaggeration to say that the Russian Orthodox émigré experience began a "second spring" for the whole Orthodox world, which is still in process of being fully elaborated to this day; a time when Orthodoxy in the old homelands (especially Russia, Romania, and Serbia) is rebuilding its structures, reopening its academies, and, like very old trees in the warmth of a rich soil, putting out vigorous green leaves afresh.

CHAPTER NINE

Recent Outstanding Orthodox Figures

ORDINARY AND EXTRAORDINARY SKETCHES

So far this book has been looking at past history, institutions, and doctrinal or ritual forms to make a picture of Orthodox life. Perhaps another way would be, as in this chapter, to look quickly at the way some recently living people have embodied the Orthodox ethos in their manner of life. Obviously I am going to skew this picture insofar as I am going to preselect some of the great and good. It would be more difficult to draw up a picture of Mrs. Sasha Ivanova of downtown Manchester (there isn't such a person as far as I know; it is just an example): an ordinary lay person living an ordinary life. As an observant Orthodox believer, such a person would surely have an icon corner in the house, would probably pray daily, perhaps morning and evening before the icons, and would attend church services. But as with most forms of Christian discipleship, for most people the faith commitment is often deeply interior. We do meet many evangelists who do their thing on vast public media or on street corners, but one suspects the proclamatory voice is not necessarily the authentic voice of the person's deepest self. There often seems to be too much agitation visible to believe such a thing. In the course of thirty years of priestly ministry, I have, for sure, known countless Sasha Ivanovas and Sergey Ivanovitches, not to mention numerous other believers whose names show no sign of a Greek or Russian original, and who were what one might call ordinary Orthodox believers. Their lives demonstrate a bewilderingly rich variety of gifts, and in terms of their spiritual lives, these too were as variegated as the personalities that formed them. But I have no doubt that the fact of being planted within a church environment shapes and forms a deep spirituality that generally does not happen in an environment devoid of the sacramental and social support that active church life provides. I have been privileged to hear many stories of the inner lives of different believers in the course of that priestly ministry, but, again, such things are not for this form of media. Once on camera I asked a Romanian nun if she would tell the viewers what transpired during her many hours of private prayer. She answered: "It would not be appropriate, or even possible, for the Bride to speak of the things whispered in the bridal chamber with the Beloved." And that, as they say, was that.

So what this chapter can offer instead is more of a set of cartoons. I don't mean they will be funny pages—more the original meaning of the word "cartoon" in the sense of a quick sketch to give an idea. At the end of it all one might say: "But there is nothing specifically Orthodox about all this. It just seems to be a picture of the Christian life demonstrated publicly." And if that is the case, then the chapter will have accomplished its task perfectly. For Orthodoxy is, simply,

Christianity; but Christianity with this vivid and pervasive sensibility that "Christ is in our midst."[1] In any case, here are three simple sketches of notable Orthodox figures of the recent past, living in Europe and chosen with an eye to what special charisms each of these remarkable characters manifests.

MOTHER MARIA SKOBTSOVA

The Russian Orthodox nun Mother Maria had begun life as a noblewoman, and even when she adopted the monastic habit she could never give up her early love of smoking cigarettes, thus scandalizing the ultra-pious on several occasions, who were more than startled to see this very robust woman in her full-length monastic habit sneaking a quiet puff whenever she could. Her life was a dramatic one full of unusual turns, but one constantly driven by a sense of her orientating herself to the light of Christ in the immediate and given circumstances of ordinary life.

She was born Elizaveta Yurieva Pilenko in Latvian Riga, in December 1891. Latvia was then an integral part of the Russian Empire. Soon after the turn of the century, when she was a teenager, her father died, and Elizaveta announced that she had embraced atheism. Her mother moved the family to the capital, Saint Petersburg, in 1904, and the richer social and intellectual life allowed the teenager to shine. She joined several literary circles and read her poetry in them, as well as belonging to some radical intellectual groups. In 1910 she married a young Bolshevik agitator, Dimitri Kuzmin-Karavaev, and they had a daughter, Gaiana, though the marriage lasted only three years.[2] Elizaveta took the child to live with her in southern Russia and started to turn back toward the Orthodoxy she had known as a child. She began to attend some church but was moved, as her poetry notes, by the profoundly loving humanity of Jesus: which she found more attractive than the transcendent majesty of his deity as emphasized in the churches. Still very active in the Party of Socialist Revolutionaries, she was moved to fury when Trotsky disbanded its assembly in January 1918 as part of the Bolsheviks' moves to suppress all alternative Marxist movements, and, like Fanny Kaplan, who had tried to assassinate Lenin, Maria started to vocalize how she would like to put a bullet in Trotsky.

Her friends quickly intervened to spirit her away to safety in the relative obscurity of the town of Anapa in southern Russia. When the Bolsheviks assumed political control, in 1918, Maria was elected deputy mayor of Anapa. The White Russian Army soon liberated the town, and when the mayor made good his escape, Maria stayed behind, assuming the mayoral office, and, as mayor, was arrested by the White Army and put on trial for being a Bolshevik. The prosecuting officer was Daniel Skobtsov, who recognized her as one of his former students when he was a prerevolutionary teacher. After hearing her case, he declared her innocent of all charges. They fell for each other and were soon married. But the hold of the White Russians was constantly being eroded, and the family had to flee from Anapa to escape the Bolshevik advance. Her mother, Sophia, Daniel, and Gaiana, the elder daughter, and Maria herself, now pregnant with her second child, made a long flight. They stopped in Georgia for the birth of her son, Yuri, and then moved through Yugoslavia, staying for a while, where her second daughter, Anastasia, was born, and finally arriving in Paris in 1923.

The family shared the difficulties of many exiled Russians in Paris. Elizaveta was drawn to social work, but her religious interests had been quickened by her return to church life, and she attached herself to the Russian Orthodox cathedral parish in Paris. She started to make a serious study of theology. In Paris in 1929 she published three studies in Russian: one on the theology of Khomiakov; another on Dostoyevsky and modernity; and a third on the idea of world-soul in the religious philosopher Solovyev.[3] The marriage with Daniel was more and more noticeably coming apart. In 1926 Anastasia died in the influenza epidemic, and Daniel and Elizaveta decided to send Gaiana to Belgium, to a boarding school there. She and Daniel separated, and Yuri opted at first to live with his father. Elizaveta moved into central Paris to undertake social work for the deprived families of the inner-city slums. She found great delight in this work. In discussions with her bishop, Metropolitan Evlogy, she asked in what way she could make this social ministry more in harmony with what she perceived as her church vocation. The bishop encouraged her to take vows as a nun: which would be possible, according to Orthodox church law, if her husband agreed to the separation. She herself was willing to follow this route but made it plain that she had no calling to an enclosed life, and only wanted a form of monasticism that was at the service of the poor and rooted in the day-to-day life of the ordinary world. The archbishop agreed, and Daniel's agreement also followed, so that in 1932 they were both granted an ecclesiastical divorce, and Elizaveta made her vows and was renamed as nun Mother Maria Skobtsova.

The priest appointed to be her confessor and spiritual guide was Father Sergius Bulgakov, the most prominent

Orthodox theologian of the age. He also had been a strong socialist advocate in his youth, and like Maria he was impassioned about correlating Orthodox tradition and values to the pressing pastoral and spiritual needs of the age of crisis they knew was now all around them. Mother Maria rented 17 rue du Lourmel in the southerly Grenelle district of Paris, to serve as her convent-house and place of work. She called it the House and Chapel of the Protection of the Mother of God. Today a marble plaque marks its spot. She made the place a house of hospitality for all the poor, especially the influx of impoverished refugees, but also the local elderly and lonely: anyone who came to her in need of any kind—for them the door was always open, and her resources were at their disposal. From the base of the house, she also started to gather intellectuals once more: this time to speak and reflect about Orthodoxy and the mission of the church in the modern age. When the work of Father Bulgakov at the Saint-Serge Institut and his international travels took more and more of his time, a new chaplain, Father Dimitri Kelpinin, a thirty-nine-year-old married priest, came to serve the liturgy at the chapel and ran a parish alongside her soup kitchen, social advice office, and training workshops. He and his family were great helpers to Mother Maria in her mission. Her own son, Yuri, also was attracted by the mission's work, as was her mother, Sophia. Mother Maria became a common sight in her cassock making her tours of the Paris markets begging for food and any other goods that were past selling, so that she could feed her growing "family." The movement grew to such an extent that, with the bishop's support, she had to rent two other buildings: one for single men and the other to house displaced families in crisis.

In 1940 another new crisis dawned. France fell to the Nazi forces. Immediately Parisian Jews started to appeal to Mother Maria for help. If they held Christian baptismal certificates, they thought, they could avoid the deportations to the camps that had already started. Mother Maria sheltered many of them and helped arrange for others to flee the country. She and Father Dimitri issued many with fake Orthodox baptismal certificates that they had printed themselves. In 1942 the Gestapo began to arrest and imprison about seven thousand of the Jews of Paris in the Vélodrome d'Hiver stadium. They were destined for transportation out to the prison camps, but conditions in that transit camp were appalling. Mother Maria gained entrance to the stadium, bringing food and medications and removing trash on her way out. In this way she was able to spirit off several Jewish children, hiding them in the exiting trash cans.

The Gestapo Paris informer networks were extensive, however. The obvious origins of Mother Maria and her family made them highly suspect to the German authorities, who had made Jews and Russians the first targets of arrests. On February 8, 1943, the Nazis made their move. The Gestapo arrived when most of the rue du Lourmel administration was out for the day, to search the complex. Yuri was present, however, and was arrested. The next day Father Dimitri celebrated his last liturgy in the house chapel with all present and went off to report to the Gestapo. He did not return that evening. The next day, when Mother Maria reported to the police, to inquire after the status of Father Dimitri and Yuri, she too was arrested, and the house was forcibly closed. She was first interned at the Romainville fort and then moved to the camp at Compiègne, where she met up again, briefly, with

Father Dimitri and Yuri. Soon afterward the two men were sent to the Nazi concentration camp at Mittelbau-Dora, a subcamp of Buchenwald that existed to supply slave labor. There, like so many others, they were worked on starvation rations, until sickness carried them to death in the winter of early 1944.

Mother Maria was sent to Ravensbrück, the vastly over-crowded women's prison camp north of Berlin. She was prisoner number 19263. For two years she survived the horrific conditions of the camp, being progressively weakened by the poor diet and the extensive diseases that ravaged the sleeping huts. She constantly strove to minister to the women, offering consolation and words of hope. Those who were unable to work, or who simply annoyed the authorities, were called out in random evening "selections." By late 1944 Mother Maria was so weakened that her many friends used to help her stand up for the 3 A.M. roll calls and hide her in the hut when inspections were made. On the morning of Orthodox Good Friday, March 30, 1945, she was selected by the guards; and just as the day turned (liturgically) into Holy Saturday, the eve of Pascha, she was led to die in the gas chamber adjacent to the crematorium, and thus entered through the doors of glory, into the paschal Resurrection of Christ.[4]

She was canonized as a saint by the patriarch of Constantinople in January 2004, along with Father Dimitri and Yuri, and the celebration of their glorification was observed in their own Alexander Nevsky Cathedral in Paris in May that same year.[5] Her deeds are recorded at the Yad Vashem memorial of the Holocaust, and she was awarded the posthumous status by the state of Israel of Righteous among the Nations. She is now known among the Orthodox as Saint Maria of Paris.

Once, when a formalist Orthodox person expressed disapproval about her smoking habits, and the apparently chaotic nature of her monastic house, which was open to everyone day and night so it did not allow her the time or the privacy to perform the usual acts of monastic piety (such as full-length prostrations in prayer), she answered with the observation that when the final judgment takes place, Christ will ask one not how many prostrations one has fulfilled in one's lifetime but whether one fed the poor and clothed the naked.[6] The dominant motif of her love for Christ was the ability to see him present in the lives of the poor and suffering, and the courage to have the generosity to respond without counting the cost. Metropolitan Anthony Bloom, the Russian archbishop of London, once called her the Orthodox "saint of our times."

PROFESSOR ELISABETH BEHR-SIGEL

When Elisabeth Behr-Sigel died in Épinay-sur-Seine, France, in 2005, her obituary in the London *Times* of December that year described her as "the Matriarch of the Orthodox Church in Western Europe." She had been born in 1907 in (then German) Alsace. Her father was Protestant and her mother was Jewish. She herself made a commitment as a young person to Protestant Christianity and was the first woman admitted to read for a theology degree at the University of Strasbourg. After graduating, with a Master's, she felt called to ministry and exercised a pastoral charge for a year, as the first woman ever to be officially commissioned as a minister by the Reformed Church of Alsace-Lorraine. It was at the end of that year, however, that she knew "something else" had to happen, even though the concept and *actualité* of ministry remained with her as a lifelong passion. It can perhaps be said that one of the dominant and guiding notions of her life's work was the central importance of the evangelical witness and work of women in the Church of Christ. Concomitant with that was her increasing awareness of how much that vital work had been stifled by social accretions over the ages, and by the short-sightedness of so many church leaders, who were content to stay inert in a mental status quo, without examining matters that surely required pressing change for a new age. Women's social and educational status had altered substantively across the centuries, Elisabeth argued, so much so that the self-evident second-class status that was given to so many women in the different ecclesial traditions was now glaringly out of harmony with the movement of the Holy Spirit in the world. She discontinued her work among the Reformed churches and moved to Paris, where she started to take advanced courses in theology. It was in Paris that she first came across the large number of Orthodox Russian exiles that had settled there after the Bolshevik Revolution. She was intrigued by their theological teachings, philosophical sophistication, and liturgical style. She took the free courses in Orthodox theology at Saint-Serge Institut, organized by the Russian clergy in exile, since at that period women were not allowed to enroll (later she would return as one of Saint-Serge's professors).

Getting to know the Russian community more closely, she came under the influence of some significant mentors: notably Metropolitan Evlogy, the archbishop in charge of the Russian exile community at the rue Daru Alexander Nevsky Cathedral. She asked to join the Russian Orthodox Church when she was twenty-four years of age and was chrismated in the Paris cathedral. Soon afterward she fell in love with a Russian engineer, André Behr, whom she met through church circles, and together they had three children.[7] By the time of the Second World War, the family was living in the town of Nancy, where Elisabeth had taken a teaching post in the public school system. She and her husband were active in the French Resistance. She would later remark that it was this time, seeing how many people of good heart banded together as one family in resistance to Nazi evil, that showed her the potential for ecumenical sharing to renew the church in the present moment.

In the civic reconstructions following the Nazi defeat, she started a long and active career in higher education. She took a post teaching theology at the Roman Catholic Institut Catholique in Paris and also lectured in the Russian Orthodox Seminary and at Saint-Serge. In this way she began what became a lifelong passion for her, to bridge the separated Catholic traditions of Christianity. The postwar era was one that was full of great hopes for ecumenical rapprochement between the churches (it is no accident that this very word at the heart of ecumenism is a French one), and much of the French Catholic theologians' work would go on in a direct way to prepare for the great opening up of mind and heart that characterized the Second Vatican Council. Elisabeth was one of the very few women theologians at the core of this movement, and certainly the only significant female Orthodox one. She forged a close friendship with a remarkable ecumenical figure of that period, Father Lev Gillet (1893–1980), an Eastern rite Catholic priest who famously joined the Orthodox clergy by accepting Metropolitan Evlogy's invitation to concelebrate the Eucharist with him. Father Lev was soon to become a major figure in ecumenical circles in Britain and lived out his life as a celibate Orthodox monk-priest, under the patronage of a very supportive Anglican Church establishment. He spent much effort serving as a retreat director and encouraging the wider knowledge of the Jesus Prayer and the mystical traditions of Orthodoxy. His and Elisabeth's ecumenical outreach was a mutual fire that inspired them both. After Father Lev's death, Elisabeth composed his spiritual biography to try to manifest the inner life of a special soul.[8] The theologians Vladimir Lossky and Paul Evdokimov were also friends and influences. Elisabeth served too as a professor giving courses at the Tantur Ecumenical Institute near Jerusalem and the Dominican College of Ottawa. She played a long-standing role on the board of the Orthodox journal *Contacts*, and through her commissions and her own writing lifted it to a significant academic level. By the end of her life she had become much sought after internationally as a lecturer and wrote extensively about Orthodox life and thought in books as well as in magazine articles, in French and German and English.

Before 1976 she had held the opinion that the admission of women to ordained priesthood in the Orthodox Church was an impossibility: something precluded by the terms of the ancient tradition. After 1976 her deep reading of the evidence had changed her mind, and she advocated for an open-minded reconsideration of the question by the church hierarchy. From this time to the end of her life she conducted a close examination of the role and status of women in the Christian Church, examining the tenets of feminism and existentialism on the way and finding them wanting in many respects. She never became bitter or angry at the slow pace of change in Orthodoxy and brought to all she did a deep and often mischievous sense of humor that had the effect of disconcerting the pompous and disarming her opponents. "I am no stylite ascetic," she told her audiences, adding, "except when the elevator in my apartment ceases to function."⁹

Many of those who dismissed the significance of women in the church found her a learning experience in and of herself. In her later years, Elisabeth first struck observers as a very frail and delicate old lady. But it soon became very apparent what a powerhouse of an intellect she had, and how deeply versed in the ancient Orthodox tradition she was: knowing it like very few of those who professed to teach it as ordained ministers. It was said that the Paris gendarmes had several times stopped her car because they could not see anyone driving it: she was so petite her eyes just peeked over the dashboard when she sat in the driving seat. Her book on the subject of female ordination remains influential, serving for the moment like a lonely shipping lamp at sea: blinking its stable existence and serving to remind a generation that the issue she addressed while most refused to will not go away.¹⁰ She has laid a foundation for others to follow in a generation of Orthodox believers still to come. One of the pressing arguments against the ordination of women was the so-called iconic one: since Christ was a male, the female priest cannot serve to iconize him properly. In her theology Elisabeth pointed out how Orthodoxy regards priesthood as one thing differentiated in three degrees: bishop, priest, and deacon. Since the ordination ritual for female deacons has existed from ancient times, it follows that Orthodox tradition already embraced the ordination of women to the priesthood (in the degree of diaconate), and to refuse it in contemporary times is actually a departure from tradition, not a maintenance of it. Moreover, Christ is properly iconized in his church, which is his own and most intimate body, not by the genetic symbols of maleness, but rather by his most characteristic signs of personal presence: his humility, his self-sacrificing love, his devotion to the Father and to suffering humanity: all the things a woman can do (and must do if she is to be authentically Christian) just as well as any man. To refuse women a full and active role in the church's ministry, she argued, was to weaken and dilute the church. She believed that one day this would be recognized. In 2000 she was one of the chief signatories of an open letter to the highest primates of the Orthodox Church calling for immediate steps to restore the ordination of women to the Orthodox diaconate.

It was a great joy to Elisabeth in 2004 to be able to witness the canonization of Mother Maria Skobtsova, whose spiritual life, wartime ministry in Paris, and final martyrial witness at Ravensbrück she had so greatly admired. Three years before her death, her birthday was celebrated by a large gathering at the French Roman Catholic Carmelite convent of Saint Elie. Present for the event were two Orthodox bishops, a Greek Catholic bishop, the vicars-general of three different Roman Catholic dioceses, and several notable Protestant clergy. It was a striking testimony to the way Elisabeth felt so at ease among the different traditions, while still being fully at home as an Orthodox, and also how her vision of ecumenism was a force in itself that brought the churches together. Shortly after returning from England, where she had delivered a talk on Father Lev Gillet, she died quietly, reading in bed, aged ninety-eight. Her life, in many ways, was marked by a brilliant light of humility. This was not a self-effacing kind of anxiety to be seen or an unease in her own self-worth—far from it. Elisabeth was a prestigiously intelligent theologian known throughout the world. It was just that whenever she talked of great things she spoke of how others around her achieved and shone. She lived out her own spiritual journey in quietness and deep assurance of the presence of Christ as the magnetic north of her whole being. It was this that grounded her and made her such a fully real person, ultimately leading her to the status of a strong prophetic voice. If she was not listened to greatly by the ecclesiastical leaders of her own day, nevertheless she will be present to a generation yet to come, as a wise and important guide: a veritable mother of the church in our own time, like the great fathers of the church, those theologians in times past who spoke prophetically to their own generations; but whose message was sometimes too uncomfortable to be immediately absorbed.

ARCHIMANDRITE CLEOPA ILIE

One of the greatest of modern Romanian spiritual leaders was born Constantin Ilie, in the village of Sulita, in the district of Botosani on April 10, 1912, fifth of ten children in a family of peasant farmers. He received a primary school education in the village but after that was apprenticed by his father, Alexandru, as the servant (and soon disciple) of the solitary hermit monk Father Paisie Olaru at the Cozancea hermitage, a cell of the great fourteenth-century Sihastria skete in the Carpathian Mountains.[11] From his earliest youth he showed a great love for the monastic life. In 1929 he and his brothers

George and Vasile went to the skete of Sihastria monastery to join as novice monks themselves.[12] Another brother would later join them. The higumen, or abbot, set Constantin to work as a shepherd caring for its flock, and over the next twelve years in this office, in following them as they grazed the wooded hills, he gained a great love for the countryside and a deep knowledge of it. During these years he used to come down from the hills on Saturday evening for the Vigil service and the Sunday liturgies on the following day. During the week, on the hillside and in his little shepherd's shack, he would immerse himself in the reading of the church fathers and spiritual masters. His monastic life was interrupted by having to fulfill his state-mandated army service in 1935, but immediately after his year was complete he returned to the monastery and was fully professed as a monk in August 1937, taking the name Cleopa (the biblical Cleophas). The community noticed how the young monk had a highly active intelligence, sharp discernment, and phenomenal memory. He was able to quote long passages by heart from both scripture and the church fathers.

In 1942 Father Ioanichie, the aging higumen of Sihastria, appointed Cleopa as his personal assistant and deputy higumen, and, because his new responsibilities required it, in December of 1944 he was ordained deacon and then in January of the following year was priested by Archbishop Galaction, who was higumen of the great Neamt monastery where Saint Paisy Velichkovsky had centered his teaching mission centuries earlier. After his ordination Cleopa took over as higumen of the skete. Two years later, in 1947, the Romanian patriarch Nicodim gave Cleopa the highest position to which monks can attain, making him an archimandrite, and established the skete as an independent monastery in its own right. His preaching career, which had begun with his ordination, now brought him increasingly to the attention of outsiders, not merely his own monastic community, who already venerated him. People would seek him out as their spiritual father and guide, what is known in the Orthodox tradition as a starets.[13] One of his foundational principles, which he often repeated to clergy and monks who were given the task of instructing others, was only to guide someone else from one's own direct and successful personal experience. He compared those who pretend to be spiritual guides, but have not lived out the spiritual truths they are inculcating to others, as "painted waterfalls on a wall" that could not offer fresh water from their wellspring.

Those who came to him across a long ministry testified that he had the gift of the common touch, able to communicate powerfully and easily (his sermons have been recorded and are widely listened to in Romania to this day). His books were numerous, addressed to the common faithful but showing a deep absorption of the fathers and the past spiritual masters, despite the fact that he had little formal education. His growing fame brought Cleopa to the attention of the new masters of Romania, the Communist secret police, the Securitate. In their zeal to establish Stalinist control of the country, this body soon became the most brutal and feared of all the Communist police establishments, outdoing even the savage Soviet NKVD. His ministry made Cleopa a marked man. In 1948 the monastery was raided after the divine liturgy, and he was taken hurriedly into prison. For five days he was locked in a basement without food or water and then just as brusquely thrown out. It was of course meant as a warning. In response Cleopa decided to have a spell as a hermit once more, and he slipped away into the wooded countryside adjacent to the monastery. He cleared out a cave and lived in it for six months with his books of prayers, wearing a sheepskin (like a local hillside shepherd in case anyone saw him) until the police lost interest. Many years later he would still wear the sheepskin coat of a shepherd over his cassock. This would be the first of several times the secret police came to arrest him, and often he would slip away into the remote mountain country that he knew so well, where he could easily outwit the city-based policemen who had no country skills at all. On several occasions, however, the Securitate did pick him up, and, like other clergy, he suffered his share of torture and beatings in their cells.

Cleopa often said that while he lived in caves, on the run, he felt it was "like living as a king." He would celebrate the divine liturgy, just himself and the angels, using an old tree stump outside his cave as his altar. This deep and extreme wilderness life spent in prayerful immersion gave him a profound understanding of how God has blessed the inner structures of the life of the natural world—so much so that it is a mistake to speak of natural and supernatural, in the way that many surface religious texts do: because God's energy and grace is so deeply permeated in the structures of creation that all things interior and exterior to the human being are hymns of praise to God. The human being is his living icon; the whole inanimate world is his sacrament: for all things constantly sing his glory by their simple being. This was a theological theme strongly present in the great patristic writers, Saints Gregory of Nazianzus and Maximus the Confessor. It was due to his constant advocacy for the beauty and God-blessed gracefulness of the world order, exemplified in the unspoiled Romanian countryside which Cleopa loved so much, that the Romanian Church after the fall of Communism became heavily involved in the ecological movement sponsored by the patriarch of Constantinople. Against the blight of heavy industry polluting the atmosphere and rivers without care, and the moronic Soviet-style architecture that had been overlaid on the beauties of Romanian Gothic styles of the medieval period (pristinely represented in so many of the monasteries), the church spoke of the need to discover the sacrament of beauty.[14] Where the Communist ideologues had taken charge of the country farms and collectivized them, throwing aside generations of peasant wisdom and local ownership, they soon brought production to all-time lows and flattened all the locally observed cycles of growth and rest, by a depressingly brutalist approach to agriculture. The constant focus of Cleopa on creation's Christ-founded beauty, along with his simplicity of heart and the humble love he presented as the keystones of the Christ life, appealed to deep and recognized resonances in the Romanian peasant soul. This was why the Communists tried several times to silence him, as they had already successfully imprisoned and tortured many other spiritual monastic leaders.

The new patriarch, Justinian, appointed under Communist control in 1948, was set the task of reordering the many Romanian monasteries in the name of rationalization—which was one of the ways the Communist authorities attempted first to reduce and then suppress the vigorous monastic life still active in Romania. Around this time Cleopa was ordered by church authorities to stop receiving pilgrims. Always careful to serve the bishops obediently, he also knew that his first duty was to the will of God: so he disregarded that instruction as emanating from hidden Communist pressure. In August 1949, the patriarch ordered Cleopa to move to serve as higumen of Slatina monastery in Suceava county, and so he went there with thirty of his own community to begin afresh. Soon afterward he established this as a stable community of just more than eighty monks. The Securitate was furious that he had, in fact, started a new and thriving monastic center, so they came again to arrest him, and this time they beat him and tortured him. Cleopa and the priest-monk Papacioc then took off once more for life in the Stanisoara Mountains between 1952 and 1954. This time he lived happily in seclusion for two years until a message from the patriarch asked him to return to lead his monastery and gave him to understand he would not be arrested.

In 1956, in the thaw of a few freedoms that followed Stalin's death, he was sent back to his first monastery at Sihastria, but two years later the Securitate unleashed a new wave of persecution against the church. At that time around one thousand five hundred clergy and active laity were imprisoned, and the patriarch was put under closer security control. Half of the monasteries in Romania were forcibly closed. Cleopa was specially targeted because of his high profile as a courageous dissident, but he again eluded the secret police by retreating to solitary life in the Carpathian Mountains. Each month a trusted forester brought him a sack of potatoes, and his main diet was one potato a day until the next delivery. For five years he lived the life of one of the ancient Christian cave dwellers, devoting his days to prayer and his nights to the recitation of the psalms. In solitude he used to spend twelve hours out of every twenty-four praying vocally, and using the silent prayer of the heart, the Jesus Prayer.

In 1964 he came out of seclusion and returned to the Sihastria monastery to serve as the *pneumatikos* of the community: the spiritual elder and confessor. He had a little skete, or small building with a chapel and an attendant monk, in the fields on the main monastery grounds. For thirty-four years he lived out his vocation here, and soon the community had to build an amphitheater outside for the increasingly large crowds of pilgrims who came to consult him and hear his preaching, and especially to seek him as a priestly confessor. As his strength began to fail and his health became a trial in his later years, he bore it with humor. He used to joke with his congregation: "I am now Uncle Mouldy. I have one foot in the grave and the other on the earth; but life is an ongoing fight against the flesh, the world, the devil, and death."[15] On December 2, 1998, Cleopa died there aged eighty-six, having told his community and congregation a short time before that he was withdrawing from public ministry in order to prepare to die. Ten thousand people gathered for his funeral, and notices of his death were carried in the world's media.

Father Cleopa consciously emulated the great Romanian spiritual master of the eighteenth century, Saint Paisy Velichkovsky.[16] He had become a person whose heart was deeply established in prayer; this he had learned from his many times in hidden seclusion, but it was equally true of the daily life of the monasteries in which he served, as well as in the incredibly busy public ministry of confessions and preaching he undertook. This latter was a ministry that grew in size immensely as soon as the Communist government collapsed in the late 1980s, and that toward the end of his life caused him considerable effort as his bodily strength ebbed away. He always spoke of his sufferings under the Communists lightly, almost as a joke, but his heart was alive to all the sufferings of others, however small or large. After the fall of the regime in 1989, and the brief armed combat in the streets that established the overthrow of the remainder of the secret police, Orthodox Christians all over Romania looked to Cleopa for spiritual guidance in the task of rebuilding Romanian society amid unaccustomed freedoms. His message remained simple and direct: retain purity of heart and learn to live a simple and open-hearted life, ever conscious of the need for repentance and humility, praying daily without fail, and being careful to receive the sacraments of the church as essential food on the journey. The streams of pilgrims who came to him en masse to hear his sermons, or individually to seek his counsel in confession, ranged from simple Romanian peasants to the new political leaders of the country. He was the spiritual father of many who are today in the highest offices of the Romanian Church, including the present patriarch, Daniel, and several other bishops.

In many ways Cleopa was a living reminder of how the early church fathers and great desert ascetics withstood the first persecutions and emerged from them with a radiant purity of heart that lit up the later centuries that would read of their exploits. He had absorbed the early fathers extensively in the long times of solitude he spent in prayer and learned from them the world of difference between professing Christianity on the lips and living it out in the heart and body. He saw God alive in the streams and mountains and above all in the needs and fears of his fellow men and women: a great mark of spiritual maturity. His innate courage and inner strength, renewed daily by his consciousness of Christ's indwelling presence, allowed him the freedom to step forward and meet people on their road. That freedom was rooted in his great simplicity of life.

CHAPTER TEN

Day-to-Day Life in an Orthodox Church

MAKING A VISIT

The simplest way to gain a flavor of life and worship activity inside an Orthodox church is to go to one some Sunday and stand at the back. If you are worried about when to stand, when to sit, what to do to "merge," just take a seat (there are always some, even though many older Orthodox churches reduce the seats considerably so as to retain the older tradition of standing throughout worship services) or just take a stance by the back wall. When you do this everyone else is in front of you, and you can just copy what they do. Most Orthodox churches welcome discreet visitors. Those few that don't are, by definition, not good representatives of the Christian Orthodox tradition. You'll know who they are immediately by the stern militaristic tone prevalent, and the ever-watchful interferers waiting for a stranger to make a mistake so they can run over and correct them in an incomprehensible language with many gesticulations. If this happens, a quick exit is in order. It is a broad sweep-of-the-brush cliché, but Greek churches are more easygoing and family-noise oriented, while Russian-tradition churches are more sober and focused. All Orthodox services are long. It is the unstated church etiquette that laity might arrive late but ought not to leave early. As a result, the churches tend to fill up increasingly as the service progresses through several hours (two to three) on a standard Sunday morning. Festival liturgies tend to take longer (three to four). It is often difficult for the visitor to know precisely when the liturgy begins, especially if it is in unfamiliar Byzantine Greek or medieval Slavonic, because most Sunday services are preceded by the hours of prayer (what are called Matins or Morning Prayer in the Western traditions); and often the eucharistic liturgy carries on straight away after Matins. It is also a confusion for visitors to know precisely when the service ends, as yet again other shorter services are often tagged on seamlessly to the end of the main service (services of prayer commemorations for deceased relatives' anniversaries and suchlike). When I was considerably younger, I attended a Greek church for the first time and tried to follow the service from the Greek text I gripped in my hand. I could never follow the line (not knowing then that a lot of the responses are in the separate choir books and are not printed in the standard lay missal). But at least I had the priest's part. But then again he regularly came out from the altar and waved his hands at the congregation (it was an Easter Eve and very noisy and happily chaotic in the church). Each time he shouted out to them "Siope! Siope!" I thought this must be a heartfelt encouragement to prayer or some such thing; but it was certainly not in the text of the liturgy. Some months afterward I found the word in the dictionary. It turned out to be "Shut up!" The poor man must have been sick of all the noise. All told, it is perhaps better to find someone in an Orthodox parish whom one knows, and ask him or her to take you to church and explain what is going on. But failing all that—here is a short chapter that tries to give a summary guide to what a visitor might expect to find if he or she wanders in off the street, through the doors of an Orthodox church, on any ordinary Sunday.

The first thing that may strike you is the brightness of the church porch, and the way in which it has a bustle about it. There will probably be candles for sale, long thin beeswax ones. It is a custom to buy two for a nominal amount, to assist church funds, in order to take them with you into the main church building. As you turn to enter the church you will notice the contrast in the lighting of the interior, which will often be very dim, lit by flickering oil lamps (called *lampadas*) that hang in front of all the icons around the walls and especially illuminate the altar area. What is called the altar in Western churches is called the holy table by the Orthodox. What the Western churches call the sanctuary area is called the altar. There is a raised set of steps immediately in front of the main doors (the royal doors) to the altar: this part is called the *bema* and is where the clergy stand for certain parts of the service, especially to read from the scriptures.

In Russian tradition churches the icon screen (iconostasis) not only stretches across the whole altar area but reaches up high into the church ceiling. In Greek tradition churches the screen is not so high. Originally it was only waist height, serving to keep the crowds of faithful away from crushing out the clergy at the holy table, but over the centuries icons were placed on it, and these became added to, so that eventually it became more of a permanent and opaque screen dividing off the altar. The Byzantine Museum in Athens, just behind Syntagma Square, has an example of such an early, and low, marble chancel screen. In some more recent Orthodox churches there has been a tendency to reduce the size of the iconostasis, so that the faithful can see more of the holy table during the eucharistic celebration. The holy table itself can be seen only when the Eucharist is being celebrated. If the divine liturgy is not taking place, the royal doors are always closed, and there is a curtain pulled across the top of them. During the course of the liturgy the royal doors are opened to symbolize the way in which Christ's sacrifice reopened the locked gates of Paradise to the world. No one ever walks through the royal doors, as they are seen as the symbols of Christ's own advent to the world. The exception to this is the priest (or bishop) who celebrates the Eucharist. But when he is not celebrating, the priest too does not walk through this door. The side doors are used instead. When clergy members first enter the altar area, for any reason, they always make three prostrations making the sign of the cross and kissing the holy table, as it is considered the very sacred symbol of Christ's tomb and contains the body of the Lord (eucharistic elements known as the holy gifts) reserved in a tabernacle, or *pyx*.

The Orthodox regard the church, which they call "the Temple" (*Naos*), as a symbolic representation (what the ancient church fathers called a "type") of the Temple in Jerusalem—but this time the Temple that is Christ's body: the fulfillment of the liturgical symbols of the Old Testament. This is why one of the first things to strike a visitor is perhaps the smell inside the church. This is either fresh or yesterday's incense. No Orthodox service takes place without the use of incense. The smell is quite different from that in Roman

Catholic or High Anglican churches, because where they tend to use pure frankincense in their devotions, the Orthodox follow the recipe for incense found in the Old Testament (Exod. 30.34), which is more fragrant—often redolent of roses. Each morning and evening incense is offered up from the holy table, which is also made square in line with the instructions given in Exodus 30.1–8. This evokes the offering of incense for evening and morning Temple service in ancient times. The psalm verses that are used when incense is offered for Vespers (Evening Prayer) recount the same liturgical use as in the ancient Temple: "Let my prayer arise as incense before you; the raising of my hands, as an evening sacrifice of praise."[1] A musical version (from the Russian Orthodox tradition) can be found on *YouTube*.[2] It has the chant style developed in later Russian times. An earlier style of close harmony Russian chant can be heard in another popular hymn to the Blessed Virgin Mary sung by the monks of Valaam monastery, also available on *YouTube*.[3] The (earlier) medieval Byzantine style of singing is held to more in the churches of the Greek tradition. A version of this form of *a cappella* choir singing, the Vesperal hymn "Let My Prayer Arise," can be heard on *YouTube* as well.[4]

The parallelism of the church with the Temple is seen too in the way the Orthodox churches are always divided into three: the outer porch (or narthex), the inner main body of the church (or nave), and the altar (that is, the sanctuary). All Orthodox churches, built as such, face eastward, to the spiritual Rising Sun, the tomb of the Lord in Jerusalem. Looking toward the altar, therefore, one is normally facing east. The clergy always face east when they celebrate the sacred prayers of the services, except on a few occasions (largely when they are particularly addressing the people). In ancient times the

narthex was the place where the unbaptized gathered for instruction, and after the scriptures were read the doors to the
nave were closed so that only the baptized would be present
for the sacraments. During the liturgy the Orthodox deacon
will still cry out before the consecration of the holy gifts (during the central prayer known as the Anaphora): "All Catechumens depart! All Catechumens depart!" and the unbaptized
used to retire to the narthex for instruction about the scripture readings they had just heard. The nave was the place of
the laity, corresponding to the court of the Israelites in the
Temple, and the altar the place of the priests and deacons.
There is a deep sense in the Orthodox Church that the presence of God palpably dwells within the holy of holies, adjacent to the holy table; and in addition, of course, the holy
gifts, the reserved eucharistic elements, are kept there in case
the sick might need them in emergency, placed upon the altar
in a special gilded vessel. The bishop, if he is present, will always commence the liturgy standing and then sitting on a
throne in the middle of the church nave, to be present with
his people, but then (after the priests have commenced the
liturgy) he will ceremonially enter the altar area to preside
over the service at the holy table.

On the holy table itself, which is always covered with several layers of cloths, the topmost being an especially rich fabric, lies the richly decorated book of the Gospels. The cover
for this is usually metal, with enamel icons set within it; it
depicts the evangelists and prophets surrounding the Crucifixion of Christ on one side and, on the other side, his Resurrection. Seven lamps (again reminiscent of the great menorah
in the Temple) stand just behind the holy table. They are always lit when a great service is taking place. There is a space

behind the holy table and the apsidal wall (or back wall) of the church, which allows for free passage of the clergy and altar servers. When the altar area is being censed, the deacon or priest will pass around the holy table before leaving through the iconostasis doors to cense the main body of the church, starting with the icons but ending with a personal censing of the faithful gathered there. It is the etiquette of the church that when the clergy cense the individual believers (because they too are the living icons of God), they in turn bow to him respectfully and make the sign of the cross over themselves. The incense comes upon them as a blessed thing, blessing them for a higher state of prayer and devout attention.

ENTERING THE BUILDING

When a person first enters the church from the narthex, by the door coming in are the two festal icons of that particular church. There is usually an icon of the Mother of the Lord holding the Savior and pointing to him. This is known as the Hodegitria icon ("She who shows the way"). Next to it will be the icon of the saint to whom that individual church is dedicated. The believers always venerate these icons as soon as they enter. A typical form of the veneration of the icons is that the person stands before them and bows twice from the waist, making the sign of the cross over himself or herself just before bowing.[5] He or she then approaches and kisses the hand of the figure depicted, and after that stands back once more to make a third bow and a final signing of himself or herself with the cross. The veneration of an icon is not an act worshipping the image. That would be a foolish idolatry. The bowing down is an act of respect (veneration in this sense) before the icon, which in that moment of faith becomes an act of the worship of the person of Christ whom that icon represents. Venerating an icon of Christ becomes an act of adoration because the veneration of the believer passes from the symbol of the presence of God directly to the Lord, whom his icon stands in for. If a believer venerates an icon of the Virgin or a saint or an angel, then the act of veneration (respect) for the icon becomes in like manner an act of venerational respect (not worshipful adoration, since that person of saint or angel is not divine) for the holy person depicted. Western contemporary attitudes among those not used to this form of devotion (especially in the Reformed tradition) are often taken aback by this form of praying: sometimes thinking incense is being offered to the icon. It is not; and it never is. It is being offered as a form of respect to the one depicted in the icon. If it is an icon of God (Christ or the Trinity), then that worshipful veneration is intended to be an act of adoration. If it is an icon of a saint, then the worshipful veneration is of a different order of respect. As we have already seen, in the Greek and Russian Orthodox traditions the terminology for all the strict degrees of veneration that are permissible, and expected, is very extensive. But ask any Orthodox children what they are doing when they venerate icons, and it will be immediately clear: the respect shown before the icon is meant to pass directly to the figure depicted therein. If it is the divine Christ, then the act of veneration becomes adoration (of Christ, of course, not the icon per se); if it is a saint or angel icon, then the act of veneration is exactly that, a deeply respectful bowing down before the heavenly saint, who receives that respectful homage (never adoration) and returns his or her blessing to the believer: for the Orthodox affirm that the saint is not dead but alive and active in the glory of the Risen Lord.

The next thing Orthodox persons will do after entering the church and venerating the icons is, usually, take the two thin taper candles they have brought with them and light one in the candle stand placed on one side of the church (near the Christ Icon) and the other in the stand, or sand tray, by the Virgin's icon. Sometimes these are together in one place, set aside. They will already be full of many glittering candles, so they cannot be mistaken. One of the candles is to symbolize the whole family's prayer for living related members and others for whom that family is specially praying. The other one is for the commemoration of, and prayer for, the departed members of the family. The Orthodox firmly believe that death, in Christ, does not separate the family and that prayer continues across the divide. The offering of the Eucharist for the departed is a constant act of loving memory in Orthodox practice. The celebrating priest will also take votive offerings of small loaves from some of the faithful who have prepared them.[6] Then from the loaves he is making ready for the Eucharist he will set some fragments aside on the paten (*diskos*), naming people both living and dead from lists of names that different families have given to him beforehand, to ask for special prayers. These fragments of bread are not consecrated but stand on the diskos during the Eucharist, and at the very end they are placed into the chalice once everyone has been communicated, with this prayer: "Wash away, O Lord, by your holy Blood, the sins of your servants here commemorated, through the prayers of the Theotokos and all your Saints. Amen." Christ's redemptive action, essentially the forgiveness of sin and its concomitant defeat of death, is felt by the Orthodox, from earliest ages, to be unrestricted by time or space. In this, it robustly contradicts the attitude of some of the Reformed traditions that maintain prayer for the dead to be either fruitless or impossible.

During divine service the Orthodox make many bows and sometimes prostrations before God if the Spirit moves them. The devout also make the sign of the cross over themselves every time they hear the phrase "Glory to the Father and to the Son and to the Holy Spirit." As this occurs many times in any service, an observer will often notice how many times the congregation members will cross themselves. Similarly, Orthodox attending other Christian services often are puzzled by how few times they see this done in other communities. Orthodox also seem to wander around the church a lot and tend to feel hemmed in by the sedentary nature of many Western churches, and by the way they seem to expect everyone to make a response at the same time throughout the liturgy. Among the Orthodox, some of the time they make a response, at other times they are off in their own prayers and disconnect with a sense of personal freedom. They are safe in the knowledge that all the official responses necessary will be performed by the choir, which sings them all at the appropriate time. There are (traditionally) no pews in an Orthodox church, and often very few chairs set at the walls for the convenience of the old and the infirm. The expectation used to be that Orthodox believers would stand to pray, as they did in ancient times. Kneeling on Sundays was forbidden by the Council of Nicaea in 325, as it is a sign of penitence for sin: acceptable on the other days of the week but deemed inappropriate for those who are sharing in the glory of the Passion and Resurrection of Christ in the Sunday Eucharist, which ought, therefore, to be clearly a glorious and radiant affair. The lack of chairs makes it possible for the faithful to move around the church during services: sometimes lighting prayer candles for others or themselves; sometimes moving to stand before particular icons to talk to the saints or to Christ or the Virgin privately; sometimes attending closely to what is happening among the clergy on the altar.

At several times the liturgy turns to specific litanies of prayer and intercession. These are always led by a deacon if one is present or by the priest if he serves alone. The deacon will come out from the altar and stand facing the Christ Icon on the iconostasis. From there he will intone the petitions of prayer and lead the faithful in the response: "Lord have mercy." In Greek this is *Kyrie Eleison*. It is one of the surviving Greek remnants of the liturgy of the Latin Church too. In Slavonic it is *Gospodi Pomilui*. In recent times some of the Greek Orthodox churches in the diaspora have introduced pews, but none of the Russian have. It is felt that while having pews may offer more comfort, it reduces the congregation more to a passive condition of recipients of the worship experience instead of being active participants. It is not the sole responsibility of the clergy to offer the Eucharist, therefore, but rather a wave of prayerful attendance on the Divine Presence that falls to each member of the church in the varying degrees of their roles, and the measure of their spiritual participation and awareness.

Even the smallest child contributes substantively; and it is touching to see Orthodox mothers and grandmothers bring in babies to church and take the children up to the icons, where they will lean out to kiss the hand of Christ or the Virgin and be entranced when the parent lights a candle that the child has been shown how to set in place. There is much truth in the adage "The things you love as a child you will love all your life long." And it is a focus of many Orthodox parents to take the children to church and show them the bright array of candles, icons, painted crosses, and other beautiful frescoes, explaining to them the intricate symbolism of the church's meanings. Orthodox children, who may also take advantage of the free floor space in the church to do their own fair share of wandering, grow up in the church in a way that makes it feel their own in a special way, deeply associated with the quest for beauty and peace in their lives. Most Orthodox families have the special icon corner in one room of their house, and so churchly prayer is also connected with personal familial prayer; the home icon shelf usually has a candle placed on it (or a lampada that can be lit) and very often a small incense burner. Devotions of prayer at home are accompanied by many of the same gestures and practices as at church: and so the children learn, from a very early age, a whole syntax of prayer that remains available to them all their lives long.

From the time of their baptism also, children are given Communion as full members of the church. Infants in arms will receive the holy gifts as a reminder to all that the presence of Christ is not restricted solely to those who are conscious of receiving but is gifted generously to all in his church. The Orthodox do not believe the holy gifts become the body of Christ by virtue of the belief of the individual but rather that they cause the belief of the individual by virtue of being the body of Christ. And this is why regular Communion is fostered as an ideal to be pursued by all the faithful of whatever age. In the Orthodox Church, the Eucharist is called "the Medicine of Immortality" and is regarded as a necessity in one's life: like antibiotics for the seriously sick, an indispensable thing for health.[7] To live a Christian life is impossible without the strength, sanctification, and Spirit's grace conveyed to the believer in the Holy Eucharist. To prepare themselves to receive this, the Orthodox attending church will have fasted from midnight the day before: so that the holy gifts will be the first food they have touched that Sunday. As soon as they have communicated they go to the side of the church and together take some more blessed bread and wine to break their fast. To look at them then, the signs of peace and joy of heart are most notable. Only the baptized and chrismated Orthodox are able to approach the chalice for the holy gifts (Communion), but visitors are always welcome to line up with the faithful and simply ask the celebrating priest for a blessing. He will often bless the person with the chalice itself. Not all the Orthodox go to Communion every week. It is a personal matter, and it involves the preparation of prayer and fasting beforehand.

Personal confession is not very prevalent in the Orthodox churches of the Greek tradition nowadays. It is often reserved for times of personal need (such as sickness) or family trouble. Confession is a much more regular part of Slavonic tradition Orthodoxy. A priest (if there is more than one priest on staff) will stand somewhere in the main body of the church while the early part of the divine liturgy is taking place. In front of him will be a high reading stand with the book of Gospels placed upon it and also a cross. The faithful will come up to him, usually a priest they know well and whom they trust as a wise guide, and after making the sign of the cross, and saying a few short prayers, make a short confession of sins before him. They do not confess to the priest; they confess to Christ, before the Gospel book, which is the iconic symbol of his living presence in that place. It is Christ who hears the confession of sins, and Christ himself who makes this a sacrament of living grace. When the confession has been made, the priest may offer some advice, or else will give some individual words of spiritual comfort and encouragement. The Orthodox believer then kneels down at his side, and the priest lays over his or her head his *epitrachelion* (the priestly stole he wears around his neck as a symbol of his spiritual office). He then lays hands upon the person's head, in one of the most ancient Christian gestures of the bestowal of the Spirit, and says a short prayer of absolution. In the Slavonic tradition it is this: "May our Lord and God, Jesus Christ, through the grace and compassion of his love for mankind, forgive you—(Name)—all your transgressions. And I, an unworthy priest, through the power given to me by Him, do forgive and absolve you from all your sins + [sign of the cross] In the name of the Father, and of the Son, and of the Holy Spirit. Amen."

If visitors happen to be present for an Orthodox baptism, they might be surprised to see how much older the babies sometimes are, compared to those baptised in Western practice. They would also note how the child (or adult convert) will be fully immersed in the water three times. The priest placing the child under the water each time says: "The Servant of God [Name] is baptized in the name of the Father [first immersion] and of the Son [second immersion], and of the Holy Spirit [third immersion]."[8] For the Orthodox, the baptismal service is composed of four indispensable parts. The first section, at the very beginning, is the renunciation of Satan and the exorcism prayers dating from very ancient times, and these culminate in the requirement of the candidate to profess the faith of the church.[9] This is essentially the recitation of the Nicene Creed. Of course, if it is a very young child being baptized the parents and godparents stand in for it here. The second part of baptism is the blessing of the oil and baptismal water in a great prayer celebrating God's power over all creation, and then the anointing of the person with the "oil of gladness," known in the West as the oil of catechumens. In ancient times oil was rubbed into the skin and scraped off with a blunt blade (a *strigillum*). This was the equivalent of our modern use of soap and water to wash. So at this stage of the catechumen's initiation (for Orthodoxy also calls baptism *photismos*, or illumination), the symbolic anointing talks of cleansing and athletic preparation to take up the duties and obligations of a Christian way of living. Again, in ancient times, athletes oiled themselves before engaging in their efforts. The third aspect of Orthodox baptism then follows, which is the immersion under the baptismal waters. This is given its symbolic explanation in the theology of the apostle Paul (Rom. 6.3–5), who connects the sign of going down under water as an initiation into the death of Christ, and the emergence as a mystical form of entrance into the Resurrection of Christ. For the Orthodox Church this cleansing of the baptismal waters forgives all past sins and strengthens the believer to follow the way of Christianity.

But the fourth and final part of baptism is equally integral; and that is the anointing of the newly baptized person with the sacred perfumed oil of *Chrisma:* on the parts of the body symbolizing the five senses. For the Orthodox, this is the moment when the baptized person is consecrated as prophet, priest, and king. The Spirit of God makes its dwelling in the newly cleansed soul. For the Orthodox there is great perplexity about the manner in which for many parts of the Western churches this fundamental and climactic part of the baptismal ceremony has fallen out of use. Converts from other Christian churches who wish to be received into Orthodoxy, if they have already been baptized with water in the threefold Trinitarian name of God, are not rebaptized therefore, but they are always chrismated before they are given the final sacrament that initiates believers into Christianity: namely, the Holy Eucharist. If there is any doubt over the earlier baptism (whether it was done in the name of the Trinity, or whether there were no immersions or at least water running over the child), the Orthodox will err on the safe side and perform an entire baptismal ceremony de novo. This is not necessary when it concerns a prior Roman Catholic or Anglican/Episcopal ritual baptism.

One of the reactions commonly felt when one visits an Orthodox church when services are in full swing is how ceremonial they are. Even in the smallest church nothing is ever simply said, all is sung or chanted, often in several voices. There are no instruments, because only the human voice (as Saint Basil said, "that instrument made by God himself") is allowed by custom in the church. The ceremonial reflects its origins in Byzantium and is meant to give a sense of something of the glory of the imperial court: acknowledging Christ as the King of Kings surrounded by his court of saints and angels. But at other times, outside a formal liturgy, the experience of an Orthodox church is quite different from this. For example, come to a Vespers service on a typical Saturday or weekday night, and one will be struck by how quiet and humble everything is. The church will be in shadows, lit by flickering lamps. The clergy will not be in gorgeous colored vestments of brocade but will be in somber black cassocks and simple stoles. The choir will recite many psalms and biblical canticles—for the services of prayer in Orthodoxy are root and branch built out of the scriptures. On Sundays there is no reading from the Old Testament given in the course of the Eucharist, but at Vespers on the preceding evening the dominant tone is set by the Old Testament readings and by the psalms. The choir performing all the responses is in the shadows, with flickering candles, while the priest stands mainly in the altar reciting prayers and blessings quietly, and offering up incense to God from the holy table, all allowing the Orthodox believer to enter into a state of intensely personal prayer and meditation. One can join in with as much of the simply chanted service as one wants or one can disengage for personal prayer, exactly as the Spirit moves. The evening services of Vespers are very different from the public, ceremonial, and illuminated liturgies—as different as their ancient origins: the one in the great imperial cathedrals of the past, the other in the small monastic chapels, designed by monks and nuns who set out to pray throughout the hours of darkness. In the modern age Vespers no longer lasts all night long; simply an hour or less. But in times long past it was designed to last through all the hours of darkness and join up seamlessly with Morning Prayer (*Orthros*) that preceded the Eucharist, which itself was begun only as the sun rose over the horizon in the east.

Many people's only experience of Orthodox worship, perhaps, is attending a wedding: a boisterous and joyful experience, culminating in the couple being garlanded with crowns. In the Russian tradition metallic royal crowns are actually used. In the Greek tradition a circlet of orange blossoms is used (symbolic of unfading freshness). The crowning ceremony was the ancient marriage ritual of the pre-Christian Roman Empire. The church took it over and gave it a new symbolic twist: now the couple are not only king and queen of love in their own household but are—by their communion together—anticipating the joy of Christ's coming Kingdom. The priest leads the Orthodox wedding couple three times in a procession around a table which has the book of Gospels and a cross laid upon it. This is the ancient manner of making a vow. It replaces the Western practice of having the bride and groom make a statement of intent.

If a visitor ever attends the Orthodox Easter services (called *Pascha* in the Orthodox Church) he or she will be overwhelmed: not only by the length of the celebration (up to three hours in a parish) but by the variety of the experience. It begins in darkness, and the winding sheet of Christ (the shroud) is lifted up and dramatically carried into the dark altar from a "tomb of Christ" that has been prepared in the middle of the church. Then a moment of complete silence descends. The church is cleared of the tomb. Candles are held by everyone, but unlit. At midnight, in the completely darkened church, a single candlelight is seen flickering in the altar. It is brought by the priest and held up high at the royal doors of the iconostasis so that everyone can see. It goes without saying that this is the vibrant symbol of Christ Risen from the Dead. The priest chants three times: "Come and Receive the Light, from the Unfading Light. And glorify Christ who has risen from the dead!" And each time the priest offers the light, and all the faithful run forward to light their candles from the single light of Christ. So the Resurrection glory spreads like fire throughout all the church. Everyone then falls into line and makes a nighttime outside procession with the candles, with incense, the Gospel book, and many icons; all the while everyone chants: "Your Resurrection O Christ our Savior, the angels in heaven sing; enable us on earth to worship you in purity of heart." Some run off during the procession to bring the "New Light" to their homes and set everything in order for the great paschal feast, which Orthodox have after the service.

Most, however, continue back inside the church, but this time when they enter all the lights have been turned on, and as they come back inside a great and solemn chant is made (the Paschal Canon) celebrating Christ's glorious victory over death and sin and corruption. Many times this is interrupted by the priest or bishop coming to the royal doors with lighted candles and incense, to incense the people as a sign of honor. He shouts out each time: Christ is Risen! (or *Christos Anesti* in Greek, *Hristos Voskresie* in Russian, *Hristos Ha Inviat* in Romanian— whatever language group is represented in the congregation), and every voice in the congregation shouts back: "He is truly Risen." All the time from Pascha to Pentecost, fifty days later, the Orthodox greet one another only with this same greeting. The Canon of the Resurrection is a mix of solemnity and festive enthusiasm. It marks the end of quite a long and severe Lenten time of fasting, and as it comes to an end, the First Eucharist of Pascha begins, culminating in almost all present in the church taking Communion. Afterward, typically, there is a paschal feast together in the parish hall.

What Role for Orthodoxy in a Postmodern Environment?

MOST people, if they think anything at all of the Orthodox Church (for it has rightly been called one of the world's great secrets and is still profoundly unknown as far as the rest of Christianity is concerned), tend to see it as a church stuck in the past. This dismissive attitude belies the fact that Orthodox Church members today number somewhere around the 250 million mark; but Orthodoxy lies outside the common experience of the vast majority of Western (Roman Catholic, Episcopal, and Protestant) believers and Western church history. The fall of Byzantium to Islamic power in the fifteenth century and the great rise of the papal monarchy after the high Middle Ages led to an understandable tendency to write out Orthodoxy from the foundational story, to dismiss the church as having lapsed into schism precisely because it refused to acknowledge those universal jurisdictional rights attributed to the pope that had become such a constitutive part of early medieval Latin Church identity. In the years after the Reformation, the Reformed churches had little desire to include Orthodoxy in their versions of church history because, although they too resisted papal centralism, they found whatever they encountered of Eastern Orthodoxy far too Catholic for their liking. Both Roman Catholic and Protestant versions of church history, therefore, even to this day, tell the story often without a nod to the Eastern Church. It has become something of an obsession of mine to write (in pencil of course) on the flyleaf of yet another church history book that thinks everything took place in Western Europe, the words "of the West" after the word "history" in the title. I was more than delighted when IVP Academic, the internationally strong evangelical publishers, commissioned me a few years back to write a universal history of the first millennial Christian Church, in which I could address this long-standing unbalance.[1]

Today it is no longer (ought not to be anyway) a case of internal apologetic fights among Christians as to who is the oldest, most authentic, or original, form of Christianity. Even though this topic is alive and well on internet blog forums, the quality of the discussion generally testifies to the sterility of the apologetic approach. That robust agnostic Voltaire does well to remind the Christian Church in this twenty-first century what is really necessary. When the hopelessly abstract philosopher Pangloss starts vapidly pontificating once again, after the series of disasters that constitute the plot of the comedy *Candide*, the young protagonist now silences him with the words that show his command of the situation: "Il faut cultiver le jardin"—we must dig the garden. This is the soil that remains to us. It is here and now. If we do not do so we shall lament the lack of harvest in winter times approaching.

This is my own estimate of Christianity's position today. It is alive and well in many parts of the world. It is growing more today than ever before in history. But equally in many parts of the world, and Western Europe in particular springs to mind, it is languishing in a high tide of secularist materialism. It has seemed to lose its spark: its spiritual lights are dimmed, and its leaders often seem tired and bureaucratic rather than fiery and prophetic. This is a day when collectively Christianity needs to "cultiver le jardin" as never before: and that means to tell its story afresh, with passion, from lived experience not hearsay, with the courage to face dispossession and an impoverished condition, instead of sheltering in the pomp of past glories. In short, with a spirit of mission rather than maintenance. In the Eastern Church territories such as Russia and Romania, Serbia and Bulgaria, the Orthodox Church is heavily engaged trying to restore the fabrics (church buildings and institutions) and syntax of Christian life (the fundamental logic and vitality of the core message of the religion) in societies that have violently tried to suppress them for generations past. The Orthodox have their work cut out for them.

In the West, however, the task is somewhat different. The great fragmentation of the Christian Church that has taken place here in the past four centuries has led to the elevation of intra-Christian apologetics as the predominant religious discourse. Being an arid conversation at the best of times, this modality has in its prolongation withered the place of religious discourse in the public forum and has allowed it to sterilize religious thought within the churches. I myself was baptized as a five-day-old baby. In that sense I am now in my seventh decade as a Christian. I don't think I have once, in all that time, heard a sermon delivered at a public worship event on the subject of deepening the practice of personal prayer. It began to puzzle me in my late teens and has gone on to disturb me throughout my later career as both professor and priest. The renowned Russian book *The Way of the Pilgrim* features as its protagonist a Russian peasant who laments the fact that there is no one to teach him how to pray. I find the plea remains indicative of the state of the need: a pressing and powerful need to fill the void in men and women's souls that materialist reductionism has brought them to.

Today, in many parts of the very wealthy and comfortable West, there is such a profound loss of spiritual consciousness that the very semantics of the Spirit are unknown. When people came asking him for spiritual advice, Archimandrite Cleopa used to ask them back: What prayers do you know by heart? What hymns from the writings of scripture or the fathers are you able to sing by heart? What habitual words do you use when you invoke the presence or the guidance of God in your lives? Often his visitors were hoping he might give them some weird and exotic "mystical" inner knowledge. But this is where he started. Il faut cultiver le jardin.

This is where a knowledge of Orthodoxy can serve to help Christianity in general today. It can make known to the Christian religion its own mystical tradition. It is one that Protestants will recognize for its immediacy and simplicity, just as Roman Catholics will, because of its richly Christocentric warmth. Both forms of divided ecclesial consciousness in the West will be able to take as their own, truly as their own, the ancient heritage of Christian wisdom, the Spirit-filled teachings of the Eastern Christian past. Orthodoxy has kept this heritage alive, even to the present. Patristic thought is not merely a side stream of medieval dogma in the Eastern Church. The fathers are still read, and are called the niptic guides: soul guides that open up levels of divine consciousness. It is in the renewal of a new and deeper consciousness of Christ and his resurrectional presence among the faithful that all other renewal will flow out in the church: a renewal that will come in the fire and quality of the common liturgies, a renewal that will be powered and fueled in the social and charitable outreach of the churches. Only after this sense of living in Christ has been renewed internally will the mission of the church be rendered actively reenergized once more. It is of no attraction whatsoever for any believers to offer to someone else what does not seem to illuminate their own hearts and minds with the radiant quality of beauty and freedom. Too often, in lieu of this, the Christian public mission has been characterized by fearfulness, cultic sectarianism, intellectual immaturity, and social hyper-conservatism. Why should we be surprised if this clammy handshake does not work?

What can Orthodox Christian thought offer to the modern man and woman outside Christian culture, who would most probably find, looking in passing at an Orthodox service, something foreign and down at heel? Well, again that is difficult, and maybe it is through the other churches that the Orthodox treasures can be translated more effectively for the West. But Orthodox religious thought turns around the axis of personalism. All things flow from the overwhelming fact that the divine Power and Word and Fire became personally incarnated within time and space: and our God was shown to us as a humble, suffering servant of mercy. This has marked Orthodoxy from the beginning to the end; from top to bottom. It sets as the goal of all Orthodox spiritual life the

quest for the believer to become a human being—and the realization that in becoming a human being, in Christ, the believer becomes deified by the grace of the indwelling presence
of the Holy. The real problem today is not that men and
women who have become secularized (nonreligious, or whatever) have lost the sense of God. The problem is that they
have lost the sense of what it is to be truly human. The fundamental character of the true human being is the self-awareness
that presses on all people that they are a transcendent reality,
and as such, profoundly strange even to themselves.

Only in the presence of God can this enigma be worked
out. It does not affect any other species in the cosmos; only us.
This is why the other life-forms in the world cannot help us in
this quintessential matter. And if we do sense our peculiar
strangeness, then there are many ways we can address this fact
that we are, basically, not at home here. It is deeply disturbing
and can lead to so many forms of avoidance therapy that ultimately hurt us and our method of living. In Orthodoxy, one
learns from generations of wise and saintly teachers the
knowledge that humility and love have been lifted up to divine
status in Christ. This saves us: for our transcendence is rooted
in the stability that our poverty has been made rich by God's
love. The individual who serves to be the place of the indwelling of Christ, through his Spirit, is a person who can stand on
the revolving planet without feeling dizzy: knowing why his
place is both here and yet not here; and why it is true that we
must cultiver le jardin; but not just the garden of our present
culture and life, also the garden of our soul. Orthodoxy has
had to learn the hard way that Christian religion is all about
humility and love, and that daily discipleship is nothing other
than walking that path with a hand always ready to reach out

to help another, precisely because we have the confidence that God will never allow us to be toppled out of balance because of the love we demonstrate.

For its own part, because the Orthodox world contains such great treasures, it must learn to offer them generously: freely and without chauvinism, without any strident apologetics of its own. The purpose of "giving freely" is not to further stock one's own coffers, so to speak, but to proclaim the living word that has been entrusted to it for the sake of sharing it, as in Matthew.[2] Orthodoxy will probably remain, for many years ahead, a minority and somewhat poor church in Western countries; but it is a church that is spiritually and intellectually rich behind the outward vesture of its poverty. If it can offer its gifts with humility they might become acceptable; and if received they have the potential to renew the Western churches profoundly and even, perhaps, lead them in this postmodern religious wilderness to a new stage of reconstituting Christianity in the West. It is an era where the damage of the Reformation divisions calls out to be healed, and perhaps a discussion can be initiated that is confident of not losing any of the deep wisdom of both sides of that old argument. The friend of Elisabeth Behr-Sigel, the humble Orthodox priest and ascetic Father Lev Gillet, spent his entire life praying for the restoration of church unity in the West because he knew that this was a prelude to the profoundest level of spiritual renewal in the churches, and that in turn would precede a great renewal of evangelical fervor. He prophetically envisaged the mediating role of Orthodoxy in this regard, not because of its great importance in anybody's eyes, but precisely because it was rather shabby and insignificant. And yet, what it could bring to the room was a certain fire that, once felt, personally experienced, and known, would undoubtedly be recognized by all believers. His words will sum up and end this essay that started out with "The Naming of Parts" and has gone on to cover two thousand years of history. He speaks here essentially of humility and love and prayer, but this was the definition of the Orthodox Church that he left us:

> O strange Orthodox Church, so poor and weak, with neither the organization nor the culture of the West, staying afloat as if by a miracle in the face of so many trials, tribulations and struggles; a Church of contrasts, both so traditional and so free, so archaic and so alive, so ritualist and so personally involved; a Church where the priceless pearl of the Gospel is assiduously preserved, sometimes under a layer of dust; a Church which in shadows and silence maintains above all the eternal values of purity, poverty, asceticism, humility and forgiveness; a Church which has often not known how to act, but which can sing of the joy of Pascha like no other.[3]

Archpriest John Anthony McGuckin
Pascha, 2019

Appendix: A Brief Commentary on the Nicene Creed (A.D. 325)

I promised earlier in the main body of the text that I would offer this longer and more focused excursus on the text and meaning of the Nicene Creed at the end. I suppose there could have been a host of other appendixes—if time and space had allowed—but this one is of preeminent importance in the matter of defining what Orthodox Christian faith is. And why? I suppose one would by now, having read the whole story, be able to conclude that Orthodoxy is the Christian faith as set out in its lineaments by the scriptures and the early authoritative writer-theologians who are called the fathers of the church. And that is true so far as it goes. But to explain that in detail and in slow motion, as it were, would have made this book a much heavier theological tome than it should have been; and the book was meant, from the outset, not to be predominantly theological in character—but rather to allow the history to make the theological underpinnings clear, according to the principles sketched out in the opening chapters, where the relation of history to theology was discussed in greater detail (how the church sees its passage through time as "salvation history").

Even so, this creed, issued in one of the most critical moments of the church, the Arian controversy, was published at the Council of Nicaea in 325 and was meant to stand as a quintessential statement of what catholic, apostolic, orthodox Christianity amounts to. It has stood the test of time as, perhaps, the sharpest and clearest summation of exactly what the Orthodox faith states. Adding to it here, along with a few commentary remarks, may allow it to be more clearly seen that for Eastern Orthodoxy, Christian faith is not expressed by scripture to which patristic theology is then added on; rather, patristic theology (the writings of the fathers and bishops assembled at the Ecumenical Councils) is itself inseparable from the scriptures, since it was from the outset meant to be nothing more than a commentary upon them. Every statement in this creed (including the one reference to Homoousion, which has often been said to be nonscriptural but isn't) is quite clearly either a paraphrastic digest of evangelical scripture, an allusion to a verse, or a direct quotation from one. The Orthodox, like the Roman Catholics and Episcopalians, have recited this creed for centuries past at every Sunday Eucharist to give voice to that sense of catholic identity. Its cardinal nature as a summation of the apostolic Orthodox faith explains why it is added here. The original text as used here can be found in Tanner, *Decrees of the Ecumenical Councils*, volume 1.

1. The Synod at Nikaia set forth this creed.
The functional purpose and motive of the whole enterprise—the Economy (Oikonomia) of salvation. Ancient thought turns largely on the distinction between *Theologia* and *Oikonomia*. The creed can fruitfully be charted in the way its premises begin from theologia—speaking about the ineffable mystery of God—and explain what that paradox might mean by its epiphany in oikonomia (God as revealed and spoken of within human limited history, thought, and language). Creation thus becomes the foundational pattern for theology; and soteriology (the understanding of what salvation means) becomes the foundational pattern (type) for Christology. In this way the creed deliberately sets out to restate basic scriptural principles of theology (revealed doctrine of God) in a Greek propositional style for the wider Gentile world that has been educated in a Hellenistic (syllogistic) culture.

2. This is the *Ekthesis* (formal statement) of the Synod at Nikaia. This, above, is the Proem of the Acts of the Council of Chalcedon, 451, which cites the creed of 325 as its chief authority after scripture.

3. We believe in (*pistevomen*) One God
What we render as "believe in" is more accurately contextualized in its New Testament usage as: have trust in; rely on; or make our stand by. It alerts us to the most probable use of this whole creedal text (at least in its embryonic stage) as a baptismal creed. But the creedal elements seem to belong only to lines 3–6, 15, 17–19, 21–23, and perhaps 24. For the remaining lines, we can note the extent of the dittography of asseverance (saying things twice for emphasis), which is probably a result of the ethos of crisis attending the council of 325. So altogether we should note three timeline elements in this creed: a second-century confessional (baptismal) prayer derived from the scriptures; a third-century reassertion using the baptismal confession as a statement probably against the Gnostics (see especially the opening verses about the Father's relation to his creation); and lastly a fourth-century conciliar reuse of the creed as a traditionalist statement in face of perceived heretical innovations of the school of Lucian in Antioch, the theological teacher of Arius of Alexandria who had sparked the controversy that immediately occasioned the Council of Nicaea.

4. The Father, All-Powerful Master (Pantokrator),
The Father-God is identified as the Lord of all power: that is, in charge of what happens on this earth—not just a random victim of other forces of chaos and evil. The line is a condensed restatement of the New Testament doctrine of the Kingdom, as seen, for example, in Ephesians 1.11. It refutes the Gnostic doctrines that suggested a good god was constantly struggling for supremacy in this world order with numerous other evil gods, or numinous forces (such as the Demiurge).

5. The Maker of things that are visible and invisible;
This is now the third restatement, in a short space of time, of the same basic point: namely, a triple denial of the fundamental Gnostic belief system that a good god could not possibly have made this visible world. The conciliar fathers state the biblical theology that God is Father of a good creation and thus Lord of all angelic powers as well as mortals (cf. Eph. 1.4–5 and 20–23; Phil. 2.9–11; and Col. 1.15–20). The evil powers (*daimones*) are under his sway, as are the good spiritual forces. The Kingdom of God, as described throughout the

New Testament, involves a certain unfinished warfare for the ascendancy of the good on earth (and in heaven), but God the Father is shepherding the good to an ultimate victory. These expressions, here based on the late Pauline creeds in the Pastoral Letters, are the late first- and early second-century embryos for what we see developed as the Nicene substrate for the creed's doctrine of Christ's salvific power.

The relation of how the Savior (who is sequentially identified from New Testament authorities via his titles as Ikon/Lord/Christ/Beloved/Exalted One/Beginning/Firstborn) stands in reference to the angelic powers is a crucial aspect of the conception of the victory of God over cosmic powers. In short, the intellectual movement from angelology to the conception of the Son's unique relation to the Father was central to the patristic answer to Gnostic subordinationist theology and was seen as crucial to the necessary restatement of New Testament Kingdom theology in the Greek world of the next generation after the apostles. This very ancient, structured apologetic is what Nicaea retains here, and reasserts, as its doctrinal substrate. One can see the importance of the Christological titles used here in the biblical texts underlying the creed both at this point and in what follows throughout. The creedal rhythm of the move from title to title is very illustrative.

6. And in One Lord Jesus Christ,
This restates the quintessence of New Testament confession about the person of Jesus (cf. Mt. 23.10; Jn. 10.30; Rom. 5.17–21; Rom. 10. 8–13; 1 Cor. 8.6). As Paul taught, "No one can confess Jesus as Lord (*Kyrios*) except in the Holy Spirit" (1 Cor. 12.3).

7. The Only Begotten (*Monogene*) Son of God,
This Christological affirmation is logically extrapolated from the naming of God as Father. The One God is entitled Father and then Maker-Lord. Jesus Christ is first entitled Lord and then Son, and thus the twin titles reflect those of the Father chiasmically—a Greek literary device that pairs statements as in a mirror. The titles begin to accumulate in the following lines to a total of six: Son, Lord, Christ, Only Begotten, God, Light. Two of these are repeated twice (God, Son), and then the sonship image is used as an explication of the divine status in what are evidently fourth-century philosophical

glosses (begotten of the being, born not created, a status of co-being with the Father). The title list, therefore, shows how the argument turns on the notion of what the term Son of God actually and precisely means. Does it mean that Jesus is just a heavenly power (in the way the Old Testament used the concept) or does it mean that he is God? This section of the creed is a careful and closely argued exegesis of scripture defending and confessing the divinity of the Son: he is Lord, not simply servant. He is God, but not the Father. Divine, and not a creature.

8. Begotten of the Father,
This phrase now prioritizes the Fourth Gospel's theology of the Only Begotten Son (*Monogenes*) following the Alexandrian Church's tradition (first seen in the *Commentary on John* by Origen and taken up by most of the archbishops of his native church after his time) of allowing Johannine Christology to be the main interpretive lens of the rest of the New Testament teachings on Jesus.

9. That is, of the being (*Ousia*) of the Father
The phrase "the being—from God" (*ek tes ousias*) was not generally received as the same teaching (at least at this period) as the "sameness or identity of being, as God" (*tautotes ousias*)—which Athanasius of Alexandria would later argue for as the intended meaning of Nicaea and as a better elucidation of the truth than the mere word "homoousion" ("selfsame being as"). The phrase is inserted here by the council fathers as a powerful supplementary commentary (or elucidation) of line 8, and as such is a supportive biblical exegesis. It is, therefore, not really correct to describe the homoousion of line 14, as has often been repeated, as the first nonbiblical term ever to enter Christian confession. Homoousion is certainly a philosophically precise keyword but is used by the bishops, even when this insertion was insisted upon by the Constantinian court, in the traditional mode of biblical exegesis. As to the meaning of the "Out of the being of the Father" (*ek tes ousias*) in situ: is it to be sought in philosophy or scripture? Does it mean identity of essence? Or insist on the real connotation of the image of divine paternity and sonship? This is a major issue of interpretation and the key to understanding the entire Arian controversy of the fourth century. There is no doubt, however, that the council fathers meant this line to insist

on the reality of the divine sonship, as against Arius's nominal or honorific interpretation of the subordinate sonship. There is also no doubt that they already intended line 14 to be the correct elucidation of the scripturally rooted lines 8 and 9. This is seen in the manner in which lines 10 through 13 serve as a crescendo of statements as to the divine stature of the Word of God, leading on directly, after line 15, to the Word's salvific role in creation and the restoration of that damaged creation (the Redemption worked within history by means of the Incarnation).

10. God from God,

This dramatically and succinctly restates the Johannine teaching of the divine Word (Jn. 1) who comes "from God" (Jn. 6.46; 7.17; 8.42; 13.3; 16.30).

11. Light from Light,

The line that follows 11 is meant as an explication of it, particularly how this doctrine does not imply there must be two gods. Light emits from Light and is not separate, nor different, from it: but one and the same energy. The analogy of light from light, or the Sun and its radiance, had been in use from the New Testament modeling of the idea in John's Gospel, right through the second- and third-century theologians, as one of the oldest images explaining the trinitarian relationships (cf. Jn. 1.9; 8.12; 9.5; 12.36; 12.46; 1 Jn.1.5; Rev.22.5). It had become a standard trope already for the second-century theologians.

12. True God from True God,

Yet again the conciliar fathers are making clear, in the third of this triplet of restatements about the manner in which the Word issues from the Father's begetting, that the relation of Son to Father is not as an independent deity in the style of the pagan lesser gods subordinate to the higher gods: gods from God. Rather, the bishops insist that the deity of the Father himself is in the Son: not any other deity. Thus there are not two Gods. The deity of the Son is within that of the Father who begets him. It is the Son's *hypostasis* (or personal instantiation), which is distinct from the Father, not his essence, since that is the selfsame being of the Father, and it is thus divine, exactly as the Father's is, since it is one and the same.

13. Begotten (*gennethenta*) not made (*poiethenta*),
The conciliar fathers return time and again, by obvious preference, to the concept of the Son and his relation to the Father, rather than to the Logos theology preferred by the third-century theologians. The two systems (Son language and Logos language) will soon merge synonymously, but the creed prefers the wider New Testament sense of sonship and applies to it the metaphysical terms elaborated by the Logos theologians: thus synthesizing for all later Christian ages the Johannine and Pauline Christologies of the New Testament. The phrase here directly attacks Arius's Christology, which taught that the Word of God was the first creature of the Father and that "there was a time when he was not." It thus makes a profound distinction between begetting and creating, which Arian thought had rendered synonymous. It also reserves the concept of the Father's begetting as a special revelation: the Son of God is Son in a different way to the manner in which his disciples and believers become sons by adoption. He is the "natural" son: his begetting is a scriptural way of connoting his essential relationship (in terms of being and nature) with God the Father.

14. The same in being (*homoousios*) as the Father;
Athanasius the Great, the staunchest defender of the Nicene Creed, would later press for a clarification of this famous phrase, to which many objected: not only the Arians but also those whom Athanasius regarded as friends of the faith. He would press for the meaning of this, as the Son has the selfsame essence as the Father (or the Son is uniquely gifted the Father's being from the Father himself, as Gregory the Theologian would later explicate it). So eventually, Athanasius came to prefer the phrase "identity of essence" (*tautotes tes ousias*) rather than the homoousion; even so he found the homoousion to be an invaluable term as a single, simple, summation of all that Nicene Orthodoxy stood for: the profession of the full divinity of the Son of God. As in Athanasius's day this single word served as a rock against which all attempts to subordinate the Son to the status of a servant messenger foundered and sank. It is to this day the catchword of Orthodoxy and the flagpole around which the faith of Nicaea flies as a standard.

15. And through him all things came to be (*egeneto*),
The statements revert, after this introduction of homoousion to more explicit restatements of New Testament Christology (see 1 Cor. 8.6; also Jn. 1.2; Col. 1.15).

16. Things in Heaven, and things on earth.
The line clarifies and parallels the line above it, now referring to the Son-Word's role in restoring creation. Accordingly, it explains the person of the Son in a parallel way to how it spoke about the Father-Creator beginning in lines 4 and 5. The Oneness of the Father-God, who is the Creator of all things, embraces the divine Son, who serves as the agent of this God's creation: the relationship being as much one as that of will and act. These lines suggest that the economy of the Son mirrors that of the Father, since the Son is the exact mirror (*ikon*, or image) of the Father. The overall concept is dependent on the hymn to Christ's work restoring the Creation in Colossians 1.15–16.

17. For us humans (*anthropous*) and for the sake of our salvation (*soterian*)
The creed now turns from the metaphysical, timeless, relations of God the Son-Word and the Father, to the role the Son played within time and space: that is, within the historic order subsequent to his incarnation as man. This sets the metaphysical Christology within its proper New Testament context: explicating salvation brought by Christ—the Economy of Salvation (*Oikonomia tes soterias*). As I have noted, almost all ancient Christian thought turns on the distinction between Theologia and Oikonomia. The first is the divine mystery, timeless and transcendent, and not open to human speculation: how God is in Himself. The second is how God reveals himself and his acts in history and through material forms: how God appears to us. The creed can clearly be seen to begin its statements from theologia and then go on from here to explain that ineffable mystery by its articulated and visible epiphany in the oikonomia of Christ's acts of salvation. Creation thus becomes the foundational pattern for theology. Soteriology becomes the foundational pattern (type) for Christology. In this way the creed exemplifies basic scriptural principles of theology (revealed doctrine of God).

18. He came down (*katelthonta*)
The verb "coming down" reflects the biblical doctrine of the *synkatabasis* of God to Israel—his stooping down in pity. It is a divine term

related to the act of compassionate salvation. The one who does this is thus given (in epiphany) as *Soter*, or Savior. This was the ultimate divine title for Hellenistic late antiquity, which here has been seamlessly translated into biblical terminology. Some, such as Harnack, have criticized this as the regrettable Hellenization of Christianity, but the Orthodox theologian Father Georges Florovsky memorably corrected him when he described it instead as the Christianization of Hellenism. In this way the church adopted the language of incarnation while carefully avoiding the many Hellenistic parallels of the stories of the enfleshed gods or the "divine men" that were common currency at the time. Christian incarnational theology has never shared that pagan imagined world of the avatar but has always been guided by the New Testament language about the humility of the Son of God, who, although he was Lord by nature, assumed the lowly status of a slave to serve and redeem humanity, through the Cross. Once again the creed reuses the New Testament terms in its theology (cf. Jn. 3.13; Jn. 6.51; Eph. 4.10).

19. And was incarnate (*sarkothenta*),

The conciliar fathers describe the act of redemption as proceeding from the descent of the Word, his merciful stooping down to earth, in the two lines that follow, using two distinct but related images. The first, here, is incarnation, or "putting on flesh." This follows the scriptural lead of John 1.4, 1 John 4.2, 1 Timothy 3.16, and 1 Peter 4.1. But in the early decades of the fourth century, immediately preceding the Arian dispute, some theologians had stressed an archaic view to rebuff Arius, arguing that Jesus's flesh was only a nominal reality; because they felt that if Christ had fully entered into human life, he would have compromised the transcendence of the Trinity. To rebuke this development the Fathers offer the next line as a qualifier of what the term incarnation means for the Church.

20. Being made man (*enanthropesanta*),

The descent into history is not a mere appearance of enfleshment, or a temporary visitation like an avatar's, but a real entrance by the Transcendent Word into the human condition: not only becoming flesh but also becoming man, with all that involves: fear, weakness, tears, sweat, and ultimately death. This apparent weakness of the Word Incarnate was a stumbling block to many ancient thinkers. It was, in a certain sense, anathema both to Jewish and to Hellenistic ideas about God, and Christianity was swimming strongly against the tide of all theological thought here. Arius had found in the New Testament teaching of the Passion of Jesus the strongest of his arguments against the Lord's personal divinity: for him, surely God could not allow himself to suffer such things? The conciliar fathers, instead of trying to avoid that scandal, embrace the paradox. The weakness of Christ, his humility, his suffering, is, in fact, his glory. Like Paul (Gal. 6.14), the fathers make their boast in the Cross. Athanasius spent many years, following the council of Nicaea, arguing how the adoption of humanity by the divine Word was the essential act of the redemption: the master strategy, of which the various other acts (teaching, suffering, dying, rising) were but the various scenes. He summated that understanding in adapting a famous phrase of the second-century theologian Irenaeus of Lyons, when he said: "He (the Word) became Man, so that Man might become god" (Athanasius. *On the Incarnation*, 54.3). The incarnation of the Lord was intended to bring fallen humanity (now chained to death and corruption) into the divine life by the exchange of grace. This approach to salvation theology has been called "deification by grace" (*theiopoiesis kata charin*) and is very frequently found in later Orthodox thinkers.

21. He suffered, and on the third day he rose up (*anastanta*), Lines 21–24 and following are notably devoid of dittography or any form of scholiast commentary. They were evidently felt to be either unarguable or not at the controversial center of the debate. The creed here quietly but carefully insists that the same personal subject of the suffering (namely, the Christ in his Passion) is the one who has been governing all the previous sentences: in other words, that the selfsame Son of God has both a transcendent and an immanent life. The Incarnation, therefore, and all the acts of the Incarnate One are just as much divine actions as his eternal agency in making the world. The selfsame person is thus immortal and mortal; is Lord and servant; is God and man. The single "he" of the subject has united divinity and humanity in himself through the Incarnation, inaugurated for the sake of remaking the human race: and thus the Resurrection is the symbol of that renewal; not only of the life of Jesus but of the human race itself as well.

22. And he ascended (*anelthonta*) into heaven.
The scheme of this descent into humility and suffering and return, not just to life but to Lordly exaltation and heavenly glory (Jn. 3.13; Jn. 20.17; Lk. 24.51; Acts 1.9), adopts the structure of descent, humility, exaltation, and glory found in the deep Pauline hymn to the redemption (which is pre-Pauline insofar as Paul himself seems to quote it rather than write it) in Philippians 2.5–11.

23. Who is coming to judge (*krinai*) both the living and the dead.
The creed states the last act of the Redemption to be the Final Judgment (2 Cor. 5.10; Mt. 13.41; Mt. 16.27; Mt. 26.64).

24. And [we believe] in the Holy Spirit.
The creed, then, has three main sections: the first deals with the doctrine of the Father-Pantokrator (lines 3–5), then the doctrine of the Son of God and his redemptive work is expounded (lines 6–23), and then line 24 finishes up with the doctrine of the Holy Spirit. It is abundantly clear that the section on the Son of God and his salvation has expanded immensely in comparison to the other two statements about Father and Spirit. The Council(s) of Constantinople in 381–382 would further elaborate the clauses concerning the Holy Spirit, which were felt to be essential statements of the apostolic doctrine—just as the Nicene Creed here has elaborated Christological statements. Accordingly, the Constantinopolitan creed simply added a few phrases on to the earlier creed and did not consider that it had altered it: though it did explicate what belief in the Holy Spirit meant, in terms of the titles of the Holy Spirit taken from the scriptures (that he is the Lord and Life-Giver; that he proceeds from the Father; that he is worshipped and glorified [as God] along with the Father and the Son; and that [in the scriptures] he has spoken through the prophets). This sense of the Constantinopolitan fathers that they had not departed from the meaning of the Nicene Creed explains the peculiarity that when Christians today say they are reciting the Nicene Creed they actually recite the creed of 381–382, not that of 325. The very sharp economy of language we find here in the original Nicene Creed's reference to the Holy Spirit reflects a strong reluctance in the earliest ages of Christianity to speak at all of the work of the Holy Spirit. This doctrine (of the Spirit's divine work in the heart of a believer) was reserved by the ancient bishops

for the baptismal candidates only at the time of their baptism, and then they were told most strictly that this was something to be kept secret by them from the scrutiny of those not of the faith (*arcana sacra*). So, only part of the confession of faith was regarded as public, or usable in the preaching offered to potential converts. To this day most of what the church believes about the Holy Spirit is still outside the creedal medium and is found elsewhere in Christian tradition—such as in the liturgical texts or the spiritual doctrines of the saints. Nicaea is content with the barest of scriptural affirmations about the Spirit (cf. Mt. 28.19).

[THE NICENE ANATHEMATA — THE EXPLICIT
DENUNCIATIONS OF ARIAN THOUGHT]

25. Whosoever shall say that "there was a time when he [*The Son of God*] was not" (*en pote oti ouk en*);

26. And that "before he was begotten he was not" (*prin gennethenta ouk en*);

27. And that "he was made of things that once were not" (*ex ouk onton egeneto*);

28. Or that he is of a different hypostasis or essence (*heteras hypostaseos e ousias*);

29. Saying that the Son of God is either subject to change or alteration (*trepton e alloioton*);

30. Such people the Catholic and Apostolic Church anathematizes. Lines 25–30 isolate six main propositions of the Arian movement against which the creed has been erected as a counter-teaching (*dogma*). To make sure that there is no room for doubt, the major positions of Arian Christology are named and rejected explicitly—but they are not addressed directly in the creed, so as to make very clear the distinction between syllogisms of heretical thought and the confession of the apostolic tradition. The former can be stated but never confessed. The latter can only be confessed in prayer. The implication here is that these six Arian propositions contradict the core and patent sense of the church's confession, as stated in lines 6–23 of the creed. For a thing to be anathema meant (originally) that

it was so sacred it was untouchable. By the Christian period the word "anathema" had become a technical term for something excommunicate, or sacrilegious and worthy of expulsion from the elect body of believers. This is the first formal, international, Christian statement that deviance in belief can be, if sufficiently extensive on central matters, enough to separate dissidents from any claim to catholicity or apostolicity—ancient terms for universally recognized harmony with the apostolic (that is, the biblical) faith. This is why the Nicene Creed has become, and remains, the touchstone of Orthodoxy: the defining charter of the Orthodox Church and all those Christians who seek to live out the catholic (universal) apostolic tradition, to this day.

Notes

PRELUDE. THE NAMING OF PARTS

1. I always registered the same point of order when any faculty member complained of confused processes of government using the pejorative adjective "Byzantine." I habitually commented on how much more efficiently organized the Byzantine palace was than our modern universities.

2. Held between 325 and 787, when Latin Christianity and Byzantine Christianity were still one undivided tradition, to establish the main features of what ought to be held doctrinally by the catholic and apostolic church internationally.

3. The Orthodox happily acknowledge plurality of churches in the Orthodox communion (such as the Greek, Russian, Romanian, Serbian, and so on) in the singularity of being the Orthodox Church. Equally, all local Orthodox churches (a church family unit of the faithful under their central ruling bishop and his council of eucharistically presiding presbyters) share in the full identity of church at the local level and thus supply their communal identity as Universal Church. The local church is not a branch of a greater corporation in Orthodox theology, like a high-street branch of a national bank: it is the Universal Church in all its fullness and authenticity. But it is more than merely local and expresses its universality by commonality of faith and doctrine with all the other local churches: a unity that is personified and symbolized by its communion with its presiding bishop, and his, in turn, with the national synod to which he belongs, and that synod's, in turn, with the supranational

synods of all the different national churches. At root, this issue of exemplifying wholeness locally, and demonstrating communion in universality, is an aspect of the eucharistic communion of worship that the church shares through the presiding eucharistic office of the local bishop.

4. The pagan persecutions had divided the church members into hostile camps, some maintaining that if a Christian denied Christ to save his or her life, he or she could not be readmitted to communion; others arguing that the church had to be the locus of active reconciliation if it was to remain faithful to its core mission.

5. By apostolic age Orthodoxy means the age of Jesus and the apostles, continuing through the New Testament era. It considers the bishops to be established in the second period of church development (as witnessed especially in the pastoral Epistles of the New Testament and the so-called apostolic fathers) as the inheritors of the apostolic charism, and thus of the teaching authority that went with that charism. Orthodoxy sees the apostolicity of the bishops as demonstrated by the corporate collegial communion of all the bishops—in synodical harmony of faith and practice. No bishop singly, however senior he may be, carries this apostolic weight personally: all bishops do so in communion. This synodical system of checks and balances to the exercise of charismatic authority in the church has always meant that Orthodoxy has put collegiality and the consensus of communion at the core of church identity and coherence.

6. "Ecumenical" is from the Greek word that means "worldwide" (*oecumene*) and implied both that the councils had global representation (in effect, this meant representation, theoretically, from across the entire Roman Empire) and worldwide applicability for all Christians.

7. Shaliachim is Hebraic for "delegates sent out." The term strongly implies people sent out as emissaries commissioned with full authority to represent the one who sent them. The word "apostle" derives from the Greek verb *apostello:* "I send out."

8. The Gospels, probably because they were addressing, in Greek, an increasingly Gentile audience, try to stress every incident where Jesus approaches, or helps, a non-Jew (the Gadarene demoniac, the Syro-Phoenician woman, the centurion with the sick servant are highlighted examples); but the fact remains clear enough that Jesus saw his mission before the Passion and Crucifixion as quintessentially addressed to the Jews, as a call to repentance and renovation of the covenant. The New Testament writings consider the mission extended to non-Jews as an

aspect of the postresurrectional grace of the Christ who is exalted to be universal Lord, now including of the Gentile world.

9. The wider assembly of New Testament writers are regarded as apostles in Orthodox tradition—extending the sense of apostolicity and apostolic authority throughout the New Testament considered as a whole, and as the authoritative (but not the sole) representation of fundamental Christian tradition. The English word "church" actually means "congregation." It is derived from the Hebrew *qahal*. The Greek word used in the ancient Septuagintal (LXX) translation of the Hebrew scriptures is *ekklesia*—"the [group] that is called out." This was adopted in the Latin language too, and gives us the adjective "ecclesiastical."

10. For a more detailed analysis of Transfiguration see McGuckin, *The Transfiguration of Christ.*

11. This and almost all other scriptural quotations in this book are taken from the Revised Standard Version.

12. Acts, the first account of Christianity by an ancient church historian, namely, Saint Luke, gives us a representative model of the post-Pentecostal preaching mission (Acts 2.14–40). It attributes it to Kephas-Peter. This is technically known as the earliest example of Christian missionary *kerygma.*

13. The Orthodox Church has kept this clear in its official title, "the Holy Orthodox Catholic Apostolic Church of the East."

14. See McGuckin, *The Orthodox Church.*

15. The publisher's blurb ridiculously adds: "The first comprehensive determination of what Jesus was, what he did, what he said." The quest had already been in process at that stage for over two centuries.

16. Hypostatic comes from the Greek *hypostasis*, meaning a "personal underlying subsistence." The church used the term to signify that the union of divine and human reality in Jesus was centered in his divine hypostasis as Second Person of the Trinity (the *Logos*), and this singleness of personhood presided over his unification of the two natures of Godhead and Manhood.

17. Further see McGuckin, "Quest of the Historical Jesus," pp. 587–589.

CHAPTER 1. ECCLESIAL FOUNDATIONS

1. Which would therefore make this part of the Gospel the earliest recorded "apostolic" sermon on record. Its moral context (paranesis— or exhortation under duress) seems to reflect an era of persecution and

the threat of confiscation of goods, which would match the conditions of the imperial persecutions.

2. Volume 1 bookends (The Sign of John the Baptist) are Mk. 1.1–8 and Mk. 6.16–29; volume 2 bookends (The Sign of Loaves) are Mk. 6.30–44 and Mk. 8.14–21; volume 3 bookends (The Sign of Blind Men) are Mk. 8.22–26 and Mk. 10.46–52; volume 4 bookends (The Sign of the Fig Tree and Temple) are Mk. 11.1–25 and Mk. 13.28–37; volume 5 bookends (The Sign of the Anointing) are Mk. 14.1–9 and Mk. 16.1–8.

3. One remembers that in the first century there were as yet no codices (bound books), only scrolls; that the Gospel of Mark would appear as a mini wallpaper roll about forty-five feet long, consisting of one long word with no sentence or word divisions and no punctuation. There were as yet no chapter or verse divisions. Readers needed division guides within the text. Archbishop Stephen Langton first made up chapter numbers to the scripture as a way of making external-ready reference in 1227. Rabbi Nathan is believed to have added the verse numbers to the Old Testament in 1448. Robertus Stephanus, the Genevan printer, is the first to have added made-up verse numbers, in his 1551 New Testament, incorporating Nathan's work into his O.T. text.

4. The Pentateuch is the title of the first five books of the Old Testament, in which the ancient Jews believed the whole substance of the Torah was contained.

5. Lk. 9.30–31. In some English versions of the Greek text the word "Exodus" (with its obvious Christological implications) is obscured by the wooden translation "departure." The evangelist meant to draw a direct line of connection between "The" Exodus (God's act of salvation of Israel bringing them to the Promised Land) and Jesus's new Exodus—his death and ascension (departure from this world to Paradise, which he had now opened to his church).

6. See further, for example, two classic studies: (a) Oscar Cullmann, *Christus und die Zeit* (Zurich: Evangelisches, 1946; trans. F. V. Filson, Louisville, Ky.: WJK Press, 1964); (b) H. Conzelmann, *Die mitte der Zeit* (Tubingen: Mohr-Siebeck, 1954; woodenly translated into English as *The Theology of St. Luke*). See also: H. J. Cadbury, "Some Lukan Expressions of Time (Lexical Notes on Luke-Acts VII)," *Journal of Biblical Literature*, vol. 82, no. 3 (Sept. 1963): pp. 272–278. A good synopsis of the way Luke uses the issue of time and its fulfillment in his Gospel is

offered by I. H. Marshall, *Luke: Historian and Theologian* (Exeter: Paternoster Press, 1970), pp. 77–102.

7. Which might also include parts of the *Gospel of Thomas*.

8. Theologians such as Clement of Rome, Ignatius of Antioch, Polycarp of Smyrna, Papias of Hierapolis, and the writers of the ancient texts: *Shepherd of Hermas, Didache, Letter of Barnabas,* and *Letter to Diognetus.*

9. The Western Catholic world traditionally elevated scripture *and* tradition as two sources of revelation, while the Reformed traditions tended to see only scripture as revelation, and tradition as at best an unreliable testimony to it.

10. Paradosis is not, of course, to be confused with any traditionalist or traditionally held belief. Further see: McGuckin, "Eschaton and Kerygma," pp. 225–271. The Sacred Tradition of Revelation then went from the New Testament back to the Old Testament texts as well—but only (for the church) insofar as these are read as themselves being an exegesis, or a foreshadowing, of the Christ-Mystery, since all things in revelation are seen as Christocentric. For a fuller expression of the tradition see Florovsky, *Bible, Church, Tradition*; Meyendorff, *Living Tradition*; McGuckin, "Eschaton and Kerygma," pp. 90–119.

11. Lk. 4.43; Lk. 8.1; Lk. 17.20–21; Mk. 1.15; Mt. 12.28.

12. This world era is called "This Age" to distinguish it from the time when God would fully reveal his power in a definitive judgment against world evil, which is called "the Next Age." The scheme is commonly used in late prophetic writing. In the canonical scriptures it is most evidently seen in the book of Daniel.

13. Schweitzer, *The Quest for the Historical Jesus*, first issued 1906; English translation 1910. Messianic apocalypticism is a radical form of the eschatological medium, focusing on destructive images of "rolling up the scroll of history" to convey the revelation (Greek: *apokalypsis*) that the world was coming to an imminent end.

14. Mk. 2.5–7; Mk. 2.17; Mk. 6.12; Lk. 5.32; Lk. 15.7; Lk. 24.47.

15. The miracle traditions written about Jesus deliberately reflect the Elijah-Elisha cycle of the Old Testament, for example.

16. A useful summation of the issue is given in Thorsteinsson, *Jesus as Philosopher.*

17. Compare Smith, *Jesus the Magician* (New York: Collins, 1978).

18. It is in the teaching that reconciliation is freely given by God and does not require great labor and transactional sacrifice to ensure

that the political sparks flew. One does not execute a poet for teaching that the lilies of the field are more lovely than Solomon. But one who challenges the political and financial ascendancy of the Jewish priestly aristocracy runs a dangerous course. Further see McGuckin, "Sacrifice and Atonement."

19. For Shaliach, Jn. 4.34; 5.24; 5.30; 5.36–37; 6.38–39; 6.44; 6.57; 7.16; 7.28–29; 7.33; 8.16–18; 8.26; 8.29; 8.42; 9.4; 12.44–45, 12.49; 14.24; 15.21; 16.5; 17.21. For shaliachim, Jn. 13.20; 17.23–25; 20.21; Mt. 10.40; Mk. 9.37; Lk. 9.48; Lk. 10.16.

20. Gender-inclusive language, which we value today, ought not to distract us from the deeper significance of the New Testament idea that Christ's glorification makes men and women "Sons of God," as Paul expressed it (Rom. 8.14, 19; Gal. 3.26); the title "Son of God" is not gender restricted in the scriptural idiom but connotes an angel. It is a transcendental promise of radical transfiguration of nature, not a gendered concept.

21. The fathers of the church use the term "anakephalaiosis," or recapitulation, to convey this mystery of how the church lives and breathes within Christ's mission; summating the purpose of history in the glorification of God.

22. Sovereignty, Power, and Domination are titles of angelic hierarchies.

23. The church spread quickly through shipping and trade to many coastal cities in late antiquity.

24. Hagiography entails the lives of the saints written for edification and instruction.

25. "Ecumenical" is the Greek word for worldwide, meaning that representatives of truly international bishops were called, and the matters they had to adjudicate were felt to be of a significance that affected the whole Christian world. The Ecumenical Synods were modeled on meetings of the Senate. The Christian emperor had the right to summon one and dismiss it, and then bring its decisions into force of Roman law, after the fourth century. He had no power to direct its business once opened, however, as only bishops were allowed to adjudicate matters of faith and worship—and they were expected to come to a unanimous decision on everything of substance. I look more closely at their working in a later chapter.

26. Later known as the Docetic heresy: Jesus only "seemed" human.

27. The hypothesis was adopted wholesale and was widely propagated in English-speaking Protestantism by C. H. Dodd in his 1936 study, *The Apostolic Preaching and Its Development.*

CHAPTER 2. SHAPING ORTHODOXY, MAPPING HERESY

1. Individuals such as Irenaeus, Polycarp, Tatian, Justin, Athenagoras of Athens, Melito of Sardis, Clement of Alexandria, Tertullian, Theophilus of Antioch, and Hippolytus of Rome. Further see McGuckin, *The Path of Christianity,* pp. 3–89.

2. The Greek and Latin churches would retain their essential unity for the first thousand years of Christian history.

3. "Prescription" is a legal term that means that only those belonging to a corporation have the right to speak for it. Tertullian argues that heretics do not properly belong to the church and therefore cannot theologize or legislate in its name.

4. Its integral catholicity. Orthodoxy has, by definition, to be the catholic faith. As the Greek Nicene creed would later put it, the church has to be one holy catholic and apostolic: *Mia hagia katholike kai apostolike.*

5. Marcion was the son of a wealthy bishop (who reportedly had already excommunicated him for his teachings) before he made his way to Rome and made a name for himself there.

6. The letters include, e.g., 1 Cor. 11.19; 2 Pet. 3.15–17; 1 Jn. 2. 18–19; 1 Jn. 4.1–3; 2 Jn. 1.7–11; Jude 1.17–19; 1 Tim. 1. 3–4,6; 1 Tim. 4.1–3, 7; 1 Tim. 6.20–21.

7. The text survives as *Dialogue with Trypho.* It can be accessed on the website of Peter Kirby, *Early Christian Writings:* http://www.early christianwritings.com/text/justinmartyr-dialoguetrypho.html.

8. Especially as the establishment of catholic consensus. Further on the significance of Law for Christians (who approach it in very different ways to the Jewish understanding of Law) see McGuckin, *The Ascent of Christian Law,* pp. 1–76.

9. Tertullian, *On the Prescription of Heretics,* 7.2–4. "The Portico of Solomon" is a pun contrasting Solomon's portico (the Temple of God) with the "Painted Portico," another word for the Stoic school. "Handed down" refers to Wisd. of Sol. 1.1.

10. Subordinationism is the notion that the Son of God was not quite the same level of divinity as God the Father.

11. "My God, my God, why have you forsaken me?" would be Ps. 22 in most modern English bibles. The Orthodox Church always cites the scripture from the Septuagint (ancient Greek) version, which often differs in one psalm number from the Hebrew numerations adopted by the Protestant world after the Reformation era.

12. "Secret" is "mystical" in Greek.

13. There were some exceptions to literal and moral readings, the most notable being those of Philo of Alexandria, whom the Christian fathers much admired for his Logo-centric reading of texts.

14. For more detail see McGuckin, *Collected Studies*, vol. 1., pp. 241–265.

15. For a literal sense, consider, for example, God's command to Moses and Joshua to slaughter all the tribe of Amalek (Exod. 17.13–16), or the peculiar incident when God apparently tries to kill Moses in a lodging house (Exod. 4.24). In a symbolic sense, Amalek, for example, is taken by the fathers of the church to be a cipher for evil: the task of Israel to root out Amalek thus becomes a foreshadowing of the role of the church to teach universal morality.

16. Origen, *Homily on Leviticus*, 7.5; *On First Principles*, 4.2.9; 4.3.4. It was an interpretative principle about sacred literature first enunciated by Xenophanes, then taken up by Plato and Philo before him.

17. Athanasius of Alexandria, *On the Incarnation of the Word of God*, 57.1–2.

18. See the fine study by Father John Meyendorff, *Living Tradition*.

19. What follows is a very condensed and abbreviated discussion of complex debates. I have treated them more extensively in McGuckin, *The Path of Christianity*, chaps. 1–4.

20. Mt. 16.13–17; Lk. 24.19 and 24.5; Jn. 8.52–58.

21. Mt. 1.22; Mt. 5.17; Mt. 8.17; Mt. 13.17; Mt. 21.4; Jn. 1.45; Acts 3.18, 24; Eph. 2.20.

22. Mt. 13.41; Heb. 1.3–14.

23. For Lord: Mt. 15.22; Mt. 20.33; Mt. 22.43–45; Lk. 1.43; Jn. 11.27; Jn. 13.13; Acts 10.36; Rom. 14.9; 1 Cor. 8.5–6. For Son of God: Mt. 14.33; Mt. 27.43; Mt. 27.54; Mk. 1.1; Jn. 3.18; Jn. 20.31; Rom. 1.3–4; 1 Jn. 4.15.

24. Phil. 2.8–11; Acts 2.33; Acts 5.30–32; Heb. 7.26.

25. Heb. 2.17; Heb. 4.14–15; Heb. 5.5–10; Heb. 9.11–12, 15; Heb. 12.24; 1 Tim. 2.5; Col. 1.20.

26. Jn. 1.1; Jn. 20.28; Phil. 2.5–11; Col. 1.13–19.

27. For a fuller survey of the early Christian doctrine of the Trinity see McGuckin, "The Trinity in the Greek Fathers," *Collected Studies,* vol. 2, pp. 317–341.

28. The term "synkatabasis" connotes the "stooping down" in mercy, like a mother bending down to her child.

29. It is this principle of the canonicity of apostolic tradition that gives rise to the derived concept of the canon of holy scripture, not the other way around as many Protestant theologians have presumed over the past five hundred years. It precedes the physical act of gathering scriptures together for use in Christian worship and provides the very impetus for that evangelical momentum.

30. *Regula fidei* in Latin or *kanon pisteos* in Greek. The trinitarian-shaped creeds develop as written examples of this from the late second century onward, though there are already examples of them in the hymnal pericopes of the New Testament Letters.

31. This was often taken in later ages (especially in the West) to be a matter of a bishop proving his lineage of ordinational descent. But at first it was far more than that: it was a matter of demonstrating that one's theology was in accord with that of the apostles by consonance with that of other episcopal teachers.

32. A diocese was an administrative political region of the Roman Empire. The early Orthodox Church simply adopted the pattern of regional, provincial, and international structures operating in its day but used them to affirm episcopal guidance over local churches; and instead of an imperial monarchy at the head, it applied a highly collegial and consensual (synodical) model of authoritative governance among the bishops, which is still followed in the modern-era Orthodox Church.

33. Jesus insists on it in Lk. 6.46–49; Mt. 5.19; Mt. 7.12, 21.

34. Further see Hadot, *Philosophy as a Way of Life.*

35. See, for example: Mt. 20–48; 1 Cor. 6–8; Eph. 4–6; Col. 3–4; 1 Pet. 1.13–4.19; 2 Pet. 1.3–11.

36. Rom. 1.7 and passim.

37. The persecutions were exceptionally savage in Africa.

38. Mk. 10.30; Mk. 10.38–39; Mk. 13.9–13; Jn. 15.20; Rom. 8.35–37; 1 Jn. 4.1–3.

CHAPTER 3. THE CLASSICAL PATRISTIC PERIOD

1. I speak, of course, as an ancient historian by profession. Taking the longer view, when the church is now two millennia old, some would regard the patristic age itself as a kind of innocent childhood, and the age of maturation and a willingness to adapt and face new challenges as something the church learns in each and every generation of its historical pilgrimage on earth.

2. Almost all meat bought from ancient urban butchers' shops had a prelife as sacrifice offerings in the pagan cults. The butchers' shops were often sited adjacent to the temples and served as their retail outlets.

3. Auspices entailed scrutinizing the livers of sacrificed birds to discern the will of the gods and their future plans. At important political moments (such as declarations of war) it was the duty of the emperor, acting as supreme high priest of the Roman religion (*summus pontifex maximus*) to preside over these religious rites as part of his role as *imperator* (commander of all the forces) of Rome.

4. From *daimones*, the lesser, terrestrial, spirits of evil. Even classifying the Roman system of gods as daimones would be seen as a sacrilegious insult by the pagan establishment.

5. Mention of the church at Nicomedia is the first time we hear in the records of a large public building known to all as a Christian church.

6. He was caesar from 296 to 305. This gave him rights of succession as emperor (augustus) of the West after Diocletian's abdication. He reigned for a very short time.

7. The garrison's raising of Constantine took place in what is now the under-crypt at York Minster in northern England.

8. Galerius had rescinded his anti-Christian policies on his death-bed, but Licinius, who gained power in the East, was highly suspicious of Christians, whom he regarded as favoring his rival, Constantine.

9. See Eusebius, *Life of Constantine*, 1.28; Lactantius, *On the Deaths of the Persecutors*, 44.

10. It was not, in that context, seen as unusual that a commander in the field should take religious auspices to forecast the result of a forthcoming battle—and a vision or divine intuition was expected by the troops.

11. The arch is adjacent to the Roman Colosseum, by the Caelian Hill.

12. The Melitian schism affecting the Church of Alexandria.

13. And thus any dissenters from unanimity would thereby reveal themselves as not being in accord with the consensus of the apostolic tradition.

14. Today the word "ecumenical" means interdenominational Christian relationships: but deriving from the Greek *oecumene* it originally meant a matter that affected or represented the entire Roman world. After Constantine it meant what was quintessentially Roman and Christian in ethos. Accordingly, it is clearly a set of refinements elaborating the details of the earlier apostolic tradition.

15. The Orthodox Church is defined by its adherence to the seven Ecumenical Councils as the core of its doctrine and the highest earthly authority in its constitution. Roman Catholicism holds to the authenticity of the seven, though it adds on numerous others it has held since the time of its separation from the Eastern churches. These later councils are not regarded as Ecumenical Councils by the Orthodox world. The Oriental Orthodox churches hold only to the ecumenicity of the first four great councils. Anglicanism (in the *Book of Common Prayer,* for example) holds to all seven while seeming to dismiss the seventh; and it generally does not attribute to them the same fundamental significance that they hold in Orthodox and Roman Catholic dogmatics. Reformed Protestantism, generally, sees the councils as merely historic moments in former ecclesial ages: not inherently inspired in and of themselves.

16. I would highly recommend as an initial review Davis, *The First Seven Ecumenical Councils,* and for a more learned immersion in them, Trostyanskiy, *Seven Icons of Christ.* Tanner, *Decrees of the Ecumenical Councils,* gives the basic texts in English.

17. The creed commonly recited at the eucharists of Orthodox, Roman Catholics, and Anglicans is actually the creed of the Council of Constantinople in 381, which poses itself as effectively the same as the Creed of Nicaea of 325. It actually has a few more clauses in it relating to the Holy Spirit.

18. See the Appendix for a closer summative analysis and commentary on this creed, which still today is the foundation of all the Orthodox and Catholic churches of Christendom.

19. Gregory of Nazianzus, *Oration 21.*

20. The Greek fathers (and the Orthodox churches following them) teach that the divine essence, or ousia, of which the Son was the hypostasis

(personal instantiation) was not a generic one but the particular essence (the *proprium* of being) belonging to the Father, which the Father thus shares by gifting it to the Son and to the Spirit, as the single Principle (*Arche*) of the Trinity.

21. See Hill, *Athanasius and the Holy Spirit.*

22. It is no coincidence that Athanasius is also called the father of the biblical canon, insofar as he drew up one of the earliest lists of what ought to be regarded as the core books of revealed scripture.

23. Nazianzus was in the eastern region of modern-day Turkey. A fuller life and times can be found in McGuckin, *St. Gregory of Nazianzus.*

24. The discourses have been called *The Five Theological Orations (Orats. 27–31).* Because of his important work Gregory was given the title "the Theologian" by the Ecumenical Council of Chalcedon in 451.

25. Gregory, *Oration 27.3* (First Theological).

26. Gregory, *Oration 27.1.*

27. Gregory, *Oration 28.3* (Second Theological).

28. Gregory, *Oration 28.4.*

29. Tentatively saying anything about the God who transcends all thought and perception is a style of theology known as apophatic, or "turning away from talking." It stands in contrast to the typical Western style of medieval scholastic theology, which advanced in terms of syllogisms and deductions. Orthodox thought does not say that nothing can be said of God; it merely points out that all human speech about the divine is tentative, since God's essence is entirely unknown, though he has revealed himself in creation and through history by means of his energies present in the world and by direct revelation, culminating in the Incarnation of the Christ.

30. The noetic consciousness is seen as the highest level of awareness, when the transcendent destiny of humankind is personally realized in a mystical apprehension.

31. Gregory, *Epistle 101 to Cledonios.* Gregory takes the phrase (to develop it more extensively) from Origen of Alexandria (*Dialogue with Heracleides,* 7; *Com. Matthew,* 12.29; *Against Celsus,* 4.19).

32. The modern word "person," with its overtones of individual mind and will and separateness, is not a good translation of this original Greek concept, which meant an instantiation or individuation of a reality: a "specific presentation" would perhaps be closest.

33. Mother of God is actually *Meter Theou* in Greek, the older title that is still found on all Orthodox icons of Mary. *Theotokos*, or God-birther, however, had a wider take-up among the Christian faithful, especially Christian women, who looked to her in prayer especially for safe childbearing. Further see McGuckin, *Theotokos*.

34. A much fuller analysis of the Council of Ephesus and Saint Cyril's Christological thought is offered in McGuckin, *St. Cyril of Alexandria*.

35. I have elsewhere offered a much more theologically weighted introduction to Orthodoxy. See McGuckin, *The Orthodox Church*.

CHAPTER 4. THE BYZANTINE IMPERIAL CHURCH

1. See Origen's third-century treatise *Contra Celsum*.

2. See Lactantius's fourth-century treatise *The Divine Institutes*.

3. Having a king interfering with church affairs—seen as worse than having a pope doing so. It is less an accurate historical term of analysis than a late Reformation apologetic concept foisted onto history, originally as an anti–Roman Catholic argument. Further see McGuckin, *The Orthodox Church*, pp. 380–398.

4. For more on care for the poor, see Miller, *The Birth of the Hospital*.

5. See Gregory the Theologican, *Oration 14, On the Love of the Poor. Patrologia Graeca*, vol. 35, cols. 857–909. For an analysis see McGuckin, *St. Gregory of Nazianzus*, 147–155.

6. Further see McGuckin, *The Ascent of Christian Law*.

7. Further see Eshel, *The Concept of the Elect Nation*.

8. The British monarchy is still rooted in the medieval ritual (borrowed from Byzantium) of the sacredly anointed monarch.

9. Today the Egyptian Church consists of: the Coptic Church, the Ethiopian Tewahedo and Eritrean churches, the Syrian (Non-Chalcedonian) Orthodox Church, the Armenian Apostolic Church, and the Malankara Indian Orthodox Church.

10. Decree of the Council of Chalcedon of 451.

11. First under the Rashidun caliphs then under the Ummayads.

12. See, for example, Chaillot, *The Dialog between the Eastern Orthodox*.

13. Further see McGuckin, "The Mia Physis Doctrine," in Chaillot, *The Dialog between the Eastern Orthodox*.

14. *Monos pros Monon* could be rendered as: *The Alone one, all for the Only One.*

15. See Athanasius the Great's *Life of Antony.* See Gregg, *Athanasius.*

16. The word "hermit" derives from the Greek *eremos,* or desert, and originally meant desert dweller, before assuming the Christian technical meaning of a solitary monastic.

17. "Cenobitic" comes from the Greek for "common life."

18. See Meyer, *Palladius,* and Wortley, *The Book of the Elders.*

19. "Rood" is an Old English word for cross, since the altar screen was always crowned with a large painted crucifix.

20. In June 813, a band of soldiers garrisoned in Constantinople forced their way into the Church of the Holy Apostles, where the imperial tombs were, and broke open the tomb of Constantine V, dramatically begging him to return to life to save the empire from its constant losses to the Islamic forces. A month later Leo V was crowned emperor and, evidently taking note of the army's opinions, began discussions to reassert iconoclasm in the face of the Council of Nicaea II.

21. The Chalke Gate was the main ceremonial gateway leading into the Imperial Palace.

22. Here reverence for one's grandfather is exactly that same "worship" mentioned in the English Church's marriage service, where the spouses are encouraged to worship one another bodily.

CHAPTER 5. THE CHURCH'S EXPANSION

1. Founded in 330 as the new capital of the empire, Constantinople was ecclesiastically dominant by the fifth century, eventually replacing Alexandria for primacy of influence in the eastern provinces after the First Council of Constantinople and challenging Rome for supremacy after the Council of Chalcedon.

2. Filioque is the creedal addition stating that the Spirit proceeds from the Father "and from the Son."

3. The book is published by Holy Cross Press, Brookline, Boston (1987).

4. Moravia is now the Czech lands.

5. Constantinople and the Slavs of Rus traded mostly in furs, amber, and wood.

6. Obolensky, *The Byzantine Commonwealth,* 238–258; Shevzov, "The Russian Tradition," 16–40.

NOTES TO PAGES 163-170

7. Martin negotiated through his representative, president of the council Cardinal Julian Cesarini, later Pope Eugene IV.

8. Vasily II, Grand Prince of the Duchy of Muscovy, reigned from 1425 to 1462.

9. The title "tsar" is a Slavic form of caesar. The Russians regarded themselves as the true successors of the Byzantine Christian imperium.

10. For a brief account see Browning, *The Byzantine Empire*, 163–183.

11. The Byzantine principalities of Mystra, Trebizond, and Epirus lasted until their own collapse in 1460, 1461, and 1479, respectively.

12. In Greek folklore his body (never recovered from the chaos) was said to have been lifted by an angel and placed in a marble tomb in a cave near the Golden Gate to the palace, waiting for the time when the capital would be restored to the Greeks and he would be brought out alive to lead the triumph. He is known in Greece as the "Marble King."

13. Patriarch Anastasios II (patr. 1450–1453) eventually took refuge on Mount Athos.

14. Mehmet had insisted first on formally bestowing on Gennadios the patriarchal crozier (*paterissa*) and cloak (*mantiya*), a ceremony that became traditional for all patriarchs under the Ottomans afterward. Three years later, in 1456, he was removed to the Church of Pammakaristos. Holy Apostles Church (the original model for Saint Mark's basilica in Venice), which had been the mausoleum church for the Byzantine emperors, was demolished in 1461, and the Fatih Jamii (Conquest Mosque) was built over the site.

15. An ethnarch is a subordinate ruler, responsible for a minority people within the Ottoman Empire.

16. The Eastern Church heroically continued with local Greek schools, teaching children their letters. Religious instruction had to be coded in terms of history lessons, but no preaching outside the churches was permitted, and proselytism of Muslims was an executable offense for both convert and Christian sponsor.

17. A church census in 1914 recorded that in Russia there were 550 men's monasteries and 475 women's monasteries, totaling 95,259 monastics.

18. A very lively read giving the past history and a gloomy view of the modern state of Orthodox and monastic affairs in the Middle East

and on Mount Athos is found in Dalrymple, *From the Holy Mountain*. Speake, *Mount Athos*, gives a much more positive report on the state of contemporary Athonite renewal.

19. The chrysobull was the most solemn level of imperial edict, granting extensive rights.

20. The fourth-century tower can still be seen within the fabric. It was funded by the empress Helena.

21. Saint John Klimakos, author of the *Ladder of Divine Ascent*, and Saints Anastasius of Sinai and Gregory of Sinai are only a few of the important figures this monastery produced.

22. The *Legenda Aurea* was compiled by Saint Jacobus de Varagine, archbishop of Genoa, circa 1260. It became the most widely read source of saints' lives through the Middle Ages and into the seventeenth century.

23. For more on the prayer of the heart see J. A. McGuckin, "The Prayer of the Heart in Patristic and Early Byzantine Tradition," in *Prayer and Spirituality in the Early Church*, vol. 2, ed. P. Allen, W. Mayer, and L. Cross, pp. 69–108 (East Melbourne: Australian Catholic University, Centre for Early Christian Studies, 1999).

24. *Klimakos* means "[author] of the ladder" in Greek.

25. See images, for example, at: https://www.alamy.com/stock-photo/mar-saba-monastery.html.

CHAPTER 6. ORTHODOX LIFE UNDER AND AFTER
ISLAMIC DOMINION

1. Text in "Filofei's Concept of the Third Rome," in *Medieval Russia: A Source Book, 850–1700*, ed. B. Dmytryshyn, 259–261 (Fort Worth: Harcourt Brace, 2000).

2. Joseph, on Sept. 9 and Oct. 18, Nil on May 7.

3. The bishops looked to Rome for protection against depredations on three sides: Islamic, Protestant, and Latin Catholic.

4. The term "Uniate" has come to be a disparagement, used by some Orthodox to designate the faithful of the Greek Catholic (Unia) tradition as schismatics. The movement is also known as the Eastern Rite Catholic Church.

5. The academy was later called the Kiev Mohyla Academy. After the fall of the Communist regime in Ukraine it was reclaimed from the Soviet Navy, to be made into the first liberal arts college, and immedi-

ately voted to restore theology to the curriculum. I was honored to be the first foreign visiting professor of patristics for a series of lectures there on ancient Christian notions of freedom.

6. Bronstrom, *Archpriest Avvakum*, p. 39.

7. The father of the church, Saint Peter of Damascus (died 775), whose writings were represented in the Russian spiritual books, had advocated the practice of using two fingers on the forehead. The standard form of the Byzantine Church after his day, however, had been to use three. This change had not been signaled to the Russians, who also, after the fall of Constantinople, tended to regard the Greeks with suspicion for compromising the faith through their (temporary) allegiance to the Western Catholics after the Council of Florence.

8. Other small liturgical deviations (such as the pre-Nikon usage of singing two alleluias as psaltic refrains, compared with Nikon's proposal to sing three, like the Greeks) were taken as matters of immense significance by the Old Ritualists: the purity of the whole faith being seen as vested in strict observance of the liturgical rubrics.

9. The movement is also called *Raskol:* the schism, or division.

10. Saint Petersburg would remain the Russian capital until that was moved back to Moscow following the 1917 Revolution.

11. Boris and Gleb were the first saints canonized (1074) in the Russian Church after its conversion.

12. His baptism made Boris a family member of the imperial house. The emperor gave him the title of prince (tsar or caesar) and recognized his suzerainty over the other nobles (*boyars*), who had previously thought the princely dominion was a movable right among their society. In 865 Boris fought off a revolt and killed fifty-two members of the old pagan aristocracy, consolidating his monarchical rule.

13. Byzantine theology regarded the single imperium of the Christian *basileus* (or king-emperor) as part of God's gifted inheritance to the Christians as the New Israel, and as such not a negotiable political factor. For the Byzantine Orthodox world to rupture the single imperium of the basileus over all Christians was a sacrilegious fracturing of the church's destiny to reconcile all humanity in one civilization. Western, non-Orthodox cultures have tended to regard politics and religion as separable. Orthodoxy on the other hand still tends to regard Christianity as the core of the political civilization it aspires to; though it does not envisage that as necessarily a theocracy or a priestocracy, since it has a

well-developed theory of the principle of subsidiarity—where civil and military politics fulfill a distinct set of duties from religion and religious authorities, the two aspects of society each operating (as we have already noted) as distinct voices in supportive harmony (*symphonia*).

14. The Mosque of Mehmet Sokollu Pasha (named after him) is one of the jewels of Istanbul today, a few hundred yards down the hill from the apsidal arch of the Hippodrome. The Christian population was forced to supply a regular quota of young boys to be Islamicized and brought up as Janissary troops in Constantinople. Sokolovic is the Serbian spelling of Sokollu.

15. The Orthodox make up 86 percent of the mainland population. The figure of three-quarters of a million in Moldova is according to the 2004 state census. Orthodoxy in Moldova, like the territory itself (now independent), is contested through historical rights' issues by the Romanian and Russian churches. The two patriarchates (Moscow and Bucharest) contend for seniority of supervision, the one via the Moldovan Orthodox Church, autonomous but subordinate to Moscow; the other through the Orthodox Church of Bessarabia, autonomous but related to the Romanian synod. Both local churches claim to be the national church of Moldova. In the 2004 census more than 93 percent of the Moldovan population declared themselves Orthodox but were not required to state which jurisdiction they felt they belonged to.

16. *Anno Domini*, for dates after the birth of Christ ("in the year of the Lord"), or *Ante Christum*, "before Christ" (hence the English abbreviation B.C.).

17. Wallachia is also known as Muntenia.

18. Among the most notable of many are the churches or monasteries at: Putna, Sucevita, Borzesti, Patrauti, Voronets, Bistrita, Iasi, and Neamt.

19. The four ancient patriarchates, and then Russia and Serbia take precedence of honor before the Romanian Patriarchate.

20. It was aimed primarily against the Bulgarian episcopate.

21. The patriarch was Saint Gregory V. His execution after the liturgy of Easter Day (April 22, 1821) was the start of a massacre of Greek Orthodox in Constantinople. His body was left hanging from the Phanar Palace gate for two days then thrown into the Bosphorus. Rescued by Greek sailors, it was buried with honor in the metropolitan cathedral in Athens. The gate of execution has been welded shut in Gregory's memory ever since.

22. About the *Philokalia*, see further McGuckin, "The Making of the Philokalia," pp. 36–49.

23. It can be read in a fine English translation by G. Palmer, P. Sherrard, and K. Ware, *The Philokalia*, 5 vols. (London: Faber and Faber, 1979–1995).

24. For Paisy's approach see further McGuckin, "The Life and Mission of St. Paisius Velichkovsky," pp. 157–173.

25. Further see McGuckin. "The Prayer of the Heart," 69–108.

26. Further see McGuckin, "Rasskaz Strannika," pp. 359–406, and McGuckin, "How the Philokalic Tradition Came to Modern America," pp. 349–370.

CHAPTER 7. ORTHODOXY UNDER THE COMMUNISTS

1. Cited by Paul Kengor, "Remembering 1917: The War on Religion," accessed at: https://www.mercatornet.com/features/view/re member-1917-communisms-war-on-religion/20435 (retrieved November 2018).

2. Stalin, *Works*, vol. 10 (Moscow, 1978), p. 132.

3. Ware, *The Orthodox Church*, p. 156.

4. The figure of eighty thousand would continue to move considerably higher. The NKVD and Cheka were the Russian security services preceding the KGB.

5. Reported by Reuters in November 1995. See Philippa Fletcher, "Inquiry Reveals Lenin Unleashed Systematic Murder of 200,000 Clergy," *Hobart Mercury* (Australia), November 29, 1995. Available at: http://www.paulbogdanor.com/left/soviet/atheism1.html (accessed November 2018).

6. On May 17, 2007, the two synods, of the ROCOR bishops and the Moscow patriarchate, signed a concordat of reconciliation that restored full communion and gave the ROCOR the status of an autonomous (self-governing) part of the Russian Orthodox Church.

7. Shevzov, "The Russian Tradition," pp. 15–40.

8. Confessor was an ancient church title for those who had been imprisoned and persecuted but had not paid the full price of their lives, in martyrdom. After the ancient persecutions, confessors were afforded great spiritual authority in the church. The bishops of Eastern Europe in the Communist era were often dismissed by Western Protestant commentators as supine; but as Gerard Manley Hopkins once wrote

about the terrors of the mind, "Hold them cheap / May he who ne'er hung there." *The Poems of Gerard Manley Hopkins*, ed. W. H. Gardner and N. H. Mackenzie (London: Oxford University Press, 1967), p. 100. The Anglican Dean of Winchester, Trevor Beeson, was kinder with his book *Discretion and Valour: Religious Conditions in Eastern Europe* (London: Fount, 1974), whose title played on Shakespeare's adage that "discretion is the better part of valour."

9. Further see Applebaum, *Iron Curtain*.

10. Churchill's speech was recorded for the BBC archives and can be heard at: https://winstonchurchill.org/resources/speeches/1946-1963-elder-statesman/the-sinews-of-peace/.

11. See Stan and Turcescu, *Religion and Politics*.

CHAPTER 8. THE TWENTIETH-CENTURY ORTHODOX DIASPORA

1. Further see Herbel, in Casiday, *The Orthodox Christian World*, pp. 164–178.

2. He was canonized as a saint by the Orthodox Church in 1977.

3. Casiday, *The Orthodox Christian World*, p. 168.

4. See Bogolepov, *Toward an American Orthodox Church*.

5. In a synodical letter of October 1970 the ROCOR hierarchs addressed the OCA hierarchy: "It is impossible for the Moscow Patriarchate, under the complete control of the Soviet atheistic regime which has set for itself the goal of destroying all religion, to do anything which could be to the overall benefit of the Church and it must be remembered that the Moscow Patriarchate cannot engage in foreign affairs without a direct order of the Soviet government. . . . It is not our intention to inflict upon you any hurt, but rather to give you again a brotherly warning of the danger now threatening you." The letter is archived at: https://orthodoxwiki.org/ROCOR_and_OCA#1970:_Autocephaly_for_the_OCA.

6. Further see T. Batrouney, in Casiday, *The Orthodox Christian World*, pp. 179–186; and also P. B. Anderson, M. H. Anderson, and O. Homburg, eds., *Eastern Orthodox in Australia* (Sydney: Australian Council of Churches, 1967).

7. Transubstantiation is the doctrine promulgated by the Fourth Lateran Council in 1215 that the eucharistic bread and wine changed sub-

stantively into the body and blood of Christ in the course of the eucharistic consecration. The English text of the decisions of Patriarch Dositheos's council in 1672 can be found online (taken from *The Acts and Decrees of the Synod of Jerusalem*, trans. and ed. J. Robertson, 1899): http://www.crivoice.org/creeddositheus.html. The bishops gathered in Jerusalem for the reconsecration of the Bethlehem basilica. While assembled they addressed the fact that many Protestants, after Patriarch Cyril Lukaris had earlier met with Calvinist theologians in Constantinople, were claiming the support of the Orthodox Church for Reformation doctrines.

8. Some Protestant theologians were claiming that their delegation to Patriarch Cyril Lukaris of Constantinople (soon afterward executed by the Ottoman Phanar) had led to his endorsing of their general positions and his alliance with them against Rome.

9. Cited in E. Carpenter, *The Protestant Bishop* (London: Longmans, Green, 1956). Cf. pp. 357–364.

10. The churches were in the City of London (1850), Bayswater (1877), and Cardiff (1906).

11. Thyateira is one of the Seven Churches of Asia mentioned in the book of Revelation. It is the custom of the Orthodox Church to appoint a diocese within its own (Eastern) area of jurisdiction with the local (Western) missionary situation reflected as an "also added" to mark respect for the diocesan boundaries that were appropriate and particular to the bishop who used to be first among equals among the Orthodox (Rome).

12. A pan-Orthodox study center, the Institute for Orthodox Christian Studies, was organized out of the University of Cambridge's external federation arrangements in 1999. Its academic faculty consists mainly of visiting professors.

13. This 11 percent of active British Christians equals an estimated 5.5 million Orthodox believers. The percentage of active British Christians who are Anglican is thought to be 21; the percentage of those who are Roman Catholic, 24. The "wider-belonging" numbers, as distinct from the numbers of regular attenders, would make the last two figures noticeably larger.

14. See Chamberlain, *Lenin's Private War*.

15. In 2014 a massive new Russian cathedral (the Holy Trinity) and cultural complex was built in Paris, near the Eiffel Tower, funded by the Russian government under the care of the Moscow patriarchate.

CHAPTER 9. RECENT OUTSTANDING ORTHODOX
FIGURES

1. It is the greeting Orthodox faithful give to other believers when in church, and the response offered is: "He is and ever shall be." At Paschal time it changes to "Christ is Risen," with the response, "He is truly Risen"; and at Christmas time it changes again, to "Christ is born," with the response: "Glorify him."

2. Dimitri Kuzmin-Karavaev: 1886–1959. He would later convert to Catholicism and was ordained to the priesthood.

3. Together the three studies were translated into English in 2016 by S. Janos, entitled *The Crucible of Doubts*. See also R. Pevear and L. Volokhonsky, trans., *Mother Maria Skobtsova: Essential Writings* (New York: Orbis Maryknoll, 2003).

4. Selection by the guards was the process of weeding out those prisoners no longer strong enough to work. At first they were shot, later they were poisoned by gas.

5. The official act of canonization noted that they were the first Orthodox saints to be canonized who had largely lived their mission in the West. Along with them were also canonized Archpriest Alexei Medvedkov and Elie Fondaminskii, a Jewish friend of Mother Maria's who asked for baptism in the camp before his death.

6. See Mt. 25.34–40.

7. André Behr died in 1968.

8. E. Behr-Sigel. "La crise et le dénouement: L'itineraire du père Lev Gillet vers l'Église Orthodoxe." See: http://www.pagesorthodoxes .net/foi-orthodoxe/temoignage-lev-gillet.htm (accessed December 2018).

9. Cited in M. Plekon, *Hidden Holiness* (Notre Dame, Ind.: Notre Dame University Press, 2009), p. 197.

10. Behr-Sigel, *The Ministry of Women*.

11. Sihastria Skete was raised to the status of an independent monastery when Cleopa was the higumen, in 1947.

12. Skete is a term designating a dependent monastic settlement. Sihastria in Romanian devolves from the Greek *hesychasterion*, literally meaning "place of quietness" and indicating a monastic community especially given over to contemplative prayer.

13. Further on Father Cleopa see Stebbing, *Bearers of the Spirit*.

14. A Google Images search for the monasteries of Voronet, Neamt, Sucevita, or Dragomirna will readily show the extraordinary

beauty of these places. See, for example, romaniatourism.com/press-romania-painted-monasteries.html.

15. Cited by F. Corley in the obituary for Father Cleopa in the *Independent* (London). December 18, 1998.

16. See Balan, *Elder Cleopa of Sihastria.*

CHAPTER 10. DAY-TO-DAY LIFE IN AN ORTHODOX CHURCH

1. Psalm 140 (141 in Western bibles).

2. https://www.youtube.com/watch?v=r8XQ-tUKLKE (accessed December 2018).

3. https://www.youtube.com/watch?v=C7vvPXz-Qes (accessed December 2018).

4. https://www.youtube.com/watch?v=bJ4Le7ANdbE (accessed December 2018).

5. The sign of the cross used to be made in the same way in both the Eastern and Western churches, but the Latin rite altered it to its present form in the early modern period. The Orthodox churches retained the earlier usage: the right hand put together the thumb and the two adjacent fingers in a joined threesome, while the remaining two fingers come together to touch the base of the thumb. This symbolizes the three persons of the Trinity in one nature and also the two natures of the Incarnate Lord made one. Held in this way the three fingers touch the forehead, the navel, the right shoulder, and then the left shoulder.

6. A visitor often wonders why so much to-ing and fro-ing is happening at one of the side doors of the icon screen, with people going up and speaking to clergy there. It is usually the handing on of small votive loaves called *prosphora* or petitions for special prayers for someone. These are written on paper with the first names of the living listed on one side and those of the departed on the other. The papers are called *diptychs.*

7. *Pharmakia tes athanasias* in Greek.

8. A baby's nose and mouth are covered by the priest's hand as, very quickly, he submerges it under the water, allowing it to take a fresh breath each time before he dips it.

9. The original meaning of the word "candidate" is "one dressed in white." It derives from the church's custom of dressing the newly baptized in celebratory white.

POSTLUDE. WHAT ROLE FOR ORTHODOXY?

1. McGuckin, *The Path of Christianity: The First Thousand Years* (Downers Grove, Ill.: IVP, 2016).

2. Mt. 10.8.

3. Father Lev Gillet, funeral homily preached in 1937 at the liturgy for Archimandrite Irenée Winnaert. Trans. T. Ware, from the French text in V. Bourne, *La quête de verité d'Irénée Winnaert* (Geneva: Labor et Fides, 1966), p. 335.

Bibliography

Appelbaum, A. *Iron Curtain: The Crushing of Eastern Europe, 1944–56*. London: Penguin, 2013.

Balan, I. *Elder Cleopa of Sihastria: In the Tradition of Saint Paisius Velichkovsky*. Lake George: Protection of the Holy Virgin Publications, 2001.

Behr-Sigel, E. *The Ministry of Women in the Church*. New York: SVS Press, 1991.

Bogolepov, A. *Toward an American Orthodox Church: The Establishment of an Autocephalous Orthodox Church*. New York: St. Vladimir's Seminary Press, 2001.

Bronstrom K. N. (trans.). *Archpriest Avvakum: The Life Written by Himself*. Ann Arbor: Michigan Slavic Publications, 1979.

Browning, R. *The Byzantine Empire*. London: Weidenfeld and Nicolson (BCA Edition), 1980.

Casiday, A. (ed.). *The Orthodox Christian World*. London: Routledge, 2012.

Chaillot, C. (ed.). *The Dialog between the Eastern Orthodox and Oriental Orthodox Churches*. Volos-Melisissiatika: Volos Academy Publications, 2016.

Chamberlain, L. *Lenin's Private War: The Voyage of the Philosophy Steamer and the Exile of the Intelligentsia*. London: St. Martin's Press, 2007.

Dalrymple, W. *From the Holy Mountain: A Journey in the Shadow of Byzantium*. Austin: Holt McDougal, 1997.

Davis, L. D. *The First Seven Ecumenical Councils (325–787): Their History and Theology*. Theology and Religious Studies, vol. 9. Wilmington, Del.: Michael Glazier, 1987.

Eshel, S. *The Concept of the Elect Nation in Byzantium*. Leiden: Brill, 2018.

Florovsky, G. *Bible, Church, Tradition: An Eastern Orthodox View*. Belmont, Mass.: Nordland, 1972.

Gregg, R. C. *Athanasius: The Life of Antony*. Classics of Western Spirituality. London: SPCK, 1980.

Hadot, P. *Philosophy as a Way of Life: Spiritual Exercises from Socrates to Foucault*. Oxford: Wiley-Blackwell, 1995.

Hill, K. D. *Athanasius and the Holy Spirit: The Development of His Early Pneumatology*. Minneapolis: Fortress Press, 2016.

Louth, A. *Introducing Eastern Orthodox Theology*. London: SPCK, 2013.

———. *Modern Orthodox Thinkers: From the Philokalia to the Present*. Downers Grove, Ill.: IVP Academic, 2015.

McGuckin, J. A. *The Ascent of Christian Law: Patristic and Byzantine Reformulations of Antique Civilization*. New York: SVS Press, 2012.

———. *The Book of Mystical Chapters: Meditations on the Soul's Ascent from the Desert Fathers and Other Early Christian Contemplatives*. Boston: Shambhala Press, 2002.

———. *Collected Studies*. 3 vols. New York: SVS Press, 2017. Vol. 1, *Witnessing the Kingdom: Studies in New Testament History and Theology*; vol. 2, *Seeing the Glory: Studies in Patristic Theology*; vol. 3, *Illumined in the Spirit: Studies in Orthodox Spirituality*.

———. *The Encyclopedia of Eastern Orthodox Christianity*. 2 vols. Oxford: Wiley Blackwell, 2010.

———. "Eschaton and Kerygma: The Future of the Past in the Present Kairos (The Concept of Living Tradition in Orthodox Theology)." *St. Vladimir's Theological Quarterly*, vol. 42, nos. 3–4 (Winter 1998): pp. 225–271.

———. "How the Philokalic Tradition Came to Modern America: And What America Made of It." In *Iosif Volotskii and Eastern Christianity: Essays Across Seventeen Centuries*, ed. D. Goldfrank, V. Nolla, and J. Spock, pp. 349–370. Washington, D.C.: New Academia Publishing, 2017.

———. *I Believe in One Lord Jesus Christ: Ancient Christian Doctrines*, vol. 2. Downers Grove, Ill.: IVP Academic, 2009.

———. "The Life and Mission of St. Paisius Velichkovsky, 1722–1794: An Early Modern Master of the Orthodox Spiritual Life." *Spiritus: A Journal of Christian Spirituality*, vol. 9, no. 2 (Fall 2009): pp. 157–173.

———. "The Making of the Philokalia: A Tale of Monks and Manuscripts." In *The Philokalia*, ed. B. Bingaman and B. Nassif, pp. 36–49. Oxford: Oxford University Press, 2012.

———. "The Mia-Physis Doctrine of St. Cyril of Alexandria and Chalcedonian Dyophysitism." In *The Dialog between the Eastern Orthodox and Oriental Orthodox Churches*, ed. C. Chaillot, pp. 39–54. Volos-Melisissiatika: Volos Academy Publications, 2016.

———. *The Orthodox Church: An Introduction to Its History, Theology and Spiritual Culture*. Oxford: Wiley Blackwell, 2008.

———. *The Path of Christianity*. Downers Grove, Ill.: IVP Academic, 2017.

———. "The Prayer of the Heart in Patristic and Early Byzantine Tradition." In *Prayer and Spirituality in the Early Church*, vol. 2, ed. P. Allen, W. Mayer, and L. Cross, pp. 69–108. East Melbourne: Australian Catholic University, Centre for Early Christian Studies, 1999.

———. "Quest of the Historical Jesus." In *The Oxford Companion to Christian Thought*, ed. A. Hastings, pp. 587–589. Oxford: Oxford University Press, 2000.

———. "Rasskaz Strannika: The Candid Tale of a Pilgrim to His Spiritual Father." In *Contemplative Literature: A Comparative Sourcebook on Meditation and Contemplative Prayer*, ed. L. J. Komjathy, pp. 359–406. Albany: State University of New York Press, 2014.

———. "Sacrifice and Atonement: An Investigation into the Attitude of Jesus of Nazareth Towards Cultic Sacrifice." In *Remembering for the Future*, vol. 1 (Oxford: Pergamon Press, 1988), pp. 648–661. Repr. in McGuckin, *Collected Studies*, vol. 1, pp. 51–88.

———. *Standing In God's Holy Fire: The Spiritual Tradition of Byzantium*. London: DLT, 2001.

———. *St. Cyril of Alexandria and the Christological Controversy: Its History, Theology, and Texts*. Leiden: Brill, 1994; New York: SVS Press, 2004.

———. *St. Gregory of Nazianzus: An Intellectual Biography*. New York: SVS Press, 2001.

———. "Theotokos: The Mother of God in the Later Patristic Period." In *The Cambridge Companion to the Virgin Mary*, ed. S. Boss., pp. 115–120. Cambridge: Cambridge University Press, 2008.

———. *The Transfiguration of Christ in Scripture and Tradition*. New York: Mellen Press, 1986.

Meyendorff, J. *Living Tradition*. Ada, Mich.: Baker Academic, 2013 [1978].

Meyer, R. T. *Palladius: The Lausiac History*. Ancient Christian Writers, vol. 34. New York: Paulist Press, 1965.

Miller, T. *The Birth of the Hospital in the Byzantine Empire*. Baltimore: Johns Hopkins University Press, 1997.

Obolensky, D. *The Byzantine Commonwealth: Eastern Europe, 500–1453*. New York: SVS Press, 1971.

Philippou, A. J. (ed.). *The Orthodox Ethos*. Oxford: Holywell Press, 1964.

Shevzov, V. "The Russian Tradition." In A. Casiday (ed.), *The Orthodox Christian World*, pp. 15–40. London: Routledge, 2012.

Speake, G. *Mount Athos: Renewal in Paradise*. New Haven: Yale University Press, 2003.

Stan, L., and L. Turcescu. *Religion and Politics in Post-Communist Romania*. Oxford: Oxford University Press, 2007.

Stebbing, N. *Bearers of the Spirit: Spiritual Fatherhood in Romanian Orthodoxy*. Cistercian Studies, vol. 201. Collegeville, Minn.: Liturgical Press, 2003.

Tanner, N. P. (ed.). *Decrees of the Ecumenical Councils: Volume 1: Nicaea I to Lateran V*. Washington, D.C.: Georgetown University Press, 2016.

Thorsteinsson, R. M. *Jesus as Philosopher: The Moral Sage in the Synoptic Gospels*. Oxford: Oxford University Press, 2018.

Trostyanskiy, S. (ed.). *Seven Icons of Christ: An Introduction to the Oikoumenical Councils*. Piscataway, N.J.: Gorgias Press, 2016.

Waddams, H. *Meeting the Orthodox Churches*. London: SCM Press, 1964.

Ware, T. *The Orthodox Church*. London: Penguin Books, 1987.

Wortley, J. *The Book of the Elders: Sayings of the Desert Fathers: The Systematic Collection*. Cistercian Studies, vol. 240. Collegeville, Minn.: Liturgical Press, 2012.

Index

INDEX